The Basics of Indian Philosophy

The Basics of Indian Philosophy

Rodinmawia Ralte

Christian World Imprints

First Published in 2025 by

Christian World Imprints
Christian Publishing & Books from India
A-71 Group, Wazirpur Industrial Area
Delhi-110052
cwidelhi2017@gmail.com
www.ChristianWorldImprints.com
Phone: +91 11 41526079

ISBN: 978-93-6065-954-7

Printed in India.

Contents

Preface

Why another book on Indian philosophy? With so many books already published and available in the market, what justifies the need for this one? I am aware of the numerous works on Indian philosophy that exist, but many of them are not accessible to beginners, particularly undergraduate students. For students from Tribal, Adivasi, and Dalit communities, Indian philosophy can seem daunting, and they often find it challenging to grasp the content of existing books. This is why I took on the challenge of writing a book that is authentic, academically rigorous, yet easy to read and understand for those just beginning their journey into Indian philosophy.

I extend my heartfelt gratitude to my good friend Sudhanshu of Christian World Imprints, a publisher of numerous Christian academic books. It was his idea to write this book, as he frequently received inquiries from students seeking an accessible introduction to Indian philosophy. His persistent reminders, encouragement, and gentle pushes kept me motivated to complete this project. Despite my demanding office and teaching responsibilities, and though I have taught this subject at the undergraduate level for several years, it took me nearly two years to finish this work.

I am also deeply thankful to my loving wife, C. Laltanpuii, who stood by me throughout the writing process. Her unwavering support, often staying up with me until the early hours of the morning, was a constant source of encouragement. The space, freedom, and motivation she provided were invaluable in bringing this book to life.

I hope this introductory book will serve as a helpful guide for students in general and, in particular, for those taking their first steps into the study of Indian philosophy.

May God be exalted in the highest.

Rodinmawia Ralte
SCEPTRE
Kolkata
February, 2025

Introduction

Indian philosophy, with its rich diversity of thought and tradition, represents a profound intellectual legacy that has shaped the spiritual, ethical, and metaphysical aspects of life for millennia. It offers multiple perspectives on the nature of existence, consciousness, and the universe, each offering a unique lens to view the world and human experience. This book, *The Basics of Indian Philosophy*, aims to provide an accessible yet comprehensive introduction to the essential philosophical systems of India, allowing readers to engage with the core ideas that have shaped this ancient tradition.

Why "Basics"?

The choice of the word "Basics" in the title is deliberate. It signifies that this work focuses on the core philosophical systems and concepts that form the bedrock of Indian philosophical thought. The term implies that the book will offer a starting point, an entry into the world of Indian philosophy, without delving into overly complex or specialized discussions. Just as the foundation of a building supports everything above it, understanding the basic philosophies of India is crucial for comprehending the diverse intellectual traditions that have emerged over centuries.

By focusing on the foundational aspects, the book intends to lay the groundwork for readers who are new to Indian philosophy, providing them with a solid grasp of its key systems and ideas. This foundational exploration will serve as a gateway for those who wish to further their studies in the subject or simply gain a deeper understanding of the philosophical outlook that has influenced countless individuals and cultures worldwide.

Aims and Scope of the Book

In this book, I have chosen to explore six key philosophical systems (*ṣaḍ-darśana*) that represent the major strands of orthodox Hindu thought, alongside other significant philosophical traditions that have contributed to the intellectual diversity of India. These include: *The Six Orthodox Schools (ṣaḍ-darśana)*: These schools of thought - Nyāya, Vaisheshika, Sāṃkhya, Yoga, Mīmāṃsā, and Vedānta - offer distinct interpretations of the nature of reality, knowledge, and liberation. Each system, while unique, contributes to a broader understanding of life's ultimate purpose and the relationship between the individual and the cosmos. *Buddhist Philosophy*: Founded by Siddhārtha Gautama, the Buddha, this philosophy introduces key concepts such as *anatta* (non-self), *dukkha* (suffering), *impermanence*, and the path to *Nirvāṇa*. While Buddhism shares cultural and historical roots with Hinduism, it presents a distinctive approach to suffering, liberation, and the nature of the self. *Jain Philosophy*: Jainism offers a unique worldview, emphasizing non-violence (*ahiṃsā*), self-discipline, and the pursuit of liberation through right knowledge, right faith, and right conduct. Jain philosophy introduces the concept of *anekāntavāda* (non-absolutism), which asserts that truth can be understood from multiple perspectives. *Cārvāka Philosophy*: This materialist school of thought challenges religious and metaphysical claims, focusing on direct perception as the only mean of knowledge. It offers a counterpoint to the more theistic and metaphysical schools, advocating for a rational, empirical approach to life. *Tribal Worldview*: The tribal philosophies of India, with their emphasis on communitarianism and interconnectedness between God, humans, and nature, provide an essential perspective on ecological balance and spiritual harmony. These worldviews often see the sacredness of the land and the interdependence of all life, providing valuable insights for addressing contemporary ecological and social issues.

The Diversity of Indian Philosophy

While Indian philosophy encompasses a wide range of systems, the common thread running through all these traditions is the search for understanding the nature of reality, the self, and the universe. From the metaphysical inquiry of the *Upanishads* to the ethical teachings of the Buddha, and from the practical philosophy of the Yoga Sutras to the social consciousness of tribal worldviews, Indian philosophy encourages deep introspection and dialogue about the most profound questions of existence. The diversity within Indian philosophy is not just a matter of different schools of thought but also reflects a broader cultural and social diversity. Each tradition emerged from different social contexts, religious practices, and intellectual discourses, yet they all share a commitment to the pursuit of wisdom and understanding. This plurality of perspectives is one of the most defining features of Indian philosophy and what makes it so rich and dynamic.

Structure of the Book

This book is organized into eleven chapters, each designed to introduce the key aspects of Indian philosophy while covering a range of diverse systems and perspectives. *Chapter one*, *An Overview of Indian Philosophy*, provides the foundational understanding of Indian philosophical thought, exploring its meaning and nature, historical development, the role of the Vedas, the place of authority and reasoning in Indian systems, and their common characteristics. The subsequent chapters focus on individual philosophical schools, beginning with *Cārvāka* in *Chapter two* which presents the materialistic approach to philosophy, emphasizing empirical experience and the rejection of metaphysical constructs. *Chapter three*, on *Jaina Philosophy*, delves into the principles of non-violence, karma, and liberation through right conduct, knowledge, and perception. *Buddhist Philosophy* is explored in *Chapter four*, where key concepts such as the Four Noble Truths, non-self (Anatta), and the path to Nirvāṇa are discussed. *Chapter five* introduces the *Nyāya* school, focusing on logic, reasoning, and epistemology, while *Chapter six* covers the *Vaiśeṣika* school, exploring atomism and the categorization of reality into distinct substances. *Chapter seven* looks at the *Sāṃkhya* school, with its dualistic understanding of the relationship between consciousness and matter, and *Chapter eight* focuses on the *Yoga* school, examining its practices and philosophy aimed at self-realization and liberation. *Chapter nine* covers *Mīmāṃsā*, which emphasizes ritual action and the interpretation of the Vedas. In *Chapter ten*, *Vedānta* is discussed through the perspectives of Sankara's *Advaita*, Ramanuja's *Viśiṣṭādvaita*, and Madhva's *Dvaita*, highlighting their varying interpretations of the relationship between the self and Brahman. Finally, the last Chapter explores the *Tribal or Indigenous Worldview*, emphasizing communitarianism and the interconnectedness of God, humans, and nature. Together, these chapters offer a comprehensive and accessible introduction to the diverse traditions of Indian philosophy.

Throughout the book, I aim to provide clear and concise explanations of the core ideas of each tradition, making the material accessible to both newcomers and those with a deeper interest in Indian philosophy. By offering a broad overview of these diverse philosophical systems, the book aims to spark further curiosity and encourage a more profound engagement with the rich intellectual heritage of India.

Indian philosophy is a vast and intricate field of study, but it is also an essential one for understanding the intellectual and spiritual foundations of human civilization. *The Basics of Indian Philosophy* serves as an entry point to the study of this tradition, offering readers a pathway to understanding the philosophical diversity that has shaped India's intellectual and spiritual life for thousands of years. By exploring the six orthodox schools, Buddhist and Jain philosophies, Cārvāka thought, and tribal worldviews, this book provides a broad and inclusive approach to the foundational ideas that continue to influence thinkers, practitioners, and spiritual seekers around the world.

This introductory exploration invites you to delve into the heart of Indian philosophical thought, gaining insights that transcend time and culture, and offering reflections on how these ideas continue to shape our understanding of the world today.

Chapter 1

An Overview of Indian Philosophy

S. Radhakrishnan said: "Philosophy is a human effort to comprehend the problem of the universe," and Indian philosophical systems are rich in this aspect. All the Indian systems are efforts of the genuine human beings to understand human problems and their solutions.

The term philosophy is commonly interpreted as the 'love of knowledge' or the 'love of wisdom'. This interpretation is more aligned with Western concepts rather than Indian ones. In the Indian context, the word predominantly used to describe philosophy is '*darśana*', which originates from the Sanskrit root '*drs*' meaning 'to see'. Etymologically, the term '*darśana*' signifies perception and can also refer to a 'view'. It represents the perception of truth or God. Additionally, it can be understood as the 'vision of truth', and it also encompasses the notions of 'critical exposition' or 'logical survey'. Therefore, '*darśana*' essentially implies 'having a direct intuitive experience of the object'. In other words this can also means "to realize it in the sense of becoming with it."[1]

This Chapter aims at introducing this *darśna* by giving a brief discussion on the Indian System of thought – what is

[1] S. Radhakrishnan, *et.al.* (Eds.), *A source book in Indian Philosophy,* (Princeton: Princeton University Press, 1967), xxvi.

the nature of Indian Philosophy? How were they developed? What are the different schools and what are their common characteristics and so on. In other words, it is an introductory note on Indian philosophy.

1. The Meaning and Nature of Indian Philosophy

By 'Indian philosophy' we mean the philosophical speculations of all Indian thinkers, ancient or modern, Hindus or non-Hindus, atheists or theists. It is to be noted here that Indian Philosophy is not synonymous with Hindu Philosophy, because, "Even in the ancient writings of the orthodox Hindu philosophers like the *sarva–darśana–saṅgraha* of Mādhavācārya which tries to present in one place the view of all schools of philosophy we find in the list of philosophies the views of atheists and materialists like *Carvakas* and unorthodox thinkers like the Buddhas and the Jainas along with those of orthodox Hindu thinkers."[2]

Due to its inherent nature, Indian philosophy possesses a broad perspective that underscores the profound commitment to the pursuit of truth. A notable characteristic of Indian philosophy is the emphasis on 'respect for others'. Within each school, there exists a profound reverence for other schools of thought and decisions are not hastily made. Instead, a thorough consideration of opposing viewpoints and their potential rebuttals takes place before arriving at any conclusive stance. For the formulation of any philosophical standpoint, a philosopher in India was obliged to begin by articulating the perspectives of their counterparts. This preliminary step is known as '*pūrvapakṣa*' or 'prior view,' a philosopher will bring forth his/her refutation (*khaṇḍana*) of this view. Only after these preceding steps would the philosopher proceed to present their own conclusion (*siddhānta*). This methodology is particularly evident when closely studying any of the schools of Indian philosophy. A comprehensive exploration of Vedanta, for instance, illuminates the meticulous examination and assessment of all other schools before the

---

[2] S. C. Cheterjee and D. M. Dutta, *An Introduction to Indian Philosophy*, (Calcutta: University of Calcutta, 1984), 4.

Vedanta philosophy itself emerged. This practice is consistently upheld across all the diverse schools of Indian philosophy. "The system thus became encyclopedic in their grasp of ideas."[3] Hence, one of the most exquisite attributes of Indian philosophy lies in its openness – the readiness to attentively consider the viewpoints of others. This very characteristic has been a source of richness and magnificence in the history of Indian philosophy, and it is a quality worth embracing and preserving in the future.

2. History of Indian Philosophy

India has several schools of philosophy, but they cannot be put into historical and chronological series. Unlike the history of the western philosophy that witnessed one school appearing after another in time, the Indian Philosophical thoughts appeared almost simultaneously. P.T. Raju observes-

> They developed through mutual criticisms by attempting to be self-consistent and comprehensive. Such developments took place during the course of centuries, each great thinker of the school contributing his own by bridging the lacunae of the argument and expanding it over areas not yet covered.[4]

Unlike Western philosophy, "Indian philosophy was a part of life." The different schools having flourished together during many centuries, pursue parallel courses of growth. As each system of thought emerged, a group of followers adopted as a philosophy of life and formed a school of that philosophy. "They lived that philosophy and handed down to succeeding generations of followers who were attracted to them through their lives and thought."[5] So slowly but steadily by constant mutual criticism various schools of philosophy along with huge philosophical literature has come into existence.

---

[3] S C. Cheterjee and D. M. Dutta, *An Introduction to Indian Philosophy*, 4.

[4] P. T. Raju, *Strutural depth of Indian thought*, (New Delhi: South Asian Publishers, 1985), 2.

[5] Cheterjee and Dutta, *An Introduction to Indian Philosophy*, 9.

Though it is not possible to be sure of the exact chronological development of Indian thought, we will try to put the period of Indian thought in a chronological way. The following are the broad chronological divisions of Indian philosophy.[6]

2.1. The Vedic Period (500 – 600 B.C.)

This covers the age of the settlement of the Aryans in India and the gradual expansion and spread of the Aryans culture and civilization. It was during this period that religious ideas coming from the forest – different thought in the form of Vedas, Brāhmaṇas and Upaniṣads were emerged. The view put forwards in this age were not philosophical in the technological sense. "It is the age of groping where superstition and thought are yet in conflict."[7]

2.2. The Epic Period (600 B.C. – 200 A.D)

This period covers the development between early Upaniṣads and the system of philosophy. The Epic – Rāmāyaṇa and Mahābhārata serves as the vehicles to convey the new message to the hungry souls. The religious traditions like Buddhism, Jainism, Śaivism, Vaiṣṇavism belong to this period. "The development of abstract thought which culminated in the schools of Indian Philosophy, the *darśanas* belonged to this period."[8] Most of the System found their early origin during this period. They developed side by side through many centuries; "yet the systematic works of the schools belonged to a later age."[9]

2.3. The Sūtra Period (from 200 A.D.)

By this period the mass of material grew so unwieldy that it was found necessary to have a summarized form and sūtras came into existence. "This sutras are unintelligible without

---

[6] This division is taken from S. Radhakrishnan, *Indian Philosophy Vol. I* (London: George Allen & Unwin Ltd., 1977), 57-59.

[7] Radhakrishnan , *Indian Philosophy Vol.*, 57.

[8] Radhakrishnan , *Indian Philosophy Vol.*, 57-58.

[9] Radhakrishnan , *Indian Philosophy Vol.*, 58.

commentaries, so much so that the latter have become more important the sutras themselves."[10] Various systems developed during this period, and it is difficult to determine which are earlier and which are later. According to Prof. Garbe, the chronological order of the six orthodox systems is as follows: *Sāṃkhya*, the oldest, followed by *Yoga*, *Mīmāṃsā*, *Vedānta*, and finally *Vaiśeṣika* and *Nyāya*.[11] It is to be noted here that there are cross-references throughout. The *Yoga* system accepts the *Sāṃkhya* philosophy, while *Vaiśeṣika* recognizes both *Nyāya* and *Sāṃkhya*. *Nyāya* refers to *Vedānta* and *Sāṃkhya*. *Mīmāṃsā* directly or indirectly acknowledges the pre-existence of all the others, as does *Vedānta*.

2.4. The Scholastic Period

It is not possible to draw a clear line between this period and the previous one. This period also starts from 200 A.D. During this time, great Indian philosophers such as Kumārila, Śaṅkara, Siddhāra, Rāmānuja, Madhva, Vācaspati, and Udayana emerged with their philosophical ideas. Commentators like Śaṅkara and Rāmānuja restated the old doctrines, and their restatements are just as valuable as new spiritual discoveries.

3. The Schools of Indian Philosophy System

The Indian schools of philosophy can be broadly divided into two classes - orthodox schools (*āstika*) and heterodox schools (*nāstika*). In Sanskrit philosophical literature, *āstika* means "one who believes in the authority of the Vedas" or "one who believes in life after death." *Nāstika* means the opposite of this. However, in modern Indian languages, *āstika* denotes 'theist' and *nāstika* stands for 'atheist.'[12] The popular *ṣaḍ-darśana* (six chief philosophical systems) belong to the first group, i.e., *āstika*. These systems are *Mīmāṃsā*, *Vedānta*, *Sāṃkhya*, *Yoga*, *Nyāya*, and *Vaiśeṣika*. They are considered orthodox for

[10] Radhakrishnan , *Indian Philosophy Vol.*, 58.

[11] Cited in S. Radhakrishnan, *Indian Philosophy, Vol.*, 58-59.

[12] Chaterjee and Dutta, *An Introduction to Indian Philosophy*, 5.

two main reasons - first, they believe in God, and second, they accept the authority of the Vedas. Although the *Sāṃkhya* school rejects the existence of God, it is included in the *āstika* category because of its acceptance of Vedic authority. These *ṣaḍ-darśana* are not the only orthodox systems; "they are the chief ones, and there are some other less prominent orthodox schools, such as the Grammarian school and the Medical school, which are also noted by *Mādhavācārya*."[13]

To the second class (heterodox schools) belong three schools, namely the materialists (*Cārvākas*), the Buddhists, and the Jains. As they do not accept the authority of the Vedas, they are called heterodox (*nāstika*).

Among the *āstika*, *Sāṃkhya* advocates dualism of '*prakṛti*' and *puruṣa* or individual self. The *Vedānta* teaches spiritualistic monism recognizes the reality of Brahman alone. The *Nyāya* and the *Vaiśeṣika* advocate the reality of God, plurality of individual souls, and the world of diverse objects. They considered the world to be composed of the eternal atoms of earth, water, fire and air existing independently of God. The *Mīmāṃsā* recognized the reality of individual selves and the self-existent material world. Yoga grafts the notion of God on the *Sāṃkhya* dualism of *prakṛti* and *puruṣa* and makes it theistic. So, sometime it is called theistic *Sāṃkhya*.

4. Place of the Vedas in Indian Philosophical System

In the development of the Indian Philosophy, Vedas play the major and prominent role either positively or negatively. Some of the system accepted the vedic authority, while other opposed it and created a system in revolt against the Vedas. System like *Cārvāka*, *Bauddha* and *Jain*a systems emerged as a rival against the vedic authority. Among those who accept vedic authority there are two groups – one group directly basing their system on the Vedas, which includes *Mīmāṃsā* and *Vedānta*. Other groups, though accepted the Vedas as authoritative, based their systems

[13] Chaterjee and Dutta, *An Introduction to Indian Philosophy*, 5-6.

not on the Vedas, but on the independent ground. *Sāṃkhya*, Yoga, Nyāya and *Vaiśeṣika* belong to this category.

Again, the systems that originated directly from the Vedas had two divisions - ritualistic (*karma*) and speculative (*jñāna*). *Mīmāṃsā*, which emphasizes the ritualistic aspect of the Vedas, belongs to the first group, whereas *Vedānta*, with its emphasis on the speculative aspect, develops a philosophy out of Vedic speculations. As both of these schools are direct continuations of Vedic culture, they are sometimes collectively referred to by a common name - *Mīmāṃsā*. For the sake of distinction, the first is called *Pūrva-Mīmāṃsā* (*Karma- Mīmāṃsā*), and the second is called *Uttara-Mīmāṃsā* (*jñāna- Mīmāṃsā*). However, the more usual names for these two are simply *Mīmāṃsā* and *Vedānta*, respectively.[14]

The various schools of Indian philosophy described above can be presented in the form of a table as follows:[15]

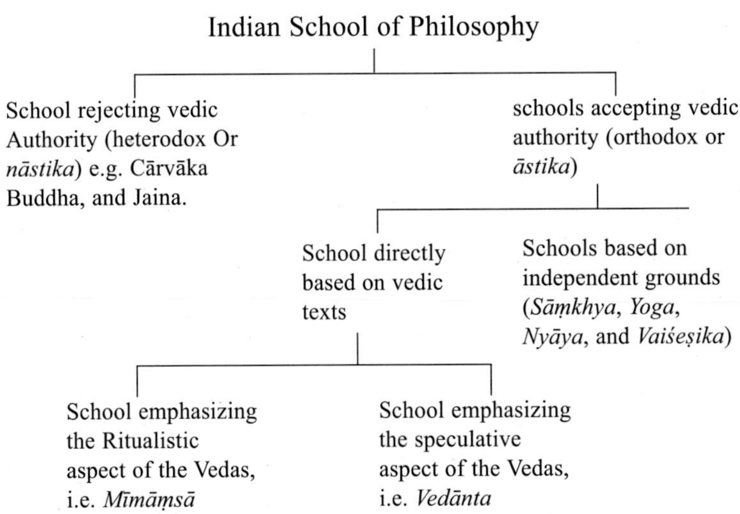

[14] Chaterjee and Dutta, *An Introduction to Indian Philosophy*, 6.

[15] This table is taken from Chaterjee and Dutta, *An Introduction of Indian Philosophy (2007)*, 7.

The *Nyāya* and *Vaiśeṣika* schools share a common philosophy regarding nature, the soul, and God, although they have minor differences. Eventually, they were merged into a syncretic school called *Nyāya-Vaiśeṣika*. This philosophy acknowledges the reality of the eternal world as independent of the perceiving selves. It advocates a dualism between matter and souls, as well as between individual souls and the supreme soul. Moreover, it recognizes the plurality of individual souls and finite objects. Therefore, it upholds realism, dualism, pluralism, and deism.

5. The Place of Authority and Reasoning in Indian Philosophy

Some of the philosophical questions, such as, what is the ultimate cause of the world? What/who is God? Does he/her/it exist? and many other metaphysical questions cannot be answered by observation. It is necessary to employ imagination and reasoning to find out answers to such questions. However such answers should be consistent with the truth already established. So, philosophy like other branches proceeds from known to unknown. "The foundation of philosophy", said Chaterjee and Dutta in their book, "is experience and the chief tool used is reason.[16] But on what experience? There are two types of views to address this question –

The first view advocates, "Philosophy should be based on ordinary, normal experience, i.e. on truth discovered and accepted by people in general or by scientists."[17] This reflects modern European philosophy, and in India, the *Nyāya*, the *Vaiśeṣika*, the *Sāṃkhya*, and the *Cārvāka* schools align with this line of thought. *Buddha* and *Jaina* philosophies are also not far from this perspective. The second group of thinkers, however, does not wish to rely on the experience of 'ordinary' or 'normal' people, holding that authentic philosophy must be based on the insights of reliable, saintly persons such as seers or prophets, as well as on scripture (since scriptures are also products of

[16] Chaterjee and Dutta, *An Introduction to Indian Philosophy*, 7.

[17] Chaterjee and Dutta, *An Introduction to Indian Philosophy*, 8.

prophets and saints). The *Mīmāṃsā* and *Vedānta* schools follow this approach. Buddhists and Jains also, to a great extent, fall into this category.

Having said this, we should also remember that reasoning has the lion's share in the process of philosophical speculation. There is often a charge leveled against Indian philosophy that its theories are not based on reasoning but on authority (scripture and reliable persons), and therefore are dogmatic. However, this is not true of the majority of Indian systems. This criticism may primarily target *Mīmāṃsā* and *Vedānta*, which are more authority-oriented than others. While it is true that these systems begin with authority, "the theories they develop are also supported by strong independent arguments that even if we withdraw the support of the authority, the theories can still stand well and compare favourable with any theories established elsewhere on independent reasoning alone."[18]

6. The Common Characters of Indian System

Though there are wide ranges of diversities in Indian philosophy, we can always observe commonalities in the midst of this. The following are the points of agreement among the different schools –

6.1. The Practical Motif Present in all System

The most striking and fundamental point of agreement, according to Chatterjee and Datta, is that "all the systems regard philosophy as a practical necessity and cultivate it in order to understand how life can be best led."[19] In India, the aim of philosophy is "not merely the satisfaction of intellectual curiosity but mainly an enlightened life led with farsight, foresight, and insight."[20] However, this does not mean that Indian philosophy is limited to practical motifs alone and lacks theoretical development. It should be remembered that Indian systems

[18] Chaterjee and Dutta, *An Introduction to Indian Philosophy*, 9.

[19] Chaterjee and Dutta, *An Introduction to Indian Philosophy*, 12.

[20] Chaterjee and Dutta, *An Introduction to Indian Philosophy*, 12.

are as comprehensive as any system in the West, especially in branches like metaphysics, epistemology, and logic.

6.2. The Source of Philosophy

Indian philosophy springs from spiritual disquiet at the existing order of things. All the systems, whether pro-Vedic or anti-Vedic, are moved by spiritual dissatisfaction, such as the sight of evils and sufferings that cast a gloom over life in this world. They seek to understand the source of these evils and sufferings, the nature of the universe, and the meaning of human life "in order to find out some means for completely overcoming life's miseries."[21]

So, Indian philosophy is spiritual in nature. It is a spiritual quest, a search for the remedy to spiritual unrest. The starting point of Indian philosophy is the helplessness of the human condition, the misery of life, and the presence of suffering in human existence. For this reason, Indian philosophy is often criticized as pessimistic. However, this pessimism is only initial and not final. Indian philosophy is pessimistic in the sense that it operates under a sense of discomfort and disquiet at the existing order of things. It recognizes and strongly asserts that life, when thoughtlessly led, is merely a sport of blind impulses and unquenchable desires, inevitably resulting in prolonged misery. However, no Indian school of philosophy stops at this tragic view of life. If Indian philosophy relentlessly points to the miseries we endure due to short-sightedness, it also discovers a message of hope. The essence of Buddha's enlightenment - the Four Noble Truths - encapsulates and articulates the core perspective of every Indian school in this regard: there is suffering, there is a cause of suffering, there is a remedy, and the remedy lies in following the Eightfold Path.[22]

---

[21] Chaterjee and Dutta, *An Introduction to Indian Philosophy*, 13.

[22] Chaterjee and Dutta, *An Introduction to In Philosophy,* 13. See also Radhakrishnan, *Indian Philosophy,* 49-50.

6.3. The Belief in an Eternal Moral Order

The concept that prevents the Indian mind from ending in despair, guarantees a brighter future, and paves the way for optimism is the so-called *eternal moral order*. Apart from the Cārvāka, all other schools firmly believe in this. "It is a common atmosphere of faith in which all these systems - Vedic and non-Vedic, theistic and atheistic - move and breathe."[23] The seers of the *Ṛg Veda* call this inviolable moral order *ṛta*. This idea gradually shapes itself into the Mīmāṃsā concept of *apūrva* - the law that guarantees the future enjoyment of the fruits of rituals performed now. This concept also gives rise to the Nyāya-Vaiśeṣika theory of *adṛṣṭa* - the unseen principle that governs even material atoms and brings about objects and events in accordance with moral principles.[24]

This eternal moral order further develops into the general concept of *karma*, which is accepted by all Indian systems. In general, the law of karma (action) asserts that all actions, whether good or bad, produce their appropriate consequences in the life of the individual who acts. In other words, all actions — past, present, or future — will yield their proper effects in this life or another life of the individual who performs the act.[25] It is akin to the saying, "As you sow, so shall you reap."

The word *karma* means both the law itself and the force generated by an action, which possesses the potency to bear fruit. The Nyāya-Vaiśeṣika school believes that the law of karma operates under the guidance of God, who creates the world in accordance with this law. In contrast, other systems such as Jaina, Buddha, Sāṃkhya, and Mīmāṃsā consider the law of karma to be autonomous, functioning independently of the will of God. The law of karma helps explain the differences among individuals - why some people are happy while others are miserable, why some are wise while others are ignorant,

---

[23] Chaterjee and Dutta, *An Introduction to Indian Philosophy,* 14.

[24] Chaterjee and Dutta, *An Introduction to Indian Philosophy,* 14-15.

[25] Chaterjee and Dutta, *An Introduction to Indian Philosophy* 15.

and why some are rich while others are poor. It is the faith in an eternal moral order that inspires and empowers people to become masters of their own destinies. This belief helps individuals understand that present suffering is the consequence of their own actions and offers hope for a better future if they strive for improvement in the present.[26]

6.4. Ignorance as the Cause of Bondage

Ignorance as the cause of bondage is a common view held by all Indian thinkers. It is the ignorance of reality that leads to suffering and bondage. Liberation from this state cannot be achieved without the proper knowledge of reality. Here, reality refers to the true nature of the self and the world. Due to this bondage, the cycle of birth and rebirth continues, which is considered a source of misery for human beings. Liberation (*mukti* or *mokṣa*) means the cessation of this cycle and the attainment of a state of perfection. Some schools, such as Jaina, Buddha, Sāṃkhya, and Advaita Vedānta, hold that this state of perfection can be attained here and now.

For liberation, knowledge is essential. This knowledge is not merely an acquaintance with the truth; rather, it is achieved through continuous meditation on the accepted truth, along with a disciplined life of self-control. As Radhakrishnan aptly states, "In India, philosophy is for life; it is to be lived. It is not enough to know the truth but to realize it, to become one with it."[27]

6.5. Meditation

Almost all Indian schools have advocated meditation as essential for liberation. An elaborate technique for meditation is explained in the Yoga system. However, meditation is not the monopoly of this system; other schools, such as Buddhism, Jainism, Sāṃkhya, Vedānta, and Nyāya-Vaiśeṣika, also incorporate this technique in one form or another. Chatterjee

---

[26] Chaterjee and Dutta, *An Introduction to Indian Philosophy,* 15.

[27] Radhakrishnan, *et.al.* (Eds.), *A source book in Indian Philosophy,* xxiv.

and Datta beautifully explain the necessity of concentration and constant meditation as follows:[28]

Our ordinary wrong beliefs have become deeply rooted in us by repeated use in the different daily situations of life. Our habits of thought speech and action have been shaped and coloured by these beliefs which in turn have been more and more strengthened by those habits. To replace these beliefs by correct ones, it is necessary to meditate on the latter constantly and think over their various implications for life.

6.6. Self Control

Self-control is necessary to remove passions that obstruct concentration, meditation, and good conduct. Since human actions are often guided by blind impulses, these impulses must be controlled for actions to follow the right path. Except for the lone Cārvāka system, all other Indian systems recognize this truth. There are impulses deeply rooted in our character that lead us away from the truth, and self-control is essential to combat these impulses. All Indian thinkers place great importance on this practice, known as *abhyāsa*. Different schools provide various descriptions of impulses, but they all agree that the chief impulses are like and dislike - love and hate. We act under the influence of these impulses when we act habitually without thoughtful consideration. Our *indriyas* (instruments of knowledge and action), including the mind, sense organs, and motor organs for movement, speech, excretion, and reproduction, have been conditioned by these blind impulses of love and hate, acquiring fixed bad habits. Our *indriyas* must be kept under the reign of reason. This is indeed a challenging task, but it is achievable through the diligent practice of self-control. It is important to note that self-control is not merely a negative practice of restraining the *indriyas*, but also a positive effort to employ them for better purposes and make them obedient to the dictates of reason.[29]

---

[28] Chaterjee and Dutta, *An Introduction to Indian Philosophy*, 19.

[29] Chaterjee and Dutta, *An Introduction to Indian Philosophy*, 20-21.

6.7. Belief in the Possibility of Liberation

All Indian philosophical systems, except the Cārvāka, accept liberation (*mokṣa*) as the ultimate goal of life. However, the interpretation of liberation varies slightly across these schools. They all agree that liberation, in its negative sense, entails the complete cessation and removal of suffering. Some schools also emphasize its positive dimension, describing liberation as a state of perfection and absolute bliss. In contrast, the Sāṃkhya School rejects this positive aspect. According to Sāṃkhya, liberation is merely the cessation of pain and suffering; it does not involve happiness or bliss because, in the absence of suffering, the concept of happiness becomes irrelevant.

6.8. Concentration upon Spirituality

One of the chief marks of Indian philosophy in general is its concentration upon spiritual matters. "Both in life and in philosophy, the spiritual motif is predominant in India,"[30] says Radhakrishnan. Except for Cārvāka, which is relatively minor, all other philosophies in India conceive human beings to be spiritual in nature and are primarily interested in their spiritual destiny. Practically all of Indian philosophy, from its beginning in the Vedas to the present day, has striven to bring about a socio-spiritual reform in the country.[31] In India, philosophy and religion are intimately connected with each other. Jadunath Sinha observes, "Philosophy is the theory of the Reality. It is an insight into the nature of Reality which leads to liberation. So, Indian philosophy is not idle theorizing but a spiritual quest."[32]

6.9. Reason and Intuition

In Indian philosophy 'reason' unquestionably and extensively used but intuition is accepted to be the only method through which the Ultimate can be known. This shows that reason,

---

[30] Radhakrishnan, *et.al.* (eds.) *A Source book in Indian Philosophy*, xxiii.

[31] Radhakrishnan, *et.al.* (eds.) *A Source book in Indian Philosophy*, xxiii.

[32] Jadunath Sinha, *Indian Philosophy Vol I,* (Delhi: Motilal Benarsidass Publishers P. Ltd., 1999), 236.

though useful, it is insufficient. To know the reality one must have actual experience of it. The words of Radhakrishnan are worth remembered when he says, "One does not merely know the truth in Indian Philosophy, one realize it." He continues, "Indian philosophy thus characterized by an ultimate dependence upon intuition along with the recognition of the efficacy of reason and intellect when applied in their limited capacity with their proper function."[33]

6.10. Value of the Study of Indian Philosophy

According to Indian thinkers, the study of Indian philosophy is of great importance, and every responsible Indian who wishes to improve the quality of human life should not shun this vital enterprise. For when we realize that we are endlessly swept along the cycle of birth and death, the rising flood of life, and the ceaseless stream of becoming, the burning question forever remains: what is the purpose of all this? According to Indian thinkers, the answer lies in Indian philosophy. Thus, Indian philosophy is a fundamental human necessity and interest. Emphasizing the importance of Indian Philosophy, Radhakrishnan says,

> The labour of the Indian thinkers are so valuable to the advancement of human knowledge that we judge their work to be worthy of study, even if we find manifest error in it…A study of Indian philosophy will conduce to the clearing up of the situation, the adopting of a more balance outlook and the freeing of the mind from the oppressing sense of perfection of everything that is ancient. This freedom from bondage to authority is an ideal worth striving at.[34]

It is claimed that the Indian philosophical tradition is humanity's oldest and the longest continuous development of speculation about the nature of reality and the place of humans

---

[33] Radhakrishnan, *et.al.* (eds.) *A Source book in Indian Philosophy*, xxvi.

[34] Radhakrishnan, *Indian philosophy,* Vol I, 54-45.

therein.[35] For Indians, the study of Indian philosophy is so vital that it alone can provide the right perspective on India's past. Philosophically, the study of Indian philosophy is important because it is a search for truth. Philosophy, as understood in India, is closely related to spiritual life. It deals with the truth about God, the world, and human beings. So, Chandradhar Sarma boldly states, "It is impossible for man (sic) to live without philosophy," because "Indian philosophy" Sarama continues, "has been…intensely spiritual and has always emphasized the need of practical realization of truth."[36] The study of philosophy is also politically important. Why? Because unity and harmony among nations cannot be achieved through political dialogue alone. Radhakrishnan is right when he claims that political unity is impossible without philosophical understanding and he says, "It is to philosophy that man (sic) must turn his hope to bring the peoples of the world together in greater mutual understanding."[37]

Concluding Remarks

Indian philosophy represents a profound and dynamic intellectual tradition that has evolved over millennia, addressing the fundamental questions of existence, knowledge, and the human condition. It is characterized by its diversity, embracing both orthodox (*āstika*) and heterodox (*nāstika*) schools, and its commitment to the pursuit of truth, spiritual liberation (*mokṣa*), and the integration of reason and revelation. The Indian philosophical tradition not only reflects a rich tapestry of metaphysical speculation and ethical inquiry but also emphasizes practical application in human life.

From the rationalism of *Nyāya* to the realism of *Vaiśeṣika*, the dualism of *Sāṃkhya* to the spiritual discipline of *Yoga*,

---

[35] Radhakrishnan, *et.al.* (eds.), *A Source book in Indian Philosophy*, xxx.

[36] Chandradhar Sarma, *A critical Survey of Indian Philosophy,* (Delhi: Motilal Benarsidass, 1979),13.

[37] Radhakrishnan, *et.al.* (eds.), *A Source book in Indian Philosophy*, xxxi.

the ritualism of *Mīmāṃsā* to the transcendental idealism of *Vedānta*, each system contributes uniquely to the comprehensive understanding of reality. The heterodox traditions like *Cārvāka*, *Jainism*, and *Buddhism* further enrich this landscape with their critical perspectives and alternative worldviews.

Indian philosophy's quest for truth is not merely speculative but is deeply intertwined with the human aspiration for liberation and harmony. Its holistic approach to knowledge - combining metaphysics, epistemology, ethics, and spirituality - continues to inspire thinkers worldwide and remains relevant in contemporary philosophical discourse. Understanding this heritage is essential not only for grasping the intellectual legacy of India but also for gaining insights into the human quest for meaning and purpose.

Chapter 2

Cārvāka Philosophy

Introduction

Cārvāka philosophy is frequently referred to as the 'materialist school' or 'materialism' due to its fundamental assertion that matter constitutes the exclusive reality. It is also recognized as *Lokāyata*, a term that essentially means "that which engages with the material world" or "that which pertains to the world." This nomenclature aptly reflects the core emphasis of Cārvāka thought, which prioritizes empirical, sensory experience over speculation and rejects metaphysical or transcendent explanations. Unlike other Indian philosophical traditions that posit the existence of an eternal soul, *karma*, rebirth, or divine order, Cārvāka boldly challenges these notions, advocating a worldview grounded solely in direct perception (*pratyakṣa*) as the valid means of knowledge.

Although it is not known who the founder of this school is, references to its teachings appear in various classical texts, often through the lens of its critics. Cārvāka is a non-Vedic Indian materialistic school of philosophy, traditionally attributed to a sage named Cārvāka, who is often considered its founder. But some believe that the founder of Cārvāka philosophy is

Bṛhaspati who is considered to be the author of some of the Vedic hymns.

The philosophy is believed to have developed around the 6th century BCE, making it one of the earliest systems of thought in India to challenge religious orthodoxy. References found in the epics and Buddhist literatures indicate that Cārvāka is a very old system of thought. Despite facing strong opposition from dominant religious and philosophical traditions such as Vedānta, Buddhism, and Jainism, Cārvāka's radical skepticism and hedonistic ethics have continued to spark interest among scholars and rationalists. While it did not garner a substantial following or survive in an institutionalized form, its influence persists in modern debates on materialism, secularism, and rational inquiry.

1. Cārvāka's Epistemology

The Cārvāka philosophy holds that perception (*pratyakṣa*) is the only source of valid knowledge. It does not accept inference and other source of knowledge generally accepted by other Indian schools of philosophy. For the materialists, whatever we can perceive through our sense organs alone is the right knowledge. It is generally accepted that there are two kinds of perception – external and internal. External perception denotes the interaction between the five senses and external objects, internal perception happens with mind. As Cārvāka do not accord the mind the status of an autonomous sense organ, leading them to dismiss the notion of internal perception via the mind.[1]

The Cārvākas reject inference (*anumāna*) as a valid source of knowledge acquisition. Their argument rests on the premise that if inference is to be deemed a valid knowledge source, it must presuppose unquestionable knowledge that accurately reflects reality. However, inference fails to meet these criteria, as exemplified in situations where one infers the presence of fire on a mountain based on the perception of

[1] M. Mostafa Kamal, "The Epistemology of the Carvaka Philosophy," *Journal of Indian and Buddhist Studies,* Vol. 46, No. 2, March 1998, 1048.

smoke. The Cārvākas contend that this inference involves an uncertain leap from the observed smoke to the unobserved fire. A counterargument might propose that such a leap is justified by our established knowledge of the consistent relationship between smoke and fire. Nonetheless, the Cārvākas dispute this stance, asserting that it would only be acceptable if the fundamental premise establishing the unwavering connection between the intermediary term 'smoke' and the major term 'fire' were beyond doubt. The Cārvākas proceed to elucidate that this invariable relationship could only be established if we possessed knowledge of all instances of smoke alongside fire. Yet, this task proves insurmountable, given our incapacity to perceive even the entirety of smoke and fire occurrences across diverse locations worldwide, both in the present and across history. Consequently, they assert that no universal invariable relationship can be conclusively established through inference.[2] Thus, according to Cārvāka the only knowledge which is undisputable is gained by means of our five sense organs. In other words, direct perception (*pratyakṣa*) is the only valid source of knowledge.

Cārvāka also rejects testimony (*śabda*) as the safe source of knowledge. It does not negate the validity of knowledge by means of hearing the words as it is knowledge gained by perception. But if these words suggest or mean things not within our perceptions, and aim at giving us knowledge of those unperceived objects, they are not free from error and doubt.[3] Therefore, according to Cārvāka, testimony (*śabda*) cannot be regarded as the true source of knowledge.

In short, we may say Cārvāka's theory of knowledge was strongly grounded in empiricism, with direct sensory perception as the primary and most reliable source of knowledge. They rejected the authority of sacred texts, the inferences drawn from

---

[2] M. Mostafa Kamal, "The Epistemology of the Carvaka Philosophy," 1048-1047.

[3] Satishchandra Chatterjee and Dhirendramohan Datta, *An Introduction to Indian Philosophy*, (Nerw Delhi: Rupa, 2007), 57.

observations, and the testimony of reliable sources, focusing solely on what can be directly observed and experienced. This emphasis on empirical knowledge set Cārvāka apart from other Indian philosophical schools that relied on a combination of direct perception, inference, scriptural authority, and logical reasoning to understand the nature of reality and existence.

2. Cārvāka Metaphysics

Cārvāka's metaphysical teachings follow its epistemology in the sense that it accepts only things that can be perceived by our senses as real. Anything that cannot be perceived by our senses, such as God, soul, life after death, heaven or hell, law of *karma*, etc. is simply false or non-existence or unreal because these are not perceptible by our senses, and their reality cannot be established beyond doubt. Matter, on the other hand, is real because it can be perceived by our senses.

According to Cārvāka, the material world, which is the only reality, is compose of four elements – air (*vāyu*), fire (*agni*), water (*ap*), and earth *(kṣiti*). Most of the Indian philosophical systems accept the fifth element, ether (*ākāśa*), as another element, but Cārvāka rejects it because its existence cannot be established by perception. So, all the living and non-living things in the world are made up of these four perceptible elements. By the combination of these four elements the world and everything in it were produced and they are reduced to it after death.[4]

Though Cārvāka does not believe in soul, it admits the existence of consciousness which is perceptible. "What people mean by a soul is nothing more than this conscious living body (*caitanya-viśiṣṭa deha eva ātmā*)."[5] A soul which is considered as non-material entity is never perceived, and thus it is non-existence. In the same manner, since there is no empirical evidence or direct sensory experience of a divine being, Cārvāka dismisses the idea of God as baseless. As there is no God who

[4] Chaterjee and Datta, *An Introduction to Indian Philosophy*, 58.

[5] Chaterjee and Datta, *An Introduction to Indian Philosophy*, 59.

is an efficient cause of creation, Cārvāka holds that the four natural elements have inherent power in themselves to create the world as we see today.

3. Cārvāka Ethics

Cārvāka, in line with its metaphysical teachings, advocates a straightforward ethical principle - to fully enjoy the material world. Since there is no future beyond this visible world and life, one is encouraged to take advantage of the present and ensure they enjoy this life to the fullest. The following ethical teachings show Cārvāka's materialistic predisposition:

(a) **Materialism**: Cārvāka philosophy was rooted in materialism, rejecting supernatural explanations for phenomena and emphasizing the primacy of the material world. According to Cārvāka, only material entities exist, and consciousness arises from the combination of material elements.

(b) **Hedonism**: Cārvāka ethics promoted hedonism, asserting that pleasure (*sukha*) is the ultimate goals of life. They believed that pleasure should be pursued and pain avoided, as long as it does not harm others or interfere with one's own long-term well-being. "A good life is a life of maximum pleasure"[6] is the main content of Cārvāka ethics.

(c) **Skepticism**: Cārvāka philosophy was marked by skepticism towards metaphysical claims, religious beliefs, and rituals. They rejected the authority of scriptures and argued that knowledge should be based on direct perception (*pratyakṣa*) rather than on faith or inference.

(d) **Ethical Relativism**: Cārvāka ethics tended towards ethical relativism, asserting that moral values are subjective and vary from person to person, society to society, and situation to situation. They believed

---

[6] Chaterjee and Datta, *An Introduction to Indian Philosophy*, 62.

that what is considered moral or immoral depends on individual preferences, social conventions, and practical considerations.

(e) **Critique of Asceticism and Sacrifice**: Cārvāka philosophers criticized ascetic practices and rituals that involved self-denial or sacrifices for religious purposes. They argued that such practices are unnecessary and often motivated by the self-interest of priests or religious elites.

(f) **Emphasis on Sensory Experience**: Cārvāka ethics emphasized the importance of sensory experience in determining what is pleasurable and desirable. They advocated indulgence in sensory pleasures and enjoyment of worldly delights as opposed to austerity or renunciation.

Concluding Remarks

Cārvāka philosophy stands out as a bold and materialistic school of thought in Indian philosophy, challenging conventional religious and metaphysical doctrines. Its epistemology prioritizes direct perception (*pratyakṣa*) as the sole reliable source of knowledge, dismissing inference, testimony, and scriptural authority as flawed and unreliable. While this emphasis on empirical observation provides a rational and pragmatic foundation for understanding the world, it arguably limits the scope of human experience, disregarding subjective and spiritual dimensions of existence that many philosophical traditions consider essential.

Cārvāka metaphysics rejects the existence of a soul, God, or any afterlife, focusing instead on the material world perceived through the senses as the only reality. While this approach provides a coherent materialist view, it raises critical questions about the nature of consciousness and the human experience, leaving little room for exploration of the inner, non-material dimensions of life that other philosophical systems address. Ethically, Cārvāka advocates for a pragmatic approach to life, encouraging individuals to seek pleasure and avoid pain as the ultimate purpose of existence. While this focus on hedonism provides a clear, accessible moral framework, it may be seen as overly simplistic and reductionist, overlooking the complexity of moral values and higher pursuits like virtue, self-discipline, or spiritual growth.

Despite its controversial stance, Cārvāka philosophy offers a valuable counterpoint to spiritual traditions, encouraging critical thinking and a focus on tangible, worldly experiences. However, its refusal to engage with questions of the metaphysical or transcendental realms may limit its broader philosophical impact, especially when contrasted with systems that address the full spectrum of human experience. In sum, while Cārvāka provides a strong, materialist critique of religious orthodoxy, its rejection of any non-empirical forms of knowledge or experience presents both a strength and a limitation in its philosophical outlook.

Chapter 3

Jaina Philosophy

Jainism, one of the ancient religious traditions of India, offers a distinctive philosophical system that significantly contributes to the broader spectrum of Indian philosophical thought. Rooted in the teachings of Tīrthaṅkaras, especially Mahavira, considered as the last Tīrthaṅkara, Jain philosophy provides a wholistic and rigorous framework for understanding reality, knowledge, and the human condition. Its approach to metaphysics, epistemology, and ethics underscores its commitment to a life of nonviolence (*aḥimsā*), self-discipline, and spiritual liberation. This chapter explores key tenets of Jaina philosophy, unraveling its profound insights and their relevance in philosophical discourse.

The Jaina theory of knowledge (*pramāṇa*) is central to understanding its epistemological perspective. Jainism categorizes knowledge into several types, emphasizing both direct and indirect means of acquiring truth. This nuanced theory accommodates human limitations while striving for the attainment of omniscience (*kevala-jñāna*), the highest form of knowledge. It underscores the interplay between empirical and transcendental realms, offering a great epistemological framework.

In the realm of metaphysics, Jainism provides a dualistic understanding of existence, dividing reality into *jīva* (sentient beings) and *ajīva* (non-sentient entities). Ajīva further comprises *pudgala* (matter), *dharma* (principle of motion), *adharma* (principle of rest), *ākāśa* (space), and *kala* (time). Together, these eternal categories shape the fabric of existence and interaction. This metaphysical schema reveals a universe that is intricately interdependent, dynamic, and governed by natural laws, devoid of any supreme creator deity.

Another hallmark of Jaina philosophy is its doctrine of *anekāntavāda*, the principle of manifoldness, which posits that reality is complex and multifaceted. This principle fosters intellectual humility and tolerance, as it acknowledges that no single perspective can fully encapsulate the truth. Complementing this is *syādvāda*, the theory of conditional predication or situational proposition, which provides a systematic methodology for articulating the relativity of truth. Together, these doctrines promote a pluralistic worldview and offer a valuable antidote to dogmatism.

The Jaina view of the bondage of the soul and its liberation forms the ethical and spiritual cornerstone of its philosophy. Bondage arises from the accumulation of *karma*, which entraps the soul in the cycle of birth and death (*saṃsāra*). Liberation, or *mokṣa*, is achieved through the purification of the soul, which entails ethical conduct, disciplined ascetic practices, and meditative realization. This spiritual journey emphasizes personal effort, aligning with Jainism's broader rejection of divine intervention in human affairs.

1. Jaina Theory of Knowledge

According to Jaina thought, there are five different type of knowledge and these are broadly divided into two categories: direct knowledge (*Pratyakṣa Jñāna*) and indirect knowledge (*Parokṣa Jñāna*). The five means of knowledge - *Mati Jñāna*, *Śruti Jñāna*, *Āvadhī Jñāna*, *Manaḥparyāya Jñāna*, and *Kevala Jñāna* - are fundamental to Jain epistemology and are detailed in several Jain scriptures such as the *Tattvārtha Sūtra* and various *Āgamas*.[1]

1.1. *Mati Jñāna* (Sensory Knowledge) - This is knowledge of the mind obtained through the five senses. It includes perception, recollection, recognition, induction, and deduction. It is the indirect knowledge which the Jīva (soul) acquires through the agency of the mind and its faculties, the senses.

1.2. *Śruta Jñāna* (Authoritative Knowledge) refers to knowledge acquired through symbols, signs, or words, encompassing all forms of verbal knowledge. This includes canonical, scriptural, or a combination of both types of knowledge. *Śruta Jñāna* is categorized into four kinds: *Labdhi* (association), *Bhāvanā* (attention), *Upayoga* (understanding), and *Nāya* (aspects of the meaning of things). It is always preceded by *Mati Jñāna*, which provides knowledge of the present moment. Unlike *Mati Jñāna*, which perceives only the present, *Śruta Jñāna* comprehends the past, present, and future aspects of an object. While *Mati Jñāna* offers knowledge by direct acquaintance, *Śruta Jñāna* provides knowledge by detailed description.[2]

1.3. *Āvadhī Jñāna* (Clairvoyant Knowledge) - This is knowledge that transcends the ordinary sensory experience, allowing perception of objects or events at a distance, both spatially and temporally. One gains this type of knowledge not through physical means such as the senses or the mind, but through his or her psychic abilities, or through clairvoyance and intuitive awareness, by overcoming the limitations of time and space. It is beyond the boundaries of our ordinary awareness

---

[1] Cf. *https://cdn.ymaws.com/sites/www.jaina.org/resource/resmgr/05042018_ENewsletter/The_Theory_of_Knowledge_in_J.pdf* (accessed 15.05.2024).

[2] Hemant Shah, "Types of Knowledge in Jainism," A paper read at a seminar on *Jain Philosophy* and Epistemology organized by the B. L. Institute of Indology, Delhi in December 1990, in *https://www.herenow4u.net/index.php?id=87104* ((15.01.2025).

and faculties and not generally available to everyone. This is direct knowledge.[3]

1.4. *Manaḥparyāya Jñāna* (Telepathic Knowledge): It is the ability to directly perceive the thoughts and mental states of others without the use of any external medium or agency. Like *Āvadhī Jñāna*, it is an extra-sensory form of perception. However, *Manaḥparyāya Jñāna* is more refined and cannot be attained by ordinary individuals. It is accessible only to persons who have reached an advanced stage of spiritual progression, known as higher *guṇa-sthāna* (spiritual purity levels). These elevated forms of knowledge reflect the Jain emphasis on the soul's potential for infinite perception and cognition.[4]

1.5. *Kevala Jñāna* (Omniscient Knowledge) - This is perfect and complete knowledge, attained by liberated souls (*kevalins*) who have eradicated all karmic obstructions and attained perfection. Hence only a *Jina* or *Kevalin* has access to it, and through him or her, others may learn it as *śruti*. By itself, this knowledge does not require any outward agency for its transmission because it is always there, in the consciousness of the soul which flowers fully in an enlightened *Jina*, unattached, unlimited and without any constraint of time and space, duality, and objectivity. Since it is transcendental, it cannot be conveyed or expressed adequately to the satisfaction of others. However, it can be obtained omnisciently in a state of perfection, when the soul becomes liberated from the bondage to the cycle of births and deaths.[5]

Jainism simplifies the classification of knowledge into two broad categories:

(a) *Pratyakṣa Jñāna* (Direct Knowledge): This refers to knowledge that is immediate and not mediated

---

[3] "The Theory of knowledge in Jainism" in *https://cdn.ymaws.com/sites/www.jaina.org/resource/resmgr/05042018_ENewsletter/The_Theory_of_Knowledge_in_J.pdf* (15.01.2025).

[4] Hemant Shah, "Types of Knowledge in Jainism,"

[5] "The Theory of knowledge in Jainism".

by any external means such as the senses or verbal testimony. It includes advanced forms of knowledge like: *Avadhi Jñāna* (clairvoyance), *Manaḥparyāya Jñāna* (telepathy), and *Kevala Jñāna* (omniscience). These forms of knowledge are considered pure and free from doubt or error, representing higher spiritual states attained through inner development.

(b) ***Parokṣa Jñāna* (Indirect Knowledge)**: This refers to knowledge acquired through external means, such as the senses, logical inference, or scriptural study. It is subdivided into: *Mati Jñāna* (sensory knowledge), *Śruta Jñāna* (scriptural knowledge). *Parokṣa Jñāna* is considered incomplete and potentially prone to error, as it relies on intermediaries like sensory perception or language.

2. Jaina Metaphysics

According to Jain Philosophy, the world comprises two fundamental realities: *Jīva* and *Ajīva* – the living and the non-living. Among the non-living (*ajīva*) entities, there are five distinct types of substances: *pudgala* (matter), *ākāśa* (space), *kala* (time), *dharma* (condition of motion), and *adharma* (condition of rest).

2.1. *Jīva* or Soul

Jiva is a conscious living substance. The soul is the knower, inherently conscious, dynamic, agent, direct experiencer, equal in scope to its own body, and distinct in each body. We can say that *jiva* is the real knower (*jñata*), the real doer (*kartā*) and the real enjoyer (*bhoktā*).[6] Contrary to the Nyāya-Vaiśeṣika viewpoint that consciousness is an accidental attribute of the soul, the Jaina school emphasizes that consciousness is the very essence of the soul. However, consciousness exists in varying degrees, depending on the form of life, from the simplest one-

[6] P. S. Daniel, "The Jaina Religious Tradition" in *Religious Traditions of India*, edited by P. S. Daniel, *at.al*, New Delhi: ISPCK, 2002), 180.

sensed beings (e.g., plants) to fully developed humans with five senses. Again, unlike certain Hindu philosophical systems that assert the permanence of the soul, Jaina philosophy posits that the soul is dynamic and subject to change. The soul is eternal but it also undergoes changes. According to Jains, the soul experiences pleasure and pain because consciousness is an intrinsic aspect of it. As a conscious entity, the soul is both the doer and the experiencer – it acts and enjoys directly. Since enjoyment is a trait of conscious entities, the soul, being conscious, inherently possesses the capacity for enjoyment. The soul knows things, performs actitivities, enjoys pleasures, suffers pain and illumines itself and other objects.[7]

Unlike the Hindu philosophical schools that propose the infinitude and omnipresence of the soul, the Jaina school contends that the soul's extent is equivalent to that of its associated body. The measure of a soul is confined to the dimensions of the body it inhabits, signifying that there exists no soul external to the body. Again, *jīva* is not infinite but co-extensive with the body; it can immediately know objects within the body not outside of it.[8] Another distinctive aspect of the Jaina understanding of the soul is its belief in the multiplicity of souls - every living being, human, animal, insect, or even microscopic life, possesses a distinct soul, resulting in a multitude of individual souls. All *jīvas,* regardless of their form, possess the same intrinsic worth and potential for liberation. This underpins Jainism's rigorous commitment to *aḥimsa* (nonviolence), as even the smallest life forms are valued and protected. The philosophy also maintains that a single body is typically associated with one soul, and a solitary soul cannot occupy multiple bodies. However, in exceptional cases, such as in *nigoda* life forms (simplest life forms), multiple microscopic souls may coexist in a single physical structure.

---

[7] Satishchandra Chaterjee & Dhirendramohan Datta, *An Introduction to Indian Philosophy*, (New Delhi: Rupa, 2023), 87.

[8] Chaterjee & Datta, *An Introduction to Indian Philosophy,* 87-88.

According to Jains, *jīva* can be dividend in to two – liberated soul (*mukta jīva*) and bound soul (*baddha* or *saṃsāri jiva*). The liberated soul (*jiva*) has attained absolute purity and perfection. It has no body and dwelt at the top of the universe and it is no longer subject to rebirth.[9] The bound souls (*jiva*), on the other hand, are the embodied soul, living in the world with bodies. They are classified into *five categories* in conjunction with their senses:[10]

(a) ***Ekendriya Jīvas*** (one-sensed beings), examples: Earth-bodied beings (soil), water-bodied beings (water), fire-bodied beings (fire), air-bodied beings (air), and plant life. They have only touch. These beings have only the sense of touch and are the simplest forms of life.

(b) ***Dvindriya Jīvas*** (two-sensed beings), examples: Worms, shellfish, leeches. They have touch and taste. These beings possess a slightly higher degree of sensory awareness.

(c) ***Trindriya Jīvas*** (three-sensed beings), examples: Ants, lice, and moths. They have Touch, taste, and smell. These beings begin to exhibit a basic ability to navigate the environment using smell.

(d) ***Chaturindriya Jīvas*** (four-sensed beings), examples: Flies, bees, mosquitoes. They have touch, taste, smell, and sight. Their additional sensory capability (sight) enables them to interact with their surroundings more effectively.

(e) ***Pañcendriya Jīvas*** (five-sensed beings) – Examples: Humans, animals, birds, and celestial or hellish beings. They have five senses - touch, taste, smell, sight, and hearing.

---

[9] P. S. Daniel, "The Jaina Religious Tradition," 180.

[10] *Tattvartha Sutra* translation with commentary by Manu Doshi (Ahmadabad: Federation of Jain Associations in North America and Shrut Ratnakar, 2007), 41-42.

Soul is said to have three qualities – consciousness (*caitanya*), bliss (*sukha*) and energy (*vīrya*). The application of *consciousness* is referred to as cognition (*upayoga*). Cognition is of two types – perception (*darśana*) that is first contact, indistinct awareness, and knowledge (*jñāna*) that is, comprehending the details of what has been perceived. The second quality, *bliss*, can be experienced by the soul through self-knowledge. But bliss is fully manifested only when the soul attains perfect purity. The third quality of the is *energy* that functions as an abstract force which energies the operation of the knowledge and perception qualities.[11]

The *jīva* is eternal and indestructible; it cannot be created or destroyed. While the soul undergoes cycles of birth and rebirth (*Saṃsāra*), its essential nature remains unchanged. A key feature of the *jīva* is its association with *karma* particles, which bind to the soul due to actions, emotions, and thoughts. This karmic bondage is the root cause of the soul's entrapment in the cycle of *saṃsāra*. Every *jīva* has the potential to achieve *mokṣa*, the state of perfect freedom and omniscience (*kevala-jñāna*). Liberation (*mokṣa*) is a personal achievement, with no external divine intervention. Jainism asserts that the enlightened soul possesses *anantajñāna* (infinite knowledge), *anantadarśana* (infinite perception), *anantasukha* (infinite bliss), and *anantavīrya* (infinite power or energy).

2.2. *Ajīva* (Non-soul)

Ajīva is what falls beyond the realm of *Jīva*. Just like *jīva*, *ajīva* is uncreated, eternal and indestructible. It encompasses five distinct types: *Pudgala, dharma*, *adharma*, *ākāśa*, and *kala*. These can be categorized into two groups: Form (*rūpi*) and Formless (*arūpi*). *Pudgala* (Matter) possesses form, while the remaining four substances (*dravya*) – *dharma*, *adharma*, *ākāśa*, and *kala* – are formless. Within the domain of *ajīva*, only matter (*pudgala*) is capable of movement, whereas the other four

---

[11] Padmanabh S. Jaini, *The Jaina Path of Purification*, (Delhi: Motilal Banarsidass, 1988), 104-105.

dravyas lack motion. Moving objects owe their mobility to the medium of motion, with *dharma* being the primary principle facilitating movement. This attribution of *dharma* as the basis of motion by Jain philosophy predates Newton's formulation of the laws of motion. The counterpart to motion is rest – *adharma*. *Adharma* assumes significance in explaining the state of rest and object immobility. Another noteworthy non-soul element is *ākāśa* (space), which accommodates all other substances. *Ākāśa* is boundless, infinite, and characterized by its non-solid, vacant nature. Within Jaina philosophy, there exist two viewpoints regarding *kala* (time): one asserts that *kala* is an integral aspect of the two realities – *jīva* and *ajīva*; the other contends that *kala* stands as an independent substance, akin to *jīva* and *ajīva*.

2.2.1. *Pudgala* (Matter)

Pudgala has four primary characteristics: (a) touch (b) taste (c) smell and (d) colour. Also sound, binding, subtlety, grossness, aggregation, division, darkness, shadow, light and glow are the properties of *Pudgala*.[12] According to Jains, sound is not an original quality like the four – touch, taste, odour and colour, it is the modification of matter. These characteristics express themselves in twenty qualities – such as, cold, hot, oily, light, heavy, soft, hard – various colours, various types of smells, various types of shapes, etc. *Pudgala* (matter) is the only substance with form; it is liable to integration and disintegration. The smallest part of matter is atom. Matter exists in gross and subtle forms. Earth, water, fire are its gross form and they can be perceived; the subtle matter is unperceivable. *Karma* is considered as subtle matter.[13]

2.2.2. *Dharma* and *Adharma*

In Jaina philosophy, *dharma* is considered a medium that facilitates movement for objects, without which motion would

---

[12] *Tattvartha Sutra 5:23-24*, translation with commentary by Manu Doshi, 92.

[13] P. S. Daniel, "The Jaina Religious Tradition," 179.

not be possible. It can assist the motion of moving objects but cannot itself move non-moving objects, much like water cannot move a fish but enables the fish to move. *Adharma,* on the other hand, is a substance that is responsible for rest. It helps matter to rest but cannot arrest the movement of a moving object. *Dharma* and *adharma* are considered eternal, formless, non-moving, pervading the whole inhabited space of the universe (*lokākāśa*).[14]

2.2.3. *Ākāśa* or Space

This is the space that provides room for all existence – soul, matter, *dharma*, *adharma* – all objects of the universe. The space containing other substances is called *lokākāśa* or cosmic space and is finite in magnitude whereas the space beyond *lokākāśa* is called *alokākāśa* or extra-cosmic space which extends infinitely.[15] *Lokākāśa* is a space where souls and other substance live and *alokākāśa* is just an empty space.

2.2.4. *Kāla* or Time

According to Jaina Scripture, *Tattvārtha Sūtra* 5:22, becoming, changing, moving, the concept of before and after are the function of *kāla* (time).[16] *Kāla* (time) is thus a vital factor for every activity, the concept 'before' and 'after' would not arise in absence of time. "Time being instrumental in those activities, they are termed the functions or *upakāras* of time."[17] Without time a thing cannot endure or continue to exist though time itself does not cause a thing to exist.

According to some Jaina writers, time (*kāla*) can be divided into two – real time (*pāramārthika kāla*) and empirical or conventional time (*vyāvahārika kāla* or *samaya*). Continuity or duration (*vartanā*) is the mark of real time which is formless and eternal. Conventional time (samaya) can be divided into

---

[14] Chaterjee & Datta, *An Introduction to Indian Philosophy,* 93.

[15] P. S. Daniel, "The Jaina Religious Tradition," 180.

[16] *Tattvārtha Sūtra 5:22*, translation with commentary by Manu Doshi, 89.

[17] *Tattvārtha Sūtra 5:22*, translation with commentary by Manu Doshi, 92.

moments, hours, days, etc. and thus limited, having a beginning and an end.[18]

Jaina metaphysics offers a profound understanding of reality through its classification of existence into *jīva* (conscious entities) and *ajīva* (non-conscious entities). This dualistic framework underscores the interdependence between life and matter while maintaining their distinct ontological nature. By emphasizing non-violence, ethical living, and the liberation of the soul from material bondage, Jaina philosophy provides a wholistic approach to understanding the cosmos and our role within it. Ultimately, it invites us to recognize the sanctity of all existence and strive for spiritual liberation through self-discipline and awareness.

3. Jaina Theory of Judgement (*Syād-Vāda*)

Syād-vāda, in Jain philosophy, is the doctrine of conditional predication that emphasizes the relativity of all judgments and knowledge. The term *syād* means 'in some sense' or 'from some viewpoint,' and it is used to qualify statements, indicating that they are true only in a limited or specific context.

According to Jain thought, only an omniscient being can perceive an object in all its infinite aspects and dimensions simultaneously. Imperfect beings, like humans, can only comprehend an object from one particular viewpoint at a time, resulting in knowledge that is partial and limited to a single aspect of the object.[19]

This concept is often illustrated by the parable of blind men describing an elephant. Each blind man touches a different part of the elephant - its legs, ears, tail, trunk, or body - and forms a judgment about what the elephant looks like. While their descriptions are accurate from their individual perspectives, their conclusions differ and seem contradictory because they each perceive only a part of the whole. Similarly, when we make judgments about objects or situations, our conclusions are

---

[18] Chaterjee & Datta, *An Introduction to Indian Philosophy,* 92.

[19] Chaterjee & Datta, *An Introduction to Indian Philosophy*, pp. 74-75.

true only in relation to the specific perspective we adopt and the aspect of the object we consider.

The purpose of *Syād-vāda* is to promote humility and open-mindedness in discussions about reality. It encourages individuals to consider different perspectives and to avoid rigid dogmatism. *Syād-vāda* aligns closely with the concept of *Anekāntavāda*, which asserts that reality is multifaceted and that no single viewpoint can capture its entirety. Both *Syād-vāda* and *Anekāntavāda* together reflect the complexity and depth of Jain philosophical thought.

4. Jaina Theory of *Anekāntavāda*

The term *Anekāntavāda* is derived from three Sanskrit words: *aneka* (many or multiple), *anta* (view or end) and *vāda* (doctrine). Thus it means the 'doctrine of manifoldness' or the 'theory of non-absolutism.' This doctrine reflects the Jain belief that reality is multifaceted and cannot be fully understood from a single, absolute perspective. *Anekāntavāda* teaches that reality cannot be fully described or understood from a single perspective or in absolute terms. Instead, reality is composed of a multitude of aspects, each contributing to a comprehensive understanding. This principle challenges the idea of a singular, absolute understanding of truth and promotes a more refined and inclusive way of thinking.

Key Aspects of *Anekāntavāda* Include

(a) Multiple Perspectives: *Anekāntavāda* asserts that reality is multi-dimensional, and different observers can have varied viewpoints about the same object or situation. Each viewpoint represents a valid aspect of the truth.

(b) Non-Absolutism: This doctrine opposes dogmatic and rigid positions, advocating instead for a willingness to consider and respect diverse viewpoints. It discourages making absolute statements that ignore the complexities of reality.

(c) Limited Understanding: *Anekāntavāda* acknowledges the limitations of human perception, language, and cognition in grasping the entirety of reality. It reminds us that our understanding is partial and subject to context.

(d) Tolerance and Harmony: By promoting understanding and respect for different perspectives, *Anekāntavāda* fosters tolerance, peaceful coexistence, and harmonious interactions among individuals with differing viewpoints.

(e) Synthesis of Opposites: *Anekāntavāda* recognizes that seemingly contradictory viewpoints can coexist in a complementary manner, leading to a more comprehensive understanding of truth.

(f) Humility and Open-Mindedness: This principle encourages humility in discussions and a willingness to learn from others. It discourages arrogance and absolutism in asserting one's viewpoint as the only truth.

Anekāntavāda is not a relativistic philosophy that denies the existence of objective truth. Instead, it offers a way to approach truth more humbly, recognizing that our perspectives are limited and that a complete understanding of reality requires the consideration of multiple viewpoints. This principle has profound implications in various aspects of Jain philosophy, ethics, and social interactions. It guides Jains in their pursuit of knowledge, empathy, and peaceful coexistence with others.

5. Bondage of Soul and Liberation

Generally speaking 'bondage' means the liability of the individual to birth and all consequent sufferings. The soul is inherently perfect. It has infinite potentiality within. The soul can attain infinite knowledge, infinite faith, infinite power and infinite bliss; but to do this it has to remove from itself all the obstacles that stand in the way. These obstacles, that is the blind cravings and passions that seek worldly satisfaction, are generated by the *karmas*. The soul is limited by the material body with which it has identified itself and became bondage in it. The passions which cause bondage are anger (*rāga*), pride (*māna*), deceitful manipulation or illusion (*māyā*) and greed (*lobha*). These are called *kaṣ*āyas i.e. sticky substance, because the presence of these in the soul makes matter particles stick to it. "The state of union of the soul (*jīva*) with matter is *bandha* or bondage."[20] Thus eight kinds of *karma* are produced: (a) *Jñānāvaraṇīya karma* (knowledge-obscuring *karma*) – it obscures the innate knowledge of the soul; (b) *Darśanāvaṇīya karma* (perception-obscuring *karma*) – it obstructs proper perception; (c) *Vedaniya karma* that causes the feelings of pleasure and pain; (d) *Mohanīya karma* (deluding *karma*) that obstructs right belief and right conduct; (e) *Āyu karma* – it is 'life span determining *karma*' that determines the length of life of an individual in a particular body; (f) *Nāma karma* that determines the kind of body which the soul will form, it decides the state of existence – whether one is born in heavenly, human, animal or infernal abode; (g) *Gotra karma* (status-determining *karma*) that is responsible to determine caste, family and social status; and (h) *Antarāyana karma* that obstructs the infinite power of the soul.[21]

According to *Tattvārtha Sūtra 8:1,* "Wrong perception, absence of restraints, indolence, defilement and undue exercise of the faculties are the causes of bondage." In *Tattvārtha Sūtra 8:2-3,* it says, "The soul assimilates the lifeless particles suitable for *karma* by indulging in defilement and that constitutes the bondage."[22]

The bound souls can be divided into four groups according to the state of existence: *devata* (gods or demons), *nara* (human being), *naraki* (hell beings), and *tiryanca* (lower animals and plants).[23]

The following image – *Svastika* shows the position of liberated souls, the three paths for liberation (Right faith, Right knowledge and Right conduct) and the position of the

[20] P. S. Daniel, "The Jaina Religious Tradition," 181.

[21] *Tattvartha Sutra 8:5* translation with commentary by Manu Doshi, 147-150.

[22] *Tattvārtha Sūtra* translation with commentary by Manu Doshi, 144, 146.

[23] P. S. Daniel, "The Jaina Religious Tradition," 180.

four different types of bound souls – *devata, nara, nāraki and tiryanca.*

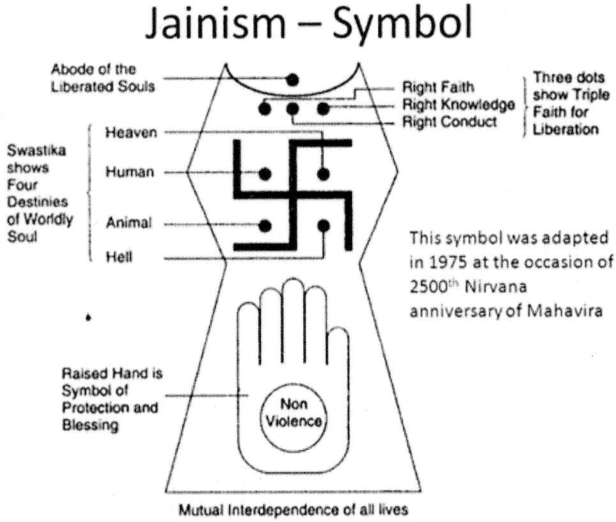

The ultimate goal of life, according to Jaina thought, is to free oneself from *karma.* This is achieved by arresting the influx of fresh *karma,* known as *saṃvara,* and annihilating accumulated *karma,* known as *nirjarā.* Upon accomplishing this, the soul attains *mokṣa* or *nirvāṇa.* According to *Tattvārtha Sūtra,* "Total destruction of all the *karmas* is liberation."[24] It is important to note that according to Jaina philosophy only human being can attain *mokṣa.* At liberation, "the soul rises till the top of the universe" *(Tattvārtha Sutra 10:5*).

5.1. The Threefold Path to Liberation

Three ways are prescribed in Jainism for liberation of soul (*jīva*): Right faith, Right knowledge and Right Conduct. These are called "three jewels" (*tri ratnas*).

---

[24] *Tattvārtha Sūtra 10:3* translation with commentary by Manu Doshi,

5.1.1. Right Faith *(Samyag darśana)*: There is a contention in regards to the exact meaning and connotation of 'right faith'. In general, it seems to mean that having a pro-attitude, a sense of respect and regard towards Jaina principle and what Jaina Tirthankaras have said and advised.[25]

Right faith has the following eight essentials: (a) absence of doubt about scriptures (*niśśankitā*); (b) absence of desire for worldly pleasures (*niḥkānkshitā*); (c) absence of doubt about attainment of spiritual path (*nirvichikitsā)*; (d) a clear and unconfusing vision about the ideal (*amūḍhadṛṣti*); (e) augmentation of spiritual qualities (*upabṛhana*); (f) re-establishing deviations from truth (*sthirikarana*); (g) sense of affection towards the followers of the right path (*vātsalya*); and (h) preaching the importance of truth (*prabhāvanā*).[26]

In essence, Right faith (*samyag-darśana*) serves as the foundation for spiritual progress in Jainism, guiding the soul toward liberation. It is not merely intellectual acceptance but an inner transformation marked by trust, clarity, and unwavering commitment to the Jain path. By cultivating these eight essentials, an individual nurtures a disposition that aligns with truth, non-attachment, and compassion, thereby paving the way for ethical conduct and true knowledge. Ultimately, right faith is the first step in overcoming delusion (*mithyātva*) and progressing toward spiritual purification and self-realization.

5.1.2. Right Knowledge (*Samyag Jñāna*): Right knowledge is the knowledge of the nature of things in the real perspective. It is the proper knowledge about the real nature of *jiva* and *ajiva*, and the distinction between the living and the non-living.[27]

Right knowledge is very much emphasized in Jainism because the root cause of bondage is identified as *ignorance*. Knowledge is said to be the real *tapas* (penance) because it

---

[25] Kedar Nath Tiwari, *Comparative Religion*, (Delhi: Motilal Banarsidass, 1992), 81.

[26] Kedar Nath Tiwari, *Comparative Religion*, 81-82.

[27] Kedar Nath Tiwari, *Comparative Religion*, 82.

burns the *karmas* to ashes. By knowledge Jainism does not mean a mere intellectual or scriptural or academic knowledge; it rather connotes inner realization. Right knowledge helps in controlling the mind and purifying the self; this is possible only by the self-realised knowledge. The wise declares knowledge to be nectar, a glory which does not depend on others. Thus, true knowledge that liberates soul is not learnt from others but it is self-knowledge and self-attained.[28]

Therefore, Right knowledge includes an accurate and comprehensive knowledge of the truth as revealed in Jaina scriptures and teachings. It requires a clear and undistorted understanding of reality. It must be aligned with right faith, ensuring that knowledge is not intellectual but spiritually transformative.

5.1.3. Right Conduct (*Samyag Cāritra*): Right faith and Right knowledge alone are not enough for liberation, Right conduct is also necessary. Right conduct is described as refraining from what is harmful and doing what is beneficial. It includes the following things:-

(a) Taking the Five Great Vows *(Pañca-mahāvrata)*

These vows includes: *Aḥimsā* (non-violence), *Satya* (truthfulness), *Asteya* (Non-stealing), *Brahmacharya* (Celibacy), and *Aparigraha* (Non-possession or non-attachment). This five vows are also emphasized in Hinduism and Buddhism, but Jainism lays much more importance on these principles and practices with much intense and rigour.

Aḥimsā (non-Violence) – This principle represents the highest rule of conduct in Jainism, where all forms of violence are strictly forbidden. Jainas often take extreme measures, such as refraining from lighting lamps or cooking meals after sunset to avoid attracting and harming insects. Similarly, Jaina monks carefully brush the ground with a soft broom as they walk,

---

[28] Kedar Nath Tiwari, *Comparative Religion*, 82.

ensuring that no small insects or worms are unintentionally harmed underfoot.

According to this principle no harm should be done to any living being, *aḥimsa* should be practiced not only in deed, but also in thought and words. Keeping ill will against some body, speaking harsh words to someone should be avoided. Causing injury to someone due to negligence, causing someone to do something against his/her will, etc. should be avoided.[29]

The laypersons or householders have to take the vow in the presence of the Jaina monk to keep the *aḥimsā* doctrine as follows:[30]

> I will desist from the knowing or intentional destruction of all great lives (souls embodied with two or more senses). As long as I live, I will neither kill nor cause others to kill. I shall strive to refrain from all such activities, whether of body, speech, or mind.

In Jainism, *aḥimsā* (non-violence) is the highest virtue, encompassing not only the avoidance of physical harm but also harm caused by thoughts, words, and actions. It advocates for universal compassion and respect for all living beings, forming the foundation of an ethical and peaceful existence.

***Satya* (Truthfulness)** – This is abstinence from falsehood, false statement or telling lie. "Truthfulness is not only speaking what is only true, but speaking what is true as well as good and pleasant."[31] Concern for the welfare of others is so much paramount in Jainism that they go to the extent of saying truth, if it is harmful to others, should be avoided. Exaggeration of fact, finding fault with others, using indecent speech are all to be avoided. The following must be avoided: (a) Denial of the existence of a thing with reference to its position, time

---

[29] Kedar Nath Tiwari, *Comparative Religion*, 83.

[30] Padmanabh S. Jaini, *The Jaina Path of Purification*, 173.

[31] Chaterjee & Datta, *An Introduction to Indian Philosophy*, 101.

and nature; (b) asserting the existence of a non-existent thing with reference to its position, time and nature; (c) representing a thing as something else, (d) reprehensible speech; (e) sinful speech; and (f) unpalatable speech.[32]

In Jaina thought, truthfulness goes beyond merely avoiding lies to encompass speaking words that are truthful, kind, and beneficial, while refraining from speech that harms others. This principle promotes ethical communication, fostering trust, harmony, and the well-being of all beings.

***Asteya* (non-stealing)** – This principle means abstaining from taking anything that does not belong to us or has not been freely given. It also includes: (a) buying a valuable article an unfairly low price, (b) taking items forgotten or left behind by someone, (c) coveting for another's property, (d) taking things with unclear or disputed ownership, (e) purchasing stolen goods, (f) engaging in illegal business activities,[33] (g) employing thieves to obtain things for him/her, (h) using false weights and measures, (i) secretly adulterating commodities, (j) gaining or storing goods without paying the required taxes, etc. All such acts of stealing are said to involve *hiṃśa* (violence), since they reflect the presence of greed. This vow allows the householder to collect water, firewood, and the likes from the public lands. However, for the mendicant, even these activities are forbidden; he may obtain such necessities, such as water, firewood, etc., only if they are gathered by others and presented to him as gift.[34]

In Jainism, *Asteya* emphasizes living with integrity and respect for the rights and possessions of others, fostering a life of honesty and self-discipline. By practicing non-stealing, individuals cultivate contentment, reduce greed, and contribute to a harmonious and just society.

---

[32] Kedar Nath Tiwari, *Comparative Religion*, 84.

[33] Kedar Nath Tiwari, *Comparative Religion*, 84-85.

[34] Padmanabh S. Jaini, *The Jaina Path of Purification*, 177.

***Brahmacharya* (Celibacy)** – While Hinduism and Buddhism also emphasize celibacy, Jainism takes this principle to a much higher level. It not only entails living a celibate life but also prohibits all forms of unlawful sexual activities. Additionally, it forbids indulging in sexual thoughts and extends to abstinence from excessive desires for any sensory pleasures. Even excessive contemplation of such enjoyment is considered a violation of this vow.

In Jainism, *Brahmacharya* signifies complete control over desires and abstinence from indulgence in physical or mental pleasures. It is a disciplined way of life that fosters spiritual growth by transcending sensual attachments and focusing on inner purity.

***Aparigraha* (Non-attachment) -** *Aparigraha* means non-possessiveness or non-attachment which is a fundamental principle in Jain philosophy. It emphasizes detachment from material possessions and the renunciation of greed. This vow encourages individuals to limit their accumulation of wealth and resources, recognizing that excessive attachment leads to bondage and suffering. It is a general attitude of non-attachment to the world. It encourages detachment not only from material possessions but also from emotional and mental entanglements. This attitude fosters inner peace, self-discipline, and a focus on spiritual growth, helping individuals transcend the temporary and fleeting nature of worldly attachments.

The Jaina scriptures often defined *parigraha* (possession) as the delusion (*mūrcchā*) of possession – having those notions as "this is mine", "I made this" and imagining that one can hold on forever to what he or she now has. Jaina monks must renounce land, houses, silver, gold, livestock, grain, servants, clothing, and all other material possessions. However, for laypersons, a limit is set on the extent to which they may possess such belongings.[35]

---

[35] Padmanabh S. Jaini, *The Jaina Path of Purification*, 177.

Aparigraha extends beyond physical possessions to include freedom from emotional attachments, desires, and dependencies. By practicing non-possessiveness, one fosters contentment, simplicity, and a balanced approach to life, which are essential for spiritual progress. This principle also promotes environmental sustainability and equitable resource distribution, reflecting Jainism's broader commitment to harmony and non-violence in all aspects of existence.

(b) Other Practices

Apart from the above five-vows, Jainas are prescribed to observe several other restraints: (a) practise extreme carefulness (*samiti*) in walking, speaking, receiving alms and other things so as to avoid doing any harm to any life; (b) practise restraint (*gupti*) of thought, speech and bodily movements; (c) practise *dharma* of ten different kinds, such as, forgiveness, humility, straightforwardness, truthfulness, cleanliness, self-restraint, austerity, sacrifice, non-attachment, and celibacy; (d) meditate on the truth concerning *jīva* and *ajīva*; (e) conquer all pains and discomforts that arise from hunger, thirst, heat, cold, and the likes; (f) attain calmness, purity, absolute greedlessness and perfect conduct.[36]

The five great vows of Jainism - *Aḥimsā* (non-violence), *Satya* (truthfulness), *Asteya* (non-stealing), *Brahmacharya* (celibacy), and *Aparigraha* (non-possessiveness or non-attachment) along with other vows - serve as the ethical and spiritual foundation for a life of purity, self-discipline, and compassion. These vows guide individuals toward liberation by minimizing harm, cultivating integrity, and detaching from worldly entanglements. Together, they reflect Jainism's profound commitment to fostering harmony within oneself, with others, and with the environment, ultimately leading to spiritual enlightenment and universal well-being.

[36] Chaterjee & Datta, *An Introduction to Indian Philosophy*, 99-100.

Concluding Remarks

Jain philosophy presents a profound and wholistic framework for understanding reality, knowledge, and the path to spiritual liberation. Its theory of knowledge emphasizes both empirical and transcendental dimensions, guiding seekers from sensory perception to ultimate omniscience. While the system's comprehensive approach to knowledge is admirable, the notion of omniscience, particularly as it pertains to the human condition, remains an ideal that seems virtually unattainable for most individuals. This raises questions about the accessibility and practical application of such an ideal for ordinary practitioners.

Jain metaphysics, rooted in the eternal interplay of the living (*jīva*) and non-living (*ajīva*), provides a dynamic vision of existence. The distinction between *jīva* and *ajīva* creates a clear framework for understanding life and the material world; however, one could critique the rigidity of this dualistic framework, which might not fully account for the interdependence and complexity of reality as understood in more integrated or wholistic worldviews. Furthermore, while the doctrines of *Syādvāda* and *Anekāntavāda* underscore the relativity and multifaceted nature of truth, they also risk becoming excessively abstract, potentially complicating the pursuit of practical wisdom and moral clarity.

Jainism's commitment to intellectual humility and openness to diverse perspectives is valuable, yet its emphasis on strict non-violence (*aḥimsā*) and self-discipline sometimes veers into an asceticism that may be seen as impractical or overly demanding in the context of modern life. The insights into bondage and liberation illuminate the journey of the soul from karmic entanglement to ultimate freedom. However, this concept of liberation can be critiqued for its highly rigorous nature, requiring an exceptional level of commitment and renunciation that may not be feasible for everyone.

Together, these principles reflect Jainism's enduring commitment to non-violence, self-discipline, and spiritual enlightenment, offering timeless wisdom for personal and collective harmony. Nonetheless, while Jainism provides a rich and intricate path to spiritual freedom, its demanding practices and ideals may seem unattainable or unrealistic for many people, limiting its practical appeal in the contemporary world. In this sense, while Jain philosophy offers a profound spiritual vision, its applicability may require re-contextualization in modern life.

Chapter 4

Baudha Philosophy

Buddhist or Baudha philosophy stands as one of the most profound and systematic approaches to understanding the nature of existence, suffering, and the path to liberation. Rooted in the teachings of Siddhartha Gautama, the Buddha, it seeks to unravel the fundamental truths of life and provide a practical framework for spiritual and moral transformation. At its core, Buddhist philosophy emphasizes introspection, ethical conduct, and the cultivation of wisdom as means to transcend the cycles of suffering and rebirth.

Central to this philosophy are the *Four Noble Truths*, which encapsulate the essence of human suffering, its origin, cessation, and the path leading to its end. These truths provide a diagnostic and prescriptive approach to life, offering insights into the human condition and a pathway to ultimate freedom. The principle of *Dependent Origination* further deepens this understanding, revealing the interdependent nature of all phenomena and the cyclical patterns that perpetuate existence and suffering.

Equally significant are the doctrines of momentariness and the denial of a permanent soul (anattā). The doctrine of momentariness challenges conventional notions of permanence, asserting that all phenomena are transient and in constant flux.

Meanwhile, the concept of no-soul dismantles the idea of a fixed, unchanging self, encouraging a realization of the interconnected and impermanent nature of existence.

Together, these philosophical insights form the foundation of Buddhist thought, offering a coherent and transformative vision of reality. This exploration aims to delve into these core doctrines, highlighting their relevance and significance in the broader context of Buddhist teachings and their enduring appeal in the quest for enlightenment.

1. Four Noble Truths

Gautama Buddha was not a metaphysician, but primarily an ethical teacher and reformer. In his teaching, there is no place for metaphysics as for him it is no cure for the miseries of life. Instead of discussing metaphysical problems as Hindu schools of philosophy often do, Buddha tried enlighten persons on the most important questions of suffering, its origin, its cessation and the paths leading to its cessation, because for Buddha the most urgent problem is to end human misery. The answers given by Buddha to these four questions have come to be known as the four noble truths or the four True Realities (*catvari arya-satyani* or *arya-sacca*).

In his first Sermon, Gautama Buddha narrated the four noble truths. They are: (a) *dukkha*, 'the painful', encompassing the various forms of pain, gross or subtle, physical or mental, that we are all subject to, along with painful things that engender these; (b) the origination (*samudaya*, i.e. cause) of *dukkha*, namely ignorance that begets craving (*tanhā* or *trsnā*); (c) the cessation (*nirodha*) of *dukkha* by the cessation of craving (this cessation is equivalent to *Nirvāna*); and (d) the path (*magga* or *mārga*) that leads to this cessation. The first sermon says that the first of the four is 'to be fully understood,' the second is 'to be abandoned,' the third is 'to be personally experienced,' the fourth is 'to be developed or cultivated.'[1]

[1] Peter Harvey, *An Introduction to Buddhism: Teachings, History and Practices, Second Edition*, (Cambridge: Cambridge University Press, 2013), 52.

1.1. The First Noble Truth: The Reality of Suffering

Buddha, in his first sermon, said:

> Now this, monks, for the spiritually ennobled, is the painful (*dukkha*) true reality (*ariya-sacca*): birth is painful, ageing is painful, illness is painful, death is painful; sorrow, lamentation, (physical) pain, unhappiness and distress are painful; union with what is disliked is painful; separation from what is liked is painful; not to get what one wants is painful; in brief, the five bundles of grasping-fuel are painful.[2]

So, all kinds of suffering both physical and mental are recognized as the truth. The five 'bundles of grasping-fuel' (*upādānakkhandha, or upādāna-skandha-Sanskrit*) are the five factors which go to make up a 'person.' Buddhism holds, then, that none of the phenomena which make up personality is free from some kind of painfulness. (a) *Rūpa* '(material) form'. This refers to the material aspect of existence. It is said to be comprised of four basic elements or forces, such as, solidity (literally, earth), cohesion (water), heat (fire) and motion (wind). From the interaction of these, the body of flesh, blood, bones, etc. is composed. (b) *Vedanā* or 'feeling'. This is the 'taste' of any experience: pleasant, painful (*dukkha*) or neutral. It includes both sensations arising from the body and mental feelings of happiness, unhappiness or indifference. (c) *Saññā* (*saṃjñā*), which processes sensory and mental objects. It is 'perception', 'cognition', 'mental labelling', recognition and interpretation – including misinterpretation – of objects. (d) The *saṃskāra*, or 'constructing activities', 'volitional activities', 'mental formations' and 'karmic activities'. These comprise a number of processes which initiate action or direct, mould and give shape to character. (e) *Viññāna* or *vijñāna*, 'discriminative consciousness.' This includes both the basic awareness of a

[2] Peter Harvey, *An Introduction to Buddhism*, 52.

sensory or mental object, and the discrimination of its aspects or parts.[3]

The First Noble Truth highlights the inescapable nature of suffering in human existence. By recognizing *dukkha* in all its forms - physical, mental, and existential - Buddhism encourages individuals to cultivate awareness of suffering as the first step toward liberation. Understanding the five aggregates (*pañcakkhandha*) as impermanent and conditioned helps one detach from clinging and misidentification with the self. This insight lays the foundation for the deeper exploration of the causes of suffering and the path toward its cessation, as outlined in the remaining Noble Truths.

1.2. The Second Noble Truth: The Cause of Suffering

In his first sermon, Buddha underlines the cause of suffering:

> Now this, monks, for the spiritually ennobled, is the originating-of-the-painful (*dukkha-samudaya*) true reality. It is this craving (*tanhā*), which leads to renewed being, accompanied by relishing and attachment, seeking enjoyment nowhere, now there; that is, craving for sense-pleasures, craving for being, craving for non-existence.[4]

According to Buddha, the existence of everything depends on certain conditions. Therefore, there must be something from which our misery originates. This understanding leads to what is called the twelve chains of causation or 'Dependent Origination' (this will be explained in details later). Suffering arises because of birth, and birth arises from other factors, ultimately leading to ignorance as the root cause of existence. Due to ignorance, humans experience craving (*tanhā*). This term literally means 'thirst' and refers to clinging desires that constantly seek gratification. It contains an element of psychological compulsion - a restless drive always searching for

[3] Peter Harvey, *An Introduction to Buddhism*, 56.

[4] Peter Harvey, *An Introduction to Buddhism*, 62-63.

new objects to focus on: "I want, I want more, I want different." The more things a person craves, the greater the opportunities for frustration (*dukkha*). Craving also leads to pain as it causes quarrels, strife, and conflict between individuals and groups. Moreover, it motivates people to perform actions that result in karmic consequences, shaping further rebirths.

1.3. The Third Noble Truth: The Cessation of Suffering

The third True Reality is described in the first sermon as follows:

> Now this, monks, for the spiritually ennobled, is the ceasing-of-the-painful true reality. It is the remainderless fading away and cessation of that same craving, the giving up and relinquishing of it, freedom from it, non-reliance on it.[5]

The end of craving - the thirst for 'the next thing' - is achieved by overcoming ignorance. When craving and its related causes come to an end, *dukkha* ceases. This cessation is equivalent to *Nirvāna* (Pali: *Nibbāna*), the ultimate goal of Buddhism. *Nirvāna* is attained only through total non-attachment and letting go. The term *Nirvāna* literally means 'extinction' or 'quenching,' akin to the extinguishing of a fire. In his first sermon, the Buddha explained the 'fires' extinguished by *Nirvāna*. He taught that everything, both internal and external to a person, is 'burning' with the 'fires' of attachment, hatred, and delusion, as well as with the fires of birth, aging, and death. These 'fires' represent both the causes of *dukkha* and *dukkha* itself.

Nirvāna in life is defined as the destruction of these three (attachment, hatred, and delusion) 'fires' or defilements. When someone who has destroyed these defilements dies, they are no longer subject to rebirth and are thus completely free from the remaining 'fires' of birth, aging, and death, having attained final *Nirvāna*.

[5] Peter Harvey, *An Introduction to Buddhism*, 73.

1.4. The Forth Noble Truth: The Path of Cessation of Suffering

In the first sermon, the Buddha has this to say on the Path:[6]

> Monks, these two extremes should not be followed … What two? That which is this pursuit of sensual happiness in sensual pleasures, which is low, vulgar, the way of the ordinary person, ignoble, not connected to the goal; and that which is this pursuit of self-mortification, which is painful, ignoble, not connected to the goal. Monks, without veering towards either of these two extremes, the Tathāgata has awakened to the middle way (*majjhimā patipadā* or *madhyama pratipad*), which gives rise to vision, which gives rise to knowledge, which leads to peace, to higher knowledge, to full awakening, to *Nirvāna*.
>
> And what, monks, is that middle way. . .? It is just this noble eight-factored (eight-fold) path. Now this, monks, for the spiritually ennobled, is the true reality which is the way leading to the cessation of the painful. It is this noble eight-factored path, that is to say, right view, right resolve, right speech, right action (conduct), right livelihood, right effort, right mindfulness, right mental unification (concentration).

The Noble Eight-fold Path is *a middle way* that avoids a life of pursuing either sense-pleasures or harsh asceticism, and it leads to the cessation of *dukkha*.

We will explain these eight-fold paths as follows:[7]

1.4.1. Right View (*Sammā-Diṭṭhi* or *Samyag-Ḍṛṣti*)

This primarily refers to a clear understanding of the four noble truths taught by Buddha. It also include correct understanding

---

[6] Peter Harvey, *An Introduction to Buddhism*, 81.

[7] Kedar Nath Tiwari, *Comparative Religion*, (Delhi: Motilal Banarsidass, 1992), 64-65; Cf. Peter Harvey, *An Introduction to Buddhism*, 83-84.

of other doctrines taught by Buddha like the principle of *Karma* and rebirth, theories of momentariness and non-soul.

1.4.2. Right Resolve or Thought (*Sammā-Sankappa* or *Samyak-Samkalpa*)

It includes possessing a pure mind free from lust, ill-will, sense-pleasure; it also requires individual to have a mind of peaceful renunciation, non-cruelty, compassion. One should be willing to give up anything that impedes his or her onward march, focusing on higher and purer things.

1.4.3. Right Speech (*Sammā-Vācā* or *Samyag-Vācā*)

This involves abstaining from false speech, divisive speech, harsh speech and frivolous (silly and foolish) speech and idle gossip. Our speech should be free from ill-will, selfish interests, dogmatic assertions.

1.4.4. Right Action or Conduct (*Sammā-Kammanta* or *Samyak-Karmanta*)

This involvers abstaining from assault on living beings, taking what is not given and wrong conduct in regard to sensual pleasures. It consists in observing the following five precepts (*panchsheel*):

- Not to kill but practice harmlessness and compassion to all
- To practice charity and generosity
- Not to commit sexual misconduct, but to practice chastity and self-control
- Not to indulge in false speech, but to practice sincerity and honesty
- Not to involve in taking intoxicating drinks or drugs, but to practice and mindfulness.

Primarily, the first three are considered the core of Right action.

1.4.5. Right Livelihood (*Sammā-Ājīva* or *Samyag-Ājīva*)

It involves making one's living in such a way as to avoid causing suffering to others (human or animal). It advocates for a just, honestly earned and undeceitful means of livelihood. It prescribes avoiding trade in weapons, living beings, meat, alcoholic drink, or poison. It refers basically to maintaining life by honest means.

1.4.6. Right Effort (*Sammā-Vāyāma* or *Samyag-Vyāyāma*)

This consists in making sincere efforts to give up bad habits and cultivate the good ones. The following are involved: (a) the effort to prevent the arising of evil which has not yet arisen; (b) the effort to eradicate evil that has already accumulated; (c) the effort to cultivate good which has not yet arisen; (d) the effort to practice the good which is already present. It is constant endeavour to maintain moral progress by banishing evil thoughts and entertaining good ones.

1.4.7. Right Mindfulness (*Sammā-Sati* or *Samyak-Smrti*)

It involves constant vigil over one's body, feelings and mind. It involves practising the four applications of mindfulness – alert, mindful observation of the qualities and changing nature of : a) body (including breathing); b) feeling; c) states of mind; d) *dhammas*: basic patterns in the flow of experience, such as: the five *khandhas* (form, perceptions, conception, volition and consciousness); the five hindrances (*nīvaraṇa*) that includes sensual desire, ill will, sloth, restlessness and worry, and skeptical doubt; the four noble truths, and the seven factors of awakening (mindfulness, investigation, energy, rapture, tranquility, concentration, equanimity).

1.4.8. Right Concentration/Mental Unification (*Sammā-Samādhi* or *Samyak-Samādhi*)

This is a states of calm, peace and mental clarity arising from intently focusing the mind on one or other meditation object. These are concentrated states, rather than the act of concentrating, which pertains more to right effort. They are states in which the mind's energies have been unified, in the form of the lucid meditative trances, culminates in the attainment of perfect equanimity and indifference or freedom from attachment. With this one reaches the goal of cessation of all suffering and attains *nirvāna*, a state of perfection.

The Eightfold Path stands as the cornerstone of Buddhist practice, offering a comprehensive framework for ethical living, mental cultivation, and the development of wisdom. It is not merely a philosophical concept but a practical guide that addresses the complexities of human existence and provides a roadmap for liberation from suffering (*dukkha*). By integrating the principles of *Right View, Right resolve, Right Speech, Right Action, Right Livelihood, Right Effort, Right Mindfulness, and Right Concentration* into daily life, one can achieve a harmonious balance between moral conduct, mental discipline, and intellectual insight. Each path is interconnected, reinforcing the other and creating a holistic approach to personal transformation and spiritual growth.

Ultimately, the Eightfold Path is not about rigid adherence to rules but about cultivating a way of life that leads to inner peace, clarity, and liberation. It is a journey of self-discovery and enlightenment, guiding practitioners toward the ultimate goal of *Nirvāna* - the cessation of suffering and the realization of profound freedom. In embracing the Eightfold Path, one embarks on a journey of wisdom, compassion, and self-mastery, contributing not only to personal well-being but also to the well-being of all beings. It is a timeless and universal teaching that continues to inspire and guide individuals on their spiritual quests.

2. Dependent Origination (*Pratītyasamutpāda*)

Dependent Origination, known as *Paticca Samuppada* or *Pratītyasamutpāda*, is a fundamental concept in Buddhist philosophy. It explains the interconnectedness of all phenomena and provides insights into the nature of suffering and the path to liberation. Dependent Origination describes the causal relationships that give rise to the cycle of birth, suffering, and rebirth (*saṃsāra*) and offers a framework for understanding how to break free from this cycle. Dependent Origination is typically presented as a chain of twelve interdependent links or factors. These links illustrate how suffering arises due to ignorance and craving, and how liberation can be attained through the cessation of these causal factors. The twelve links are divided into three groups: the past, the present, and the future.[8]

(a) *Ajñāna* (Ignorance) - The cycle begins with ignorance, the lack of understanding of the true nature of reality, the impermanence of phenomena, and the law of cause and effect. Ignorance leads to distorted perceptions and views.

(b) *Samskāra* (Formation) - Ignorance leads to the formation of mental and physical activities or volitional formations. These are the intentions, thoughts, and actions that arise based on ignorance. *Samskāra* are the forces generated by the past karmas.

(c) *Vijñāna* (Consciousness) – It is awareness or perception of sensory experiences and mental objects.

(d) *Nāma-rupa* (*Name and form*) - Consciousness gives rise to name and form, which represent the mental and physical aspects of existence. Name refers to mental factors, while form refers to the physical body.

(e) *Sadāyatana* (Six sense organs) - eye, ear, nose, tongue, body, and mind. Mind is considered in Buddhism as one of the sense organs. These are the faculties through which we perceive the world.

(f) *Sparsha* (Contact) - that is, the interaction between the six sense bases and external objects leads to contact. Contact is the meeting of sense organs, sensory objects, and consciousness, resulting in sensory experience.

[8] Cf. Kedar Nath Tiwari, *Comparative Religion*, 55-56.

(g) *Vedanā* (Feeling) – feeling or sensation derived from actual sense-enjoyment.

(h) *Tṛṣnā* (*Craving*) - thirst for enjoyment or craving for enjoyment.

(i) *Upādāna* (Clinging) – Craving for sense enjoyment leads to clinging on to sensory enjoyment, where one clings to sensory experiences, desires, and views. Grasping is the deepening of attachment.

(j) *Bhava* (Becoming or will to be born) - Grasping leads to becoming, which refers to the emergence of a self-identity, the sense of "I" and "mine," and the creation of karmic tendencies that influence future existences.

(k) *Jati* (Birth) - Becoming leads to birth, the entry into a new existence, whether it is a physical birth or a birth in a mental realm.

(l) *Jaramarana* – Birth leads to suffering in the form of old age and death. Birth inevitably leads to aging, decay, and death, completing the cycle of suffering. As long as birth, there will be suffering.

The purpose of understanding Dependent Origination is to recognize the causes of suffering and break the cycle of rebirth by addressing the root causes of ignorance, craving, and attachment. By eliminating ignorance and realizing the impermanent and interconnected nature of all phenomena, one can attain *Nirvāṇa* (*Nibbāna* in Pali), the state of complete liberation from suffering.

3. Doctrine of Momentariness (*Kṣaṇikavāda*)

According to the teachings of Buddha, every aspect of the phenomenal world is characterized by impermanence. Subsequently, Buddhist philosophers expanded upon this concept, giving rise to the doctrine of momentariness (*kṣaṇikavāda*). Buddhist logicians, led by Dharmakirti who played a pivotal role in Buddhist logic, assert that everything within the phenomenal realm undergoes a constant state of change - coming into existence in one moment and ceasing to exist in the next. Why does this occur? Dharmakirti contends that for something to genuinely qualify as an existent entity, it must possess causal efficacy (*artha-kriyā kāritva*), meaning that it has the capacity to bring about an effect. Put more succinctly, 'to be' or 'to exist' implies 'to act' or 'to accomplish.' However, as elucidated in the subsequent paragraph, a prerequisite for possessing causal efficacy is momentariness. Hence, it logically ensues that, in accordance with the Buddhist viewpoint, anything that exists and possesses causal efficacy must inherently possess momentariness as well.[9]

If an object possesses the ability to cause effects and simultaneously remains non-momentary, implying that it is enduring, it would entail having contradictory attributes. However, the presence of contradictory qualities within an object contradicts the very identity of that object. Consequently, in order to maintain logical coherence, we must acknowledge that for an entity to exert causal influence, it must be transient. For instance, consider a non-momentary entity like a seed that exhibits causal efficacy by giving rise to another entity, such as a sprout. Let's assume that at one moment (moment one), the seed is not the cause of the sprout, but at another moment (moment two), it becomes the cause of the sprout. Given that the seed at *moment two* serves as the originator of the sprout, it logically implies that the seed at *moment one* must differ from the seed at *moment two* (to maintain that they are identical would be too absurd). Consequently, we are compelled to accept that in order for something to possess causal efficacy, it must exist momentarily.[10]

The doctrine of momentariness (*kṣaṇikavāda*) presents a radical yet rigorous philosophical stance on the nature of existence, emphasizing the transient and ever-changing nature

---

[9] Rita Gupta, "The Buddhist Doctrine of Momentariness and Its Presuppositions: Dharmakīrti's Argument in Hetubindu", *Journal of Indian Philosophy*, Vol. 8, No. 1, March 1980), 47.

[10] Rita Gupta, "The Buddhist Doctrine of Momentariness and Its Presuppositions: Dharmakīrti's argument in Hetubindu", 48.

of reality. By establishing causal efficacy as the defining criterion of existence, Buddhist logicians argue that nothing persists beyond a single moment. This insight has profound implications not only for Buddhist metaphysics but also for epistemology and the understanding of selfhood, reinforcing the central Buddhist idea that clinging to permanence is an illusion that leads to suffering.

4. The Doctrine of Not-Soul (*Anatta*)

The doctrine of not-soul, known as '*anatta*' in Pali or '*anātman*' in Sanskrit, is a direct consequence of the doctrine of momentariness (*kshanikavada*). This doctrine holds a central place within Buddhist philosophy, challenging the concept of a permanent, unchanging, and independent self or soul (*ātman*). It serves as a foundational principle in Buddhist thought, offering essential insights into the nature of existence, suffering, and the path to liberation.

"Not-soul" does not mean that Buddhists are annihilationist, who denied the existence of soul and thereby reject rebirth and afterlife. "Buddhism does not deny a self in the empirical sense but in ultimate reality. The Buddhist teaching of *anattā* does not proclaim the absence of individuality or self; it only says there are no permanent and individuality and unchanged self."[11] This doctrine proclaims that everything which comes into being vanishes away in the same moment (*sarvaṃ anityaṃ, sarvaṃ kṣaṇikam*).

According to this doctrine, what is commonly referred to as the 'soul' or 'self' is not an enduring and unalterable reality, but rather a continuous sequence of changing movements of consciousness. Analogous to a flame that burns throughout the night or a river that flows as a single body of water, the soul undergoes change in every moment while maintaining an unchanging and enduring essence. Just as the river or the flame is not identical in consecutive moments, a consistent and

[11] Nguyen Quy Hoang, "The Doctrine of Not-self (*anattā*) in Early Buddhism," in *International Review of Social Research,* Vol. 9, No. 1, 2019, 20.

unbroken continuity is preserved. This continuity is akin to how the present moment gives rise to the next, ensuring an unbroken flow.

We may ask: If there is no permanent soul (*ātman*), what then transmigrates from one body to another? A Buddhist response would emphasize that it is not a fixed, unchanging self that undergoes rebirth, but rather a continuous flow of consciousness. Upon a person's death, the final conscious moment (*citta*) of their current life gives rise to the initial conscious moment of their next life, maintaining an unbroken continuity in the cycle of existence (*saṃsāra*). This process, often likened to the flame of a lamp lighting another without the original flame being transferred, ensures the seamless transition of consciousness from one existence to another. While no static entity transmigrates, the causal chain of mental and karmic impressions (*saṃskāra*) carries forward, sustaining the thread of life across successive moments.

5. *Karma-Saṃsāra* and *Nirvana*

The term *saṃsāra* literally means 'continuing on' or 'wandering on,' signifying the repetitive cycle of birth, aging, death, and rebirth. This concept underscores the transient and impermanent nature of existence, marked by a constant process of change.

Both Buddhism and Hinduism share the idea of rebirth, yet they differ significantly in their interpretations. In Hinduism, rebirth involves the transmigration of a 'permanent' soul - a conscious entity that leaves one body upon death and assumes another. This soul is seen as eternal and unchanging, navigating through different bodies in its journey. In contrast, Buddhism rejects the notion of a permanent soul (*ātman*) and views rebirth not as the migration of a conscious entity but as the recurring process of existence. There is continuity between lives, but no fixed or permanent self transmigrates. Instead, rebirth is understood as the re-arising of conditioned phenomena, propelled by past actions (*karma*).

Karma plays a central role in this cycle. In Buddhism, *karma* refers to the natural law of cause and effect, where every intentional action - whether through thought, speech, or deed - produces corresponding consequences. This law governs not only the outcomes within a single lifetime but also the conditions of rebirth. Actions rooted in wholesome intentions lead to positive outcomes, while unwholesome actions result in suffering. Buddhism teaches that the process of *karma* is cumulative, shaped by experiences from both previous lives and the present one. As such, who or what we become in the next life is a direct consequence of our actions and intentions in this life, just as our current existence reflects past actions. Importantly, the individual in the next life is not the same as in previous lives, yet there is a continuity influenced by *karma*.

In essence, *karma* is the thread that weaves through all of existence, reflecting the moral essence of human life. The Buddhist emphasis on ethical conduct, mindfulness, and wisdom highlights the potential to shape one's future through intentional action, ultimately breaking free from *saṃsāra* and attaining liberation, *Nirvāṇa*.

Nirvāṇa is the ultimate goal in Buddhism, signifying liberation from the cycle of *saṃsāra* and the cessation of suffering. It is achieved by extinguishing the three poisons - greed (*lobha*), hatred (*dosa*), delusion (*moha*) and uprooting ignorance and craving, which are the causes of *karma* and rebirth. *Nirvāṇa* is described as the cessation of all conditioned phenomena and the realization of ultimate truth. It is not a place but a state of being, free from attachment, aversion, and ignorance - a state of perfect peace and unconditioned bliss.

It is to be noted here that in Baudha philosophy, *Karma-Saṃsāra* doctrine is not the most important one. Peter Harvey maintains,

> While teachings on karma and rebirth are an important part of Buddhist belief, they are not the most crucial, nor the most specifically Buddhist. They act, though, as the lead-up to, and motivator for,

> the most important teachings, those on the four True Realities for the Spiritually Ennobled. When teaching laypersons, the Buddha frequently began with a 'step-by-step discourse': that is, (i) talk on giving, talk on moral virtue, talk on the heaven worlds; (ii) he made known the danger, the inferior nature of and tendency to defilement in sense pleasures, and the advantage of renouncing them … When the Blessed One knew that the householder Upāli's mind was ready, open, without hindrances, inspired and confident, then he expounded to him the elevated *Dhamma*-teaching of the *Buddhas*: the painful, its origin, its cessation, the path.[12]

The Buddhist understanding of *saṃsāra*, *karma*, and *nirvāṇa* presents a profound view of existence that emphasizes impermanence, ethical responsibility, and the possibility of liberation. While the doctrine of *karma* and rebirth serves as a framework for understanding continuity across lifetimes, it is ultimately a means to a higher goal - the realization of the Four Noble Truths and the path to *Nirvāṇa*. Unlike Hinduism, which upholds the notion of an eternal self, Buddhism maintains that liberation is attained not through the journey of an unchanging soul, but through the cessation of suffering and the dissolution of conditioned existence. In this sense, the teachings on *saṃsāra* and *karma* are not ends in themselves but stepping stones toward the ultimate awakening that transcends the cycle of birth and rebirth.

Concluding Remarks

Buddhist philosophy offers a profound and comprehensive framework for understanding the nature of suffering, its causes, and the path to liberation. The *Four Noble Truths* provide the foundation for recognizing the inevitability of suffering, its origins in craving and attachment, and the possibility of its

[12] Peter Harvey, *An Introduction to Buddhism*, 48.

cessation through the cessation of craving. While this framework is deeply insightful, one could argue that the emphasis on detachment and the cessation of desire can lead to an overly ascetic view of human existence, potentially neglecting the value of positive desires and attachments that can contribute to meaningful, compassionate lives.

The doctrine of *Dependent Origination* further elucidates the interconnectedness of all phenomena, demonstrating that all conditions arise in dependence on other factors, emphasizing the impermanence and interdependent nature of existence. While this view highlights the fluid and dynamic nature of reality, it may also lead to an overly complex and abstract understanding of causality, making it difficult for some practitioners to apply in everyday life. The *theory of momentariness* reinforces the transient nature of all things, reinforcing the idea that nothing in the universe is fixed or permanent. While this understanding promotes impermanence as a key insight into human suffering, it may also cause existential uncertainty, as it challenges the possibility of finding any lasting meaning in the world.

The *doctrine of not-soul* challenges the notion of a permanent, unchanging self, advocating instead for the understanding of a dynamic, ever-changing process of becoming. This radical view on the self is an important aspect of Buddhist philosophy, yet it raises questions about personal identity and continuity. If the self is merely a collection of changing phenomena, the notion of personal responsibility and moral accountability might be complicated. The interplay of *Karma*, *Saṃsāra*, and *Nirvāṇa* underscores the cyclical nature of existence, where ethical actions and wisdom can break the cycle of rebirth, leading to the ultimate liberation. While the promise of liberation from suffering is compelling, the complexity of *karma* and the prolonged path to *Nirvāṇa* may seem overwhelming or inaccessible for many.

Together, these teachings encourage mindfulness, ethical conduct, and the cultivation of wisdom to transcend suffering and attain *Nirvāṇa*, the state of peace and liberation from the cycle of existence. However, while Buddhist philosophy offers a profound path to liberation, its emphasis on renunciation and detachment might not resonate with those who seek a more integrated approach to life's joys and struggles. The ideal of *Nirvāṇa*, while deeply aspirational, may seem elusive or unattainable to many, raising concerns about its practical applicability in the face of the challenges of contemporary existence. In this sense, Buddhist philosophy provides invaluable insights into the nature of suffering, but its path to liberation can be critiqued as overly rigorous and demanding for ordinary individuals navigating the complexities of modern life.

Chapter 5

Nyāya School of Philosophy

The Nyāya School of philosophy, *Nyāya Darśana*, is one of the six orthodox systems (*ṣaḍ-darśanas*) of Indian philosophy. It was founded by Gautama (Gotama) who is also known as Akṣapāda. Accordingly Nyāya School of philosophy is also known as 'Akṣapāda System.' It is primarily a system of logic and epistemology, focusing on the means of acquiring valid knowledge (*pramāṇa*) and its application to philosophical and practical problems. Because of its emphasis on critical thinking, Nyāya is also called *Tarkashāstra* or the science of reasoning; *Pramānashāstra* or the science of logic and epistemology; *Hetuvidyā* or the science of causes; *Vādavidyā* or the science of debate; and *Ānvīksikī* or the science of critical study.[1] In fact, the term *Nyāya* can be translated as 'to rule,' 'logic,' or 'method,' reflecting the system's emphasis on reasoned argumentation and critical inquiry.

The foundational text of the Nyāya School is the *Nyāya Sūtras* by Gautama (Akṣapāda). This work systematically outlines the principles of logic, epistemology, and metaphysics. Subsequent commentators, such as Vātsyāyana, Udayana, and

[1] Chandradhar Sharma, *Indian Philosophy: A Critical Survey*, (New York City: Barnes & Noble, Inc. 1962), 179.

Gaṅgeśa, enriched the tradition with their interpretations and expansions.

1. Epistemology: The Sources of Knowledge (*Pramāṇas*)

The Nyāya school recognizes four *pramāṇas* as valid means of knowledge: (a) Perception (*Pratyakṣa*): direct sensory experience, considered the primary source of knowledge; (b) Inference (*Anumāna*): knowledge derived through logical reasoning; (c) Comparison (*Upamāna*): knowledge gained by analogy or comparison ; and (d) Verbal Testimony *(Śabda):* knowledge derived from trustworthy sources, including scriptures and reliable authorities.

We will explain these *four sources* of valid knowledge briefly.

1.1. Perception (*Pratyakṣa*)

The founder of this school Gautama (or Gotama) defines Perception (*Pratyakṣa*) as 'non-erroneous cognition which is produced by the intercourse of the sense-organs with the objects, which is true or unerring. According to Nyāyaikas (followers of Nyāya), there are several ways of classifying Perception. We can divide Perception into two – *laukika* or ordinary perception and *alaukika* or extraordinary Perception. We have *laukika* when senses come in contact with object. *Alaukika* happens when the presence of object is conveyed through an unusual medium. Again, there are two different type of *laukika* perception – external (*bāhya*) and internal (*mānasa*) perception. *Bhāya* is due to the external senses of sight, hearing, touch, taste and smell whereas *mānasa* perception is brought about by the mind's contact with psychical states and processes. Thus, we have six different types of *laukika* or ordinary Perception: visual (*cākṣusa*), auditory (*śrautra*), tactual (*spārśana*), gustatory (*rāsana*), olfactory (*ghrāṇaja*), and the internal or mental (*mānasa*).[2]

---

[2] Satishandra Chaterjee and Dhirendramohan Datta, *An Introduction to Indian Philosophy*, (New Delhi: Rupa, 2007), 160-161.

Alaukika or extraordinary Perception is of three different types: *First, sāmānyalakṣaṇa* – this is a combination of two words: *sāmānya*: universals or general characteristics that are shared by a class of objects (e.g., the property of 'cow-ness' shared by all cows); and *lakṣaṇa*: the distinguishing mark or characteristic by which an object or class is identified. Thus, *sāmānyalakṣaṇa* perception involves recognizing an individual object not only as itself but also as belonging to a broader category or class based on shared properties. *Second, jñānalakṣaṇa* – this is also a combination of two words: *Jñāna*: Knowledge or cognition and *lakṣaṇa*: the distinguishing feature or characteristic. It refers to a type of perception that arises due to the recognition or association provided by previous knowledge. It is not a direct sensory experience but is mediated by the cognitive grasp of something based on memory or inference. For example, when I say, "I see a piece of fragrant sandalwood," I may not actually smell the fragrance at that moment, yet I conclude that the sandalwood I see is fragrant. This is an example of *jñānalakṣaṇa pratyakṣa* because it involves perceiving a property (fragrance) that is not directly accessible to the sense organs at that time but is inferred through prior knowledge and cognitive association. The Third one is *yogaja* – it is the intuitive perception of all objects – past and future, hidden and infinitesimal – by people who possess some supernatural power in the mind. *Yogaja* Perception is possessed by those who attained spiritual perfection (*yokta*).[3]

Perception (*Pratyakṣa*) in the Nyāya school is a foundational epistemological category that encompasses both direct and extraordinary modes of cognition. The classification into *laukika* (ordinary) and *alaukika* (extraordinary) Perception highlights the diverse ways in which knowledge is acquired, whether through direct sensory contact or through cognitive processes influenced by universals, prior knowledge, or spiritual insight. This systematic approach not only underscores the

---

[3] Chaterjee and Datta, *An Introduction to Indian Philosophy*, 162-163.

depth of Nyāya epistemology but also reflects its commitment to a rational and structured understanding of reality.

1.2. Inference (*Anumāna*)

The second sources of knowledge is Inference (*anumāna*) which is the combination of two words – '*anu*' meaning 'after' and '*māna*' meaning 'knowledge'. Thus, it refers to a knowledge which follows some other knowledge. Examples – "There is fire on the hill because there is smoke", "Ram is mortal because he is a human."

In Inference there are three constituent terms:

Pratijñā (Proposition): The statement to be proved (the conclusion).
Hetu (Reason): The reason or evidence supporting the proposition.
Vyāpti (Universal Concomitance): The invariable relationship between the reason and the conclusion.

We can put this using syllogism which is the typical Nyaya Syllogism:[4]

(a) This hill has fire (*pratijnā*).
(b) Because it has smoke (*hetu*).
(c) Whatever has smoke has fire.
(d) This hill has smoke which is invariably associated with fire (*upanaya*).
(e) Therefore this hill has fire (*nigamana*).

In this syllogism, *firs*t proposition asserts something (hill has fire); the *second* proposition gives a reason for this assertion (because there is smoke); the *third* proposition is concerning the universal fact, showing connection between the asserted fact and the reason (wherever there is smoke, there is fire); the *fourth* proposition applies the universal fact to the present case (the hill has smoke). In the *final* proposition we have the concluding

[4] Chandradhar Sharma, *Indian Philosophy: A Critical Survey*, 186.

result which follows from the preceding propositions (thus, the hill has fire).

There are *three things* involved here – *first*, the knowledge of smoke in the hill; *second*, there is recollection of the invariable relation between smoke and fire; *third*, we have the resulting knowledge of the presence of fire in the hill though we do not perceive it with our senses. In this inference the hill is the *pakṣa* (minor term); as fire is the subject which we want to prove, it is called *sādya* (major term); and the smoke which is the sign indicating the presence of fire is called the *liṇga* (middle term), sometimes it is also called *hetu* or *sādhana*.[5]

Thus, by means of Inference we established the presence of fire on the hill though we do not see the fire. This is possible because of the presence of 'smoke' and the 'universal relationship' (universal concomitance) between fire and smoke.

We can give another example:

(a) Lal is mortal (*pratijñā*)
(b) Because he is a human (*hetu*)
(c) All humans are mortal (*udāharaṇa*)
(d) Lal also is a human (*upanaya*)
(e) Thus, lal is mortal (*nigamana*)

Thus, through inference, we establish the presence of fire on the hill or the mortality of Lal, even though they are not directly perceived. This is made possible by the existence of a 'universal relationship' (universal concomitance) - such as the invariable connection between fire and smoke or between Lal and the mortality shared by all humans.

Nyāya philosophy highlights Inference (*anumāna*) as a powerful tool for acquiring knowledge beyond direct perception. By relying on universal concomitance and logical reasoning, inference enables individuals to establish truths that are not immediately evident. This systematic approach reflects the intellectual rigor of Nyāya, showcasing its emphasis on

[5] Chaterjee and Datta, *An Introduction to Indian Philosophy*, 166.

rationality and precision in epistemology. Inference thus serves as a cornerstone of Nyāya's contribution to Indian philosophy, bridging the gap between observable phenomena and abstract understanding.

1.3. Comparison (*Upamāna*)

In Nyaya philosophy, comparison (*upamāna*) is recognized as one of the four valid means of knowledge (pramāṇas). *Upamāna* is the process of acquiring knowledge about an unknown object based on its similarity to a known object. It involves recognizing a relationship of resemblance between two entities and using that resemblance to identify or understand something unfamiliar.

For example, a man who has never seen a gavaya or a wild cow and does not know what it is, is told by a person that a wild cow is an animal like a cow, subsequently comes across a wild cow in a forest and recognizes it as the wild cow, then his knowledge is due to *upamâna*. He has heard the word 'gavaya' and has been told that it is like a domestic cow and now he himself sees the object denoted by the word 'gavaya' and recognizes it to be so.[6]

It is worth noting that most Indian philosophical schools reject *upamāna* (comparison) as an independent and distinct source of knowledge. The Buddhists subsume *upamāna* under perception and testimony, while the Sāmkhya and Vaiśeṣika schools consider it a form of inference. The Jainas interpret it as recognition (*pratyabhijñā*). Although Mīmāṁsā acknowledges *upamāna* as a separate means of knowledge, its understanding and acceptance of it differ significantly from that of Nyāya.

In Nyāya philosophy, comparison (*upamāna*) serves as an essential method for acquiring knowledge of the unknown through analogy. By recognizing similarities between familiar and unfamiliar objects, *upamāna* allows individuals to understand new concepts based on existing knowledge. This process of analogical reasoning enriches the philosophical toolkit of Nyāya, highlighting the importance of relational

[6] Chandradhar Sharma, *Indian Philosophy: A Critical Survey*, 191.

thinking in human cognition. As a valid means of knowledge, comparison facilitates the expansion of understanding, bridging the gap between experience and abstraction in the quest for truth.

1.4. Testimony (*Śabda*)

In Nyāya philosophy, *śabda* (verbal testimony) is recognized as one of the four valid means of knowledge (*pramāṇas*). It is defined as the statement of a trustworthy person (*āptavākya*) and involves understanding the meaning of that statement. A sentence is described as a collection of words, and a word is defined as an entity capable of conveying meaning. According to Nyāya, testimony (*śabda*) is based on the words of a reliable source, whether human or divine. Testimony is categorized into two types: scriptural (*vaidika*) and secular (*laukika*). Scriptural testimony, such as the Vedas, is considered perfect and infallible because it is believed to be spoken by God. Secular testimony, on the other hand, originates from human beings who are prone to error. Its validity depends on the reliability of the speaker. Of the two, only secular testimony that comes from a trustworthy source should be regarded as valid.[7] Thus, while scriptural testimony is inherently infallible, secular testimony requires the credibility of the speaker to be deemed reliable.

In recognizing verbal testimony (*śabda*) as a valid means of knowledge, Nyāya underscores the importance of trust and communication in the epistemic process. By distinguishing between scriptural (*vaidika*) and secular (*laukika*) testimony, it offers a perspective that accommodates divine authority and human reliability. *Śabda* not only broadens the scope of knowledge but also emphasizes the need for the credibility of the speaker in ensuring validity. This approach demonstrates Nyāya's balanced and pragmatic outlook, reinforcing its significance in the philosophical discourse on knowledge.

Nyāya epistemology offers a comprehensive and systematic approach to understanding the nature of knowledge and its

---

[7] Chandradhar Sharma, *Indian Philosophy: A Critical Survey*, 192.

acquisition. By recognizing four distinct means of knowledge -Perception (*pratyakṣa*), Inference (*anumāna*), Comparison (*upamāna*), and Verbal testimony (*śabda*) - Nyāya provides a balanced framework for validating human cognition. Each *pramāṇa* is carefully defined, emphasizing logical reasoning, empirical observation, and trustworthy communication. Through this – epistemological structure, *Nyāya* not only defends the reliability of human knowledge but also underscores the importance of reasoning, evidence, and authority in the pursuit of truth. Its influence on Indian philosophy remains profound, shaping the discourse on knowledge and logic for centuries.

2. Nature of Physical World

Nyāya accepts the metaphysics of Vaiśeṣika including its theory of the physical world. The physical world is made up of the atoms of the four substances – earth, water, fire and air. The atoms of these substances are eternal and unchanging. The physical world "contains all the composite products of these atoms, and their qualities and relations, including organic bodies, the senses, and the sensible qualities of things."[8] The physical substance of *ākāśa* (ether) is also considered part of the physical world. In contrast, the non-physical and infinite substances, such as *kāla* (time) and *diśa* (space), serve to encompass and interconnect all physical entities and events in diverse ways.

In the Nyāya concept of the physical world, mind (*manas*) and self (*ātman*) play critical roles beyond the physical elements like earth, water, fire, and air. The mind is a subtle, atomic substance that acts as a mediator between the senses and the self, enabling cognition and perception. The self, an eternal and non-physical substance, is the locus of consciousness and experiences the physical world through the body and mind. While the physical substances provide the objective foundation, the mind bridges the physical and non-physical, and the self transcends them as the conscious experiencer.

[8] Chaterjee and Datta, *An Introduction to Indian Philosophy*, 190.

3. Individual Self and Its Liberation

The Nyāya, like the Vaiśeṣika, upholds a teleological view of creation. The material causes of the universe are the eternal atoms of earth, water, fire, and air, while God serves as the efficient cause. The infinite individual souls and the eternal atoms coexist with God, all being co-eternal and beyond creation or destruction. God is external to both atoms and souls and cannot create or destroy them. Consequently, God is not the true creator in the sense of being the material cause of the universe but functions as the guiding force behind its formation.[9]

The self, according to Nyāya, is imperishable, eternal, infinite, and not constrained by time or space. Unlike Vedānta, which regards consciousness as the very essence of the self, Nyāya asserts that consciousness is not the self's essence but rather an attribute of the self. Consciousness arises in the self only when it is in association with the mind, senses, and external stimuli.

The soul, in Nyāya philosophy, is a real knower, real enjoyer, real agent, and an eternal substance. Unlike transcendental consciousness, it is distinct from God, who is regarded as the Supreme Soul. Each soul possesses a *manas* (mind) during its empirical existence, but the soul is separated from the mind upon liberation. The soul is also distinct from the body, senses, and mind. Bondage arises from ignorance and *karma*, while liberation is attained through knowledge and the destruction of *karma*. The Vedas, being the work of God, hold absolute authority according to Nyāya.[10]

To attain liberation one must acquire a true knowledge of the self and all other objects of experience (*tattva-jñāna*). He or she must realize the self as distinct from the body, the mind, the senses, etc. For this Nyāya prescribes the following things:

(a) Listening to the scriptural instructions about the self (*śravana*)

---

[9] Chandradhar Sharma, *Indian Philosophy: A Critical Survey*, 195.

[10] Chandradhar Sharma, *Indian Philosophy: A Critical Survey*, 195-196.

(b) To firmly establish the knowledge of the self my means of reasoning (*manana*)
(c) Meditating on the self in conformity with the principles of yoga (*nididhyāsana*)

These help one to know the true nature of the self and destroy the wrong knowledge (*mithyā jñāna*) – "I am the body and mind." This leads one to cease to be moved to action (*pravṛtti*) by passion and impulses (*doṣa*). When a man or woman achieved this, his or her past *karmas* are exhausted by producing the effects; the individual has to undergo no more birth in this world. The cessation of birth means the end of connection with the body and the end of pain and suffering (*duḥkha*). This is liberation.[11]

Nyāya School of Philosophy presents the individual self (*ātman*) as an eternal, conscious, and distinct entity, separate from the body, mind, and senses. The self is bound by ignorance and *karma*, which shape its experiences and actions in the empirical world. Liberation, in Nyāya, is achieved through the acquisition of true knowledge (*jñāna*) and the destruction of accumulated *karma*, leading to freedom from the cycle of birth and rebirth. For liberation to happen, Nyāya suggested the listening to the scriptural instruction and meditation with the principles of yoga.

4. Arguments for the Existence of God

Before we come to the discussion of Nyāya's argument for the existence of God, let us discuss about God in Nyāya system.

The Nyāya conception of God can be considered inadequate in presenting a fully developed theistic framework, as it falls short of embodying the ideals of true theism. For the Nyāya philosophers, God is regarded as the ultimate cause responsible for the creation, maintenance, and destruction of the world. However, God does not create the universe out of nothing or from His own substance. Instead, He arranges eternal atoms,

[11] Chaterjee and Datta, *An Introduction to Indian Philosophy*, 194.

which have existed alongside God from eternity, into an orderly universe. This portrayal positions God not as the creator of the fundamental building blocks of reality but as the arranger of pre-existing entities. Thus, it is difficult to say God as a Creator. Consequently, in the Nyāya framework, God is seen as the efficient cause of the universe, orchestrating its order, but not as the material cause from which the universe is made. This distinction underscores the limitations of the Nyāya view in presenting a fully developed theistic understanding of God.

According to the Nyāya School, God is eternal, infinite, omnipotent, and omniscient, possessing eternal consciousness. However, consciousness is not regarded as the very essence of God but rather as an attribute of God. He is not only the creator of the world but also its preserver, and He assumes the role of destroyer when necessary.

Udayana, a prominent Nyāya philosopher, in his *Nyāyakusumāñjali*, presents strong arguments for the existence of God that have become foundational for classical theism. These arguments, which remain highly influential, can be briefly summarized as follows. He offers nine key points to establish the existence of God:[12]

(a) The world is an effect and hence it must have an efficient cause. This intelligent agent is God. The order, design, co-ordination between different phenomena comes from God (*kāryāt*).

(b) The atoms being essentially inactive cannot form the different combinations unless God gives motion to them. The Unseen Power, the *adṛṣta*, requires the intelligence of God. Without God it cannot supply motion to the atoms (*āyojanāt*).

(c) The world is sustained by God's will. Unintelligent *adṛṣta* cannot do this. And the world is destroyed by God's will (*dhrtyādeh*).

[12] Chandradhar Sharma, *Indian Philosophy: A Critical Survey*, 197-198.

(d) A word has a meaning and signifies an object. The power of words to signify their objects comes from God (*padāt*).

(e) God is the author of the infallible Veda (*pratyayaṭaḥ*). As Vedas are infallible, whatever they say should be considered true.

(f) The Veda testifies to the existence of God (*śruteḥ*).

(g) The Vedic sentences deal with moral injunctions and prohibitions. The Vedic commands are the Divine commands. God is the creator and promulgator of the moral laws (*vakyāt*).

(h) In Nyāya-Vaiśeṣika philosophy, the size of a dyad (a pair of atoms) is not due to the tiny size of each atom, but rather because it is made up of two atoms. The concept of 'one' is directly perceived, but other numbers, like 'two' or more, are formed by the mind as concepts. Numerical conception is related to the mind of the perceiver. At the time of creation, the souls are unconscious. And the atoms and the Unseen Power and space, time, minds are all unconscious. Hence the numerical conception depends upon the Divine Consciousness. So God must exist (*san-khyāvishesāt*).

(i) We reap the fruits of our own actions. Merit and demerit accrue from our actions and the stock of merit and demerit is called *adṛṣta*, the Unseen Power. But this Unseen Power, being unintelligent, needs the guidance of a supremely intelligent God (*adṛṣtat*)

The Nyāya philosophy, particularly as articulated by Udayana in his *Nyāyakusumāñjali,* provides a systematic and rational basis for the belief in the existence of God (*Īśvara*). Through its nine-point argument, Udayana establishes God as the ultimate cause of the universe, addressing both cosmological and teleological aspects. These arguments emphasize the necessity of an intelligent and omniscient being to account for creation, order, and the moral governance of the world. By invoking logical reasoning and inference, the Nyāya school bridges the gap between metaphysics and empirical experience, grounding its theistic conclusions in rational inquiry. God is not only the efficient cause but also the moral governor who ensures justice and the fruition of *karma*. This perspective complements the Nyāya-Vaiśeṣika commitment to logical rigor while affirming the spiritual truths central to Indian philosophical traditions.

5. The Unseen Power (*Adṛṣṭa*)

The Nyāya-Vaiśeṣika philosophy introduces the concept of *Adṛṣṭa* (the Unseen Power), which refers to an invisible force or latent potency that governs the results of actions (*karma*) and explains phenomena that cannot be directly perceived. Sometimes, it is called 'the will of God,' through which God creates and sustains the universe from the eternal atoms of air, water, fire, and earth. Though non-conscious, yet used by God, *Adṛṣṭa* is responsible for the moral order of the cosmos, ensuring that good and bad actions yield appropriate consequences even if their effects are not immediately observable. It also accounts for seemingly inexplicable events, such as the movement of atoms, destiny, and the continuity of life across births. Thus, *Adṛṣṭa* serves as a crucial link between metaphysics, ethics, and cosmology in Nyāya-Vaiśeṣika thought.

6. Ethics

Nyāya philosophy is primarily focused on logic, epistemology, and metaphysics, but it also offers important ethical insights. Although Nyāya does not have an elaborate ethical system like some other Indian philosophies, it presents key principles regarding human behaviour, moral actions, and the pursuit of virtue. The ethical concepts in Nyāya may be discussed as follows:

Nyāya assumes the power of initiative, selection and choice implying that the soul or self has freedom to do whatever he or she likes though the ultimate controller is God. All acts have their motive – that is, the desire to obtain pleasure (*sukhaprāpti*) and avoid pain (*duhkhaparihāra*). The highest good is deliverance from pain and not enjoyment of pleasure because pleasure is always mixed up with pain. *Saṁsāra* bring pain to human and the highest good is to escape from *saṁsāra*. Pain (*duḥkha*) is the result of birth (*janma*) and birth is the result of activity (*pravṛtti*). All activities, good or bad bind to *saṁsāra* and leads us to some kind of birth, lower form or higher form. Activity is due to the defects of aversion (*devaṣa*), attachment (*rāga*) and stupidity (*moha*). Aversion includes anger, hatred, envy, etc.; attachment includes lust, avarice, covetousness; stupidity includes misapprehension, suspicion, deceit and carelessness. The cause of all these defects is false knowledge (*mithyājñāna*) about the nature of soul, pain, pleasure, etc. To attain freedom, we have to end the chain which begins with false notion and ends with pain. When false knowledge passed away, faults disappeared resulting into cessation of birth. When there is no birth, there is no pain and the soul attains eternal bliss.[13]

The adoption of virtuous activities will enable one to discriminate the soul from the body and the senses. But the true knowledge cannot be acquired from books, but only through meditation and increase of righteousness. The Naiyāyika prescribes yoga practice in addition to study and reflection of the Vedas. Scriptural studies, philosophic thought and meditation are prescribed for liberation. To refrain from worldly pleasure, renounce all desires, retire to the forest for meditation, and to practice *Bhakti* are also recommended for the liberation of soul in Nyāya School.[14]

Concluding Remarks

Nyāya philosophy, with its rigorous approach to logic and reasoning, makes its most significant contribution to epistemology, the theory of knowledge. By identifying and elaborating on the various means of valid knowledge - perception, inference, comparison, and verbal testimony –

[13] S. Radhakrishnan, *Indian Philosophy Vol. II*, (New York: The Macmillan Company, 1958), 160-162.

[14] Cf. Radhakrishnan, *Indian Philosophy Vol. II*, 263-264.

Nyāya provides a sophisticated framework for understanding how humans acquire knowledge and distinguish truth from falsehood. This emphasis on rational inquiry and the scientific method of gaining knowledge marks Nyāya as a foundational school in the development of Indian philosophy, particularly in its exploration of how knowledge functions within human experience and the natural world.

However, in the area of metaphysics, Nyāya's conception of God appears somewhat limited. While it acknowledges the existence of a divine being (*Īśvara*) as the efficient cause of the universe, it portrays God more as a controller and arranger of eternal atoms, which have existed alongside God from eternity and were not created by Him. This view contrasts with more expansive theistic conceptions found in other philosophical traditions. In its understanding of God, Nyāya falls short of presenting a strong and fully developed theistic framework, making its conception of the divine relatively weak compared to other schools that assert a more personal and all-encompassing God.

Furthermore, Nyāya follows the Vaiśeṣika School in its metaphysical teachings, particularly in its atomistic view of the material world. Both schools agree that the universe is composed of eternal, indivisible atoms that combine to form the objects we experience. This shared belief in atomism shapes the Nyāya understanding of the physical world, although Nyāya's primary focus remains on epistemological and logical concerns.

In summary, Nyāya philosophy excels in its contribution to the theory of knowledge, establishing clear and systematic methods of understanding and reasoning. However, its metaphysical doctrines, especially in terms of the conception of God, and its reliance on Vaiśeṣika for certain metaphysical teachings, suggest that Nyāya's philosophical system is more concerned with logic and epistemology than with developing a comprehensive theological or metaphysical worldview.

Chapter 6

Vaiśeṣika School of Philosophy

The Vaiśeṣika School of philosophy is one of the six classical systems of Indian philosophy. It is often grouped with the Nyāya School under the collective category of "Nyāya-Vaiśeṣika," as the two schools share significant similarities and are frequently regarded as a unified philosophical tradition. Vaiśeṣika was founded by the sage Kaṇāda, he was also known as Ulūka. So, the Vaiśeṣika philosophy is known as Kaṇāda or Aulukya Syatem. The Vaiśeṣika system is primarily concerned with the nature of the physical world and the categories of existence, focusing on the analysis of substances, qualities, actions, and their interrelations.

The Vaiśeṣika philosophy recognizes only two sources of valid knowledge: Perception (*pratyakṣa*) and Inference (*anumāna*). Unlike the Nyāya School, which accepts four *pramāṇas*, Vaiśeṣika subsumes the other two - Comparison (*upamāna*) and Testimony (*śabda*) - under Perception and Inference, considering them extensions of these primary means of knowledge. This distinction highlights a significant divergence between Vaiśeṣika and Nyāya philosophies in their approach to epistemology.

Our discussion will focus on the two most significant contributions of the Vaiśeṣika to Indian philosophy: its theories on Categories of Existence, and Atomism.

1. Categories of Existence (*Padārtha*)

The main purpose of Vaiśeṣika School is to explain the Categories (*padārtha*) and to unfold the atomistic pluralism. *Padārtha* literally means 'the meaning of a word' or 'the object signified by a word'. All that is real comes under the object of knowledge and is called a *padārtha*. So, *padārtha* means an object which can be thought (*jñeya*) and named (*abhidheya*).

Originally the Vaiśeṣika held that there are six categories and the seventh, that is, *abhāva* or 'negation', was added later on. Kaṇāda himself spoke of *abhāva*, but he did not give it the status of a category, the later Vaiśeṣikas added it to the list of category (*padārtha*). The Vaiśeṣika divides all existent reals which are all objects of knowledge into two classes - *bhāva* or being and *abhāva* or non-being. Six categories come under *bhāva* and the seventh is *abhāva*. All knowledge necessarily points to an object beyond and independent of it. The seven *padārthas* are: (a) substance (*dravya*), (b) quality (*guṇa*), (c) action (*karma*), (d) generality (*sāmānya*), (e) particularity (*viśesa*), (f) inherence (*samavāya*), and (g) non-being (*abhāva*). We will explain in brief one by one:

1.1. Substance (*Dravya*)

A *dravya* or substance is that in which a quality or an action can exist, but which is distinct from both.[1] Substance signifies the self-subsistence, the absolute and independent nature of things. In the Vaiśeṣika system, the category of substance vividly illustrates its pluralistic realism. Substance is the substratum of qualities and actions. Substance serves as the foundation for qualities and actions, as these cannot exist independently or float freely but must reside within a substratum. It provides

[1] Satishandra Chaterjee and Dhirendramohan Datta, *An Introduction to Indian Philosophy*, (New Delhi: Rupa, 2007), 213.

the grounding for qualities and actions, whether actual or potential, present or future. At the same time, substance itself cannot be fully defined apart from its association with qualities and actions. Ultimate substances are eternal, independent and individual and are either infinite or infinitesimal. The *dravyas* are nine and include material as well as spiritual substances. The nine substances are: (a) earth (*prthivi*), (b) water (*āp*), (c) fire (*tejas*), (d) air (*vāyu*), (e) ether (*ākāśa*), (f) time (*kāla*), (g) space (*dik*), (h) spirit (*ātman*), and (i) mind or the internal organ (*manas*).[2]

The earth (*prthivi*), water (*āp*), fire (*tejas*), and air (*vāyu*) are considered the fundamental elements, comprising the eternal, indivisible, and partless atoms, which are both individual and infinitesimal. Ether (*ākāśa*), on the other hand, is not atomic but infinite and eternal. These five are known as the elements (*bhāta*), and they are physical in nature. Time (*kāla*) and space (*dik*) are also eternal (*nitya*) and all-pervading (*vibhu*). They are imperceptible, infinite, and indivisible substances. Time facilitates our perception of past, present, and future, as well as the concepts of youth and age. Space (*dik*) enables our understanding of directions - east and west, here and there, near and far, and so on. The soul (*ātman*) is an independent, eternal, and all-pervading spiritual essence. Countless souls exist, each individual, eternal, and atomic. Consciousness is not the essence of the self; rather, it is an attribute of the self. There are two kinds of soul – the individual soul (*jīvātma*) and the Supreme Soul (*Paramātmā* or *Īśvara* or God). Every self possesses a mind (*manas*), which serves as the organ through which the self interacts with objects. The existence of the mind is inferred from the fact that the self must perceive internal states - such as cognition, desire, and volition - through an internal sense, just as it perceives external objects through external senses.[3]

---

[2] Chandradhar Sharma, *Indian Philosophy: A Critical Survey*, (New York City: Barnes & Noble, Inc. 1962), 164-165.

[3] Chandradhar Sharma, *Indian Philosophy: A Critical Survey*, 165-166.

1.2. Quality (*Guṇa*)

Kaṇāda, the founder of Vaiśeṣika School defines *guṇa* (quality) as "that which inheres in a substance, which does not possess quality or action, which does not produce any composite thing, and which is not the cause of conjunction and disjunction like an action" (*Vaiśeṣikasûtra* I, 1.16). It is a non-material cause of things and it determines only their nature and character but not their existence. It is not eternal but independent reality. Quality is static and permanent.

According to Kaṇāda, there are seventeen qualities to which Prashastapāda added seven more and now we have twenty four (24) different types of qualities. They are: *rūpa* or colour, *rasa* or test, *grandha* or smell, *sparśa* or touch, *śabda* or sound, *saṅkhyā* or number, *parimāṇa* or magnitude, *pṛthaktva* or distinctness, *saṁyoga* or conjunction, *vibhāga* or disconjunction, *paravata* or remoteness, *aparavata* or nearness, *buddhi* or cognition, *sukha* or pleasure, *duḥkha* or pain, *icchā* or desire, *dveṣa* or aversion, *prayatna* or effort, *gurutva* or heaviness, *dravatva* or fluidity, *sneha* or viscidity, *saṁskāra* or tendency, *dharma* or merit, and *adharma* or demerit.[4]

1.3. Action (*Karma*)

It is physical movement or action. Like quality, *Karma* belongs to and inheres in a substance and cannot exist separately from it. But while a quality (*guṇa*) is a static and permanent feature of a substance, an action (*karma*) is a dynamic and transient feature of it. It is the cause of conjunction and disjunction. Action (*Karma*) is said to be of five kinds: (1) upward movement (*utkṣepaṇa*), (2) downward movement (*avak-ṣepaṇa*), (3) contraction (*ākunchana*), (4) expansion (*prasāraṇa*), and (5) locomotion (*gamana*).[5] While most actions are perceptible, some cannot be directly perceived. For example, the movement of the mind (*manas*) or the motion of elements like earth, water, and light are not observable.

---

[4] Chaterjee and Datta, *An Introduction to Indian Philosophy*, 218.

[5] Chandradhar Sharma, *Indian Philosophy: A Critical Survey*, 167.

1.4. Generality (*Sāmānya*)

Sāmānya refers to the universal or common characteristic that is present in multiple individual entities, allowing them to be grouped into a single class or category. It is the basis for the recognition of similarity among diverse objects. Generality enables us to identify objects as belonging to a specific class or type. For example, the generality of 'cowness' (*gotva*) is what allows us to recognize different cows as part of the category 'cow,' despite individual differences among them like colour, etc. "It is because there is one common essence present in different individuals that they are brought under a class and thought of as essentially the same."[6] According to Vaiśeṣika, generality is not just an abstract idea but has a real, objective existence. It is not created by the mind but exists inherently in the objects themselves.

1.5. Particularity (*Viśeṣa*)

Viśeṣa is the opposite of *Sāmānya*. It refers to the intrinsic uniqueness of an entity that makes it irreducibly distinct from every other entity. "Through *viśeṣa* things are perceived as diverse… this difference must be due to the existence of some specific differences amongst the atoms themselves."[7] *Viśeṣa* (particularity) is considered to be eternal.

1.6. Inherence (*Samavāya*)

Inherence (*Samavāya*) is a fundamental category in Vaiśeṣika philosophy that explains the inseparable and eternal relationship between entities that cannot exist independently of each other. It is the inseparable relationship of inherence, through which two distinct entities - such as substance and attribute, substance and action (*karma*), substance and generality (*sāmānya*), cause (*kāraṇa*) and effect (*kārya*), or atoms and particularity (*viśeṣa*) -

---

[6] Chaterjee and Datta, *An Introduction to Indian Philosophy*, 223.

[7] S. N. Dasgupta, *A History of Indian Philosophy: An Introduction to the Eight Major Philosophies of Ancient India*, Vol. 1, (Cambridge: Finger Print Classic, 2024), 367.

are so intimately connected that they appear as a unified whole or an indivisible and inseparable reality.[8]

1.7. Non-existence (*Abhāva*)

While the above six categories are positive, the Non-existence (*abhāva*) is negative. It explains the absence or negation of entities in specific contexts. There are four kinds of *Abhāva*: (a) antecedent non-existence (*prāgabhāva*) - the non-existence of a thing before its production, (2) subsequent non-existence (*pradhvaṁsābhāva*) - the nonexistence of a thing after its destruction, (3) mutual non-existence (*anyonyābhāva*) - the non-existence of a thing as another thing which is different from it, and (4) absolute non-existence (*atyantābhāva*) - a pseudo-idea, the absence of a relation between two things in the past, the present and the future.[9]

The Categories of Existence (*padārtha*) form the foundational framework of the Vaiśeṣika school of Indian philosophy, providing a comprehensive classification of all that exists in reality. These categories are designed to explain the nature of the world and its diverse phenomena systematically. Vaiśeṣika identifies seven *padārthas*, which include: Substance (*Dravya*), the material basis of existence; Quality (*Guṇa*), the attributes inherent in substances; Action (*Karma*), the movement or activity associated with substances; Generality (*Sāmānya*), the universal properties shared by multiple entities; Particularity (*Viśeṣa*), the unique individuality of eternal entities;. Inherence (*Samavāya*), the inseparable relationship binding two entities into a unified whole; and Non-existence (*Abhāva*), the absence or negation of entities. Together, these categories offer a logical and ontological framework that explains both the physical and metaphysical aspects of reality, bridging perception, cognition, and existence. This system is integral to Vaiśeṣika's pluralistic worldview, which seeks to analyze the complexity of the universe through a structured and reasoned approach.

---

[8] S.N. Dasgupta, *A History of Indian Philosophy*, 367.

[9] Chandradhar Sharma, *Indian Philosophy: A Critical Survey*, 170.

2. Atomism

The Vaiśeṣika School stands as the foremost champion of atomism in Indian philosophy. From as early as the 7th century BCE to the 17th century CE, its proponents, through numerous commentaries and independent works, diligently developed and refined their atomic theory, establishing it on a strong logical foundation while countering critiques from anti-atomist schools. Rooted in a systematic framework of atomism, the Vaiśeṣika philosophy explains the cosmic process as one in which the soul is integrally involved, offering a profound metaphysical perspective on the nature of reality and its underlying principles.[10]

Atoms in the Vaiśeṣika system are classified into four types: earth, water, fire, and air. These atoms differ from one another in both quantity and quality, each possessing a unique particularity and existing as a distinct reality. The atoms of earth, water, fire, and air are distinguished by their inherent, eternal qualities. Air atoms are the finest and have the quality of touch. Fire atoms possess touch and colour, water atoms exhibit touch, colour, and taste, while earth atoms embody touch, colour, taste, and smell. In addition to these qualities, all atoms share attributes such as velocity, number, and distinctness. The qualities of composite objects in the world arise from the qualities of the constituent atoms. Atoms are co-eternal with the soul and serve as the material cause of the world. However, they are inherently inactive and motionless, becoming active only during creation. During dissolution, they remain in a state of inactivity.[11]

Motion is imparted to atoms by the Unseen Power (*adṛṣṭa*) arising from *dharma* (merit) and *adharma* (demerit), which reside in individual souls and seek to manifest in the form of enjoyment or suffering. These atoms are supra-sensible and imperceptible. Their combinations follow a geometrical progression, not an arithmetic one, meaning they increase

---

[10] Ashok K. Mishra, "Atomism of Vaisesika-Nyaya V. S. Jainism – A Scientific Appraisal" in *Indian Journal of History of Science*, (Vol. 42, no. 2, 2006), 248.

[11] Chandradhar Sharma, *Indian Philosophy: A Critical Survey*, 171.

by multiplication rather than simple addition. When set into motion by *adṛṣṭa*, the atoms begin to vibrate (*parispanda*) and immediately transform into *dyads* (*dvyaṇuka*). A dyad is formed by the conjunction of two atoms. The atoms serve as its inherent cause (*samavāyikāraṇa*), their conjunction (*saṁyoga*) as its non-inherent cause (*asamavāyikāraṇa*), and the Unseen Power (*adṛṣṭa*) as its efficient cause (*nimittakāraṇa*). An atom is indivisible, spherical, and imperceptible. A dyad is minute (*aṇu*), short (*hrasva*), and also imperceptible. Three dyads combine to form a triad (*tryaṇuka*), which is great (*mahat*), long (*dīrgha*), and perceptible. This process continues in a geometrical progression until the gross elements of earth (*pṛthivī*), water (*āp*), fire (*tejas*), and air (*vāyu*) come into existence.[12]

The Vaiśeṣika atomism is not materialistic because it acknowledges the existence of spiritual substances, including souls and God, alongside its theory of physical atoms. The school also recognizes the *Law of Karma*, integrating moral and spiritual dimensions into its philosophy. While atoms serve as the material cause of the physical world, God acts as the efficient cause, assisted by the Unseen Power (*adṛṣṭa*), which originates from the accumulated merits and demerits of individual souls. The physical world is thus intertwined with a moral order, as the process of evolution and creation is driven by the karmic forces of these souls, which manifest as experiences of joy or suffering. This connection between material and spiritual realms underpins the Vaiśeṣika worldview, distinguishing it from purely materialistic philosophies.[13]

Vaiśeṣika's atomism offers a unique synthesis of metaphysical, physical, and spiritual elements, emphasizing the interplay between material atoms and the moral order of the universe. Unlike materialistic atomism, it integrates the roles of God, souls, and the Law of Karma, presenting a holistic view of creation and dissolution. The eternal and indivisible atoms form the foundation of the physical world, while the Unseen

[12] Chandradhar Sharma, *Indian Philosophy: A Critical Survey*, 171-172.

[13] Chandradhar Sharma, *Indian Philosophy: A Critical Survey*, 172.

Power (*adṛṣṭa*), sometimes called "the will of God" "gives direction of all such unions in harmony with the principle of a 'moral government of the universe,' so that only such things are produced as can be arranged for the due disposal of the effects of *karma*."[14] This approach not only explains the material cosmos but also aligns it with ethical and spiritual principles, highlighting the interconnectedness of matter and morality in its philosophical framework.

Concluding Remarks

The Vaiśeṣika philosophy, though frequently discussed alongside Nyāya due to their shared metaphysical and epistemological frameworks, occupies a distinctive position in Indian philosophy with its unique focus on the Categories of Existence and Atomism. The seven categories (*padārthas*) - substance, quality, action, generality, particularity, inherence, and absence - offer a systematic and detailed framework for classifying all that exists. These categories not only provide a comprehensive ontology but also reflect the School's commitment to a logical and structured understanding of reality, setting it apart as a meticulous and analytical tradition. However, one might critique Vaiśeṣika's reliance on a rigid categorization of existence, which, while systematic, can sometimes appear overly abstract and disconnected from lived, practical experience. This framework risks reducing the rich diversity of the world to a set of discrete, objective entities, potentially missing the fluidity and interconnectedness found in more dynamic philosophical traditions.

The atomistic theory of Vaiśeṣika adds another layer of uniqueness, presenting the material world as composed of eternal, indivisible atoms (*aṇus*) corresponding to the elements of earth, water, fire, and air. These atoms combine through geometrical progression, driven by the Unseen Power (*adṛṣṭa*), which is rooted in the karmic forces of individual souls. Governed by divine will, this process intertwines the physical

[14] S. N. Dasgupta, *A History of Indian Philosophy*, 376.

cosmos with moral and spiritual dimensions. The explanation of creation and dissolution through atomic interactions reflects not just a scientific approach to the material world but also its moral and spiritual underpinnings, connecting the material and ethical realms in a cohesive manner. However, the concept of Unseen Power (*adṛṣṭa*) may be seen as speculative, lacking empirical grounding. It introduces a metaphysical force that, while offering an elegant solution to the interaction between the physical and moral realms, can appear difficult to substantiate through direct observation or rational deduction. This introduces a potential gap in the philosophy's explanatory power when compared to more empirically grounded systems.

While the epistemological aspects of Vaiśeṣika, primarily Perception and Inference, are aligned with Nyāya, and much of its metaphysical teachings share similarities with Nyāya, the Vaiśeṣika School's unique emphasis on categories and atomism ensures its distinct identity. By focusing on these two critical contributions, the Vaiśeṣika School enriches the Nyāya-Vaiśeṣika tradition and offers a comprehensive lens to view the interplay between material, moral, and spiritual realities. However, one could argue that the atomistic model, in its focus on material elements, may neglect the complexity of subjective experiences and consciousness, which are central to other philosophical systems in India. This leaves Vaiśeṣika's approach somewhat limited in its ability to account for the full scope of human existence and experience.

Despite these potential limitations, Vaiśeṣika's ability to integrate these diverse elements into a coherent philosophical framework underscores its enduring significance in the broader landscape of Indian thought. The School's rigorous approach to categorizing and understanding the world continues to influence modern debates in metaphysics and epistemology, offering insights into the nature of reality that remain relevant even today.

Chapter 7

Sāmkhya School of Philosophy

Sāmkhya (or Sāṅkhya), one of the six classical systems of Indian philosophy, is a profound and ancient tradition that offers a dualistic framework for understanding the nature of reality and human existence. The great sage Kapila is the founder of this School. He wrote *Sāṃkhya-sūtra* which became the foundation of this School. The other significant works that shaped the Sāṃkhya School of Philosophy include, Gaudapada's *Sāṃkhya-kārikā-bhāṣya*, Vācaspati's *Tattvakaumudī*, Vijñānabhikṣu's *Sāṃkhya-pravaccana-bhāṣya-vrtti.* This school emphasizes the interplay between two fundamental realities: *Puruṣa* (the conscious self) and *Prakṛti* (the unconscious material nature). Sāmkhya's teachings are deeply rooted in a rational and analytical exploration of the universe, prioritizing knowledge and discernment as the path to liberation (*mokṣa*).

Sāṃkhya and Yoga are often regarded as closely related traditions due to their shared epistemological and metaphysical foundations. Yoga philosophy is frequently referred to as 'theistic Sāmkhya,' while Sāṃkhya is characterized as 'atheistic Sāṃkhya.' The distinction lies in their stance on the existence of God: the Yoga school acknowledges and emphasizes the role of God, whereas Sāṃkhya rejects the necessity of a divine being in its framework.

Sāṃkhya is undoubtedly one of the oldest systems of Indian Philosophy. We find references to the Sāṃkhya-Yoga doctrines in some of the Upanisads, e.g., in the *Chhāndogya*, the *Praśna*, the *Kaṭha* and particularly in the *Shvetāshvatara*. We also find references in the *Mahābhārata*, in the *Gīta*; and in the *Smṛtis* and the *Purānas*. Bādarāyana, the author of the *Vedānta-sūtra*, repeatedly refers to the view whether the Sāṃkhya can be regarded as the teaching of the Upaniṣads and rejects it.[1]

This Chapter will explore the essential tenets of Sāmkhya, including its epistemology, its challenges to theistic beliefs, and its comprehensive exposition of *Puruṣa* and *Prakṛti*. By doing so, it will highlight the enduring relevance of Sāmkhya as a philosophical system that addresses fundamental questions about existence, knowledge, and liberation.

1. Theory of Knowledge

Sāṃkhya recognizes three independent sources of valid knowledge (*pramāṇa*): Perception (*pratyakṣa*), Inference (*anumāna*), and Testimony (*śabda*). These three are considered sufficient to encompass all forms of knowledge, and Sāṃkhya does not acknowledge additional sources of knowledge as independent or distinct. Some Indian philosophical systems recognize other *pramāṇas*, such as Comparison (*upamāna*), Postulation (*arthāpatti*), and Non-recognition or absence (*anupalabdhi*). However, Sāṃkhya subsumes these under the three primary *pramāṇas* rather than treating them as separate and autonomous sources of knowledge.

In any valid knowledge, there are three factors – the subject (*pramātā*), the object (*pramey*) and the ground or source of knowledge (*pramāṇa*). The self who is a conscious being is the subject (*pramātā*). The object presented to the self through modification is the *prameya*. The modification (*vṛtti*)

---

[1] Chandradhar Sharma, *Indian Philosophy: A Critical Survey*, (New York City: Barnes & Noble, Inc. 1962), 137.

of the intellect through which the self knows an object is called *pramāṇa*.[2]

According to Sāṃkhya, experience belonged to *Puruṣa*, the self. *Buddhi* (intellect), *ahaṁkāras* (self-sense), *manas* (mind), and the senses constitute the apparatus by means of which the external object is apprehended by the subject. When an object excites the senses, the *manas* arranges the sense-impressions into a percept, the *ahaṁkāras* (self-sense) refers it to the self and the *buddhi* forms the concept.[3] This is how knowledge of an object is gained.

1.1. Perception (*Pratyakṣa*)

In Sāṃkhya philosophy, perception (*pratyakṣa*) is defined as the direct cognition of an object through the contact between the senses and the object. It is considered the most immediate and reliable source of knowledge in the realm of empirical experience. When objects, such as a table or a tree, come within the range of our sensory organs - for example, the eyes - they come into direct contact with the sense organ. This contact produces certain impressions or modifications in the sense organ, which are then processed further by the *manas* (mind). The mind plays a crucial role in analyzing and synthesizing these sensory impressions, integrating them into coherent knowledge. This is how we become aware of and perceive the presence of the table or tree in front of us.[4] Again, a thing like jar comes within the range of vision buddhi is so modified so as to assume the form of the jar, finally the soul becomes aware of the existence of the jar.[5]

Perception is classified into two types: indeterminate (*nirvikalpaka*) and determinate (*savikalpaka*). According to

---

[2] Satishandra Chaterjee and Dhirendramohan Datta, *An Introduction to Indian Philosophy*, (New Delhi: Rupa, 2007), 258.

[3] S. Radhakrishnan, *Indian Philosophy Vol. II*, (New York: The Macmillan Company, 1958), 294.

[4] Chaterjee and Datta, *An Introduction to Indian Philosophy*, 258.

[5] S. Radhakrishnan, *Indian Philosophy Vol. II*, 297-298.

Vācaspati Miśra, when the *buddhi* (intellect) comes into contact with an external object through the senses, the initial moment of perception does not involve any interpretation or identification of the object's specific features. At this stage, we experience *indeterminate perception*, where the mind merely registers the presence of sensory data without categorizing or recognizing the object. As the mind (*manas*) processes, analyzes, and synthesizes the sensory impressions, it discerns the object's true nature, leading to *determinate perception*.[6] This refined perception involves the mind forming a clear concept of the object, allowing the individual to recognize and identify it. In this way, indeterminate perception precedes determinate perception, with the latter representing a more advanced stage of cognitive processing.

1.2. Inference (*Anumāna*)

Inference is a cognitive process in which knowledge about one term (that is not directly perceived) is derived based on its *invariable relation* to another term (that is directly perceived). In this process what is perceived leads to knowledge of what is not perceived through the knowledge of a universal relation (*vyāpti*) between the two.[7] We deduce the present of fire on the hill (not perceived) by observing the smoke (perceived) due to the invariable relation between fire and smoke.

Two types of Inference are recognized in Sāṁkhya – affirmative (*vīta*) and negative (*avīta*). *Vīta* is based on affirmative concomitance and *avīta* is based on the negative concomitance. That means, vīta involves drawing conclusions based on the presence of one thing always being associated with another (positive relationship) whereas *avīta* involves drawing conclusions based on the absence of one thing always being associated with the absence of another (negative relationship). The *vīta* is subdivided into the *pūrvat* and the *sāmānyatodṛṣṭa*. *Apūrvat* inference is based on the observed uniformity of

---

[6] S. Radhakrishnan, *Indian Philosophy Vol. II*, 298.

[7] Chaterjee and Datta, *An Introduction to Indian Philosophy*, 260.

concomitance between two things. For example, we infer the presence of fire on the hill from smoke because smoke is always accompanied by fire. *Sāmānyatodṛṣṭa* inference is not based on directly observing the invariable relationship between the middle term and the major term. Instead, it is based on the similarity of the middle term to other facts that are always connected to the major term. For example, Cows eat grass, so horses (which are similar to cows) must also eat grass. Here, the middle term (horses) is not directly observed to have a relationship with the major term (eating grass). Instead, the inference is made based on the similarity between horses and cows, which are known to eat grass.[8]

The other kind of inference, *avīta* is also called *śeṣavat* or *pariśeṣa* inference which consists in providing something to be true by elimination of all other alternatives to it. For example, we argue that sound must be a quality because it cannot be a substance or an activity or a relation or anything else.

In regards to the form of syllogism, Sāṁkhya admits Nyāya five-membered syllogism as the most convincing form of inferential proof.[9]

The five-membered syllogism of Sāṁkhya may be illustrated as follows:

Proposition (*Pratijñā*)	:	The self is distinct from the body.
Reason (*Hetu*)	:	Because the self is eternal, while the body is not.
Example (*Udāharaṇa*)	:	Just as the body undergoes birth, growth, and decay, but the self remains unchanged.
Application (*Upanaya*)	:	The self cannot be identical to the body, since it is not subject to change.
Conclusion (*Nigamana*)	:	Therefore, the self is distinct from the body.

[8] Chaterjee and Datta, *An Introduction to Indian Philosophy*, 261.

[9] Chaterjee and Datta, *An Introduction to Indian Philosophy*, 261.

1.3. Testimony (*Śabda*)

The third *pramāna* gives the knowledge which cannot be known by Perception and Inference, it is Testimony or *Śabda* which is constituted by authoritarian statement (*āptavacana*). In Indian epistemology, *Śabda* is normally divided into two – *laukika* and *vaidika. Laukika* is the testimony of ordinary trustworthy persons which is not recognized by *Sāṁkhya* as a separate *pramāna*, since it depends on Perception and Inference. The second one, *vaidika*, the testimony of *Śruti* or the Vedas is the third separate *pramāna* admitted by the *Sāṁkhya*. The Vedas give us true knowledge about realities which cannot be known through Perception and Inference.[10] The Vedas are not composed by human beings since there are not any persons who can be the author. The Vedas, on account of their non-personal authorship, is free from doubts and discrepancies, and is regarded as self-evident validity. The scriptural statements are tested and lived by the *muktas* or the liberated, who passed them on to others. But the Vedas are not considered eternal since they possess the character of effects.[11]

Sāmkhya epistemology provides a comprehensive framework for understanding knowledge acquisition through its recognition of *three valid* means of knowledge: Perception (*pratyakṣa*), Inference (*anumāna*), and Testimony (*śabda*). By emphasizing the reliability of perception as direct and immediate knowledge, inference as logical reasoning based on observed patterns, and testimony as the wisdom of authoritative sources, Sāmkhya integrates empirical, rational, and scriptural approaches. This epistemological model is deeply intertwined with Sāmkhya's metaphysical dualism, aiming to illuminate the distinction between *puruṣa* (consciousness) and prakṛti (*matter*). Through this, Sāmkhya epistemology not only serves as a guide for philosophical inquiry but also supports its ultimate goal of

[10] Chaterjee and Datta, *An Introduction to Indian Philosophy*, 262

[11] S. Radhakrishnan, *Indian Philosophy Vol. II*, 301.

liberation (*mokṣa*) by fostering clear and accurate understanding of reality.

2. Sāṃkhya Metaphysics

Sāmkhya offers a dualistic understanding of reality that seeks to explain the nature of existence, the process of creation, and the ultimate goal of liberation. At its core, Sāmkhya distinguishes between two fundamental principles: *Prakṛti* (the material, unconscious nature) and *Puruṣa* (the individual consciousness or soul). This dualistic framework provides a foundation for its metaphysical theories, especially its theory of causation, where the world is seen as emerging from the interaction of these two principles. In the Sāmkhya system, *Prakṛti* is the primal cause, a dynamic, evolving force governed by the three *guṇas* (qualities) – *sattva*, *rajas*, and *tamas*. The theory of causation explains how these *guṇas* shape the material world through their inherent qualities and their constant interplay. *Puruṣa*, on the other hand, represents the pure consciousness, which is passive and unaffected by the changing world of *Prakṛti*.

The ultimate goal of the Sāmkhya system is liberation (*mokṣa*), which is achieved by the realization of the distinction between *Puruṣa* and *Prakṛti*, leading to freedom from the cycles of birth, death, and rebirth. In this context, the problem of the existence of God is addressed, not through theistic belief but through an understanding of *Puruṣa* and *Prakṛti* as the primary forces of reality, where the concept of God is not central to the metaphysical framework.

2.1. Theory of Causation

Sāṃkhya theory of causation is the foundation of its doctrine of *Prakṛti*. The basic question involved in any theory of causation is: "Does the effect pre-exist in its material cause?" Those who answer this question in the negative are called *Asatkāryavādins* - Nyāya, Vaiśeṣika, Buddhism, Cārvāka, and some followers of Mīmāṃsā belong to this group. According to the *Asatkāryavādins*, the effect is a new creation, a real beginning.

The effect (*kārya*) does not pre-exist (*asat*) in its material cause. They argue: if the pot already exists in the clay, then why should the potter exert himself in producing the pot out of the clay? On the other hand, those who answer it in the affirmative are called *Satkāryavādins*. The followers of the Sāṃkhya School are *Satkāryavādins* who believe that the effect pre-existed in the cause. All material effects are the modification (*pariṇāma*) of *Prakṛti*. They pre-exist in the eternal bosom of *Prakṛti* and simply come out of it at the time of creation and return to it at the time of dissolution. There is neither new production nor utter destruction. Production means development or manifestation (*āvirbhāva*); *destruction* means envelopment or dissolution (*tirobhāva*).[12]

Sāṃkhya gives five arguments in support of *Satkāryavāda*:[13]

(a) If the effect does not pre-exist in its material cause, no amount of the effort on the part of any agent could bring it into existence. Can anyone turn blue into read? Sugar into salt? Thus, when an effect is produced from the material cause, it was pre-existed in the cause.

(b) There is an invariable relation (*upādānagrahaṇāt*) between a material cause and its effect. A material cause can produce only that effect with which it is causally related. Hence the effect must exist in the material cause before it is actually produced.

(c) Everything cannot be produced out of everything. Pot can be produced only from clay, not form milk. This shows that the effect before its manifestation, is implicit in its material cause (*sarvasambhavābhāvāt*). Otherwise, curd could be produced from water, cloth from reeds, and oil from sand particles.

(d) Only an efficient cause can produce that for which it is potent. This suggests that the effect, prior to its manifestation, is potentially contained in its material

---

[12] Chandradhar Sharma, *Indian Philosophy: A Critical Survey*, 139-140.

[13] Chaterjee and Datta, *An Introduction to Indian Philosophy*, 239-240.

cause. This shows that the effect exists in the cause in an unmanifested form before its production or manifestation. Production is merely the actualization of this potential (śaktasya śakyakaraṇāt).

(e) We see that the effect is not different from, but essentially identical with its material cause. If the cause exists the effect also must exist. A cloth is not really different from the threads of which it is made, the oil inherent in the oil-seeds, and the curd in the milk. The effect pre-exists in its material cause *(kāraṇabhāvāt)*.

(f) If the effect be really non-existent in the cause, then we have to say that, when it is produced, the non-existent comes into existence, which is absurd.

Therefore, the effect exists in the material cause even before its production or manifestation.

2.2. *Prakṛti*

Sāṃkhya offers a dualistic framework to understand the universe and human existence. It posits two eternal, independent, and coexistent realities: *Puruṣa* (pure consciousness) and *Prakṛti* (primordial matter). Among these, *Prakṛti* holds a central position as the material cause of the phenomenal world, serving as the basis for all physical and mental manifestations.

Prakṛti, often translated as 'nature' or 'primordial matter,' is the unconscious, non-intelligent, and dynamic principle that creates the universe through its transformations. It is eternal, unmanifest (*avyakta*), and consists of the three *guṇas* (qualities or attributes): *sattva* (balance or purity), *rajas* (activity or dynamism), and *tamas* (inertia or darkness). These *guṇas* are the fundamental constituents of *Prakṛti*, whose interplay gives rise to the diversity and complexity of the world.

This theory of causation forms the foundation of the concept of *Prakṛti* as the source and cause of the world of objects in *Sāṃkhya* philosophy. According to this, all worldly effects are latent in this uncaused cause, which is known as *Prakṛti*. It is called *Pradhāna*, the first principle of this universe. It is referred to as *Avyakta*, the unmanifested state of all effects; it is called *Anumāna*, the extremely subtle and imperceptible entity inferred only from its products; it is termed *Jada*, the unintelligent and unconscious principle; and it is called *Śakti*, the ever-active and unlimited power. The products of *Prakṛti* are caused, dependent, relative, manifold, and temporary, as they are subject to birth and death or production and destruction. However, *Prakṛti* itself is uncaused, independent, absolute, singular, and eternal, being beyond both production and destruction.[14]

Sāṃkhya gives five proofs for the existence of *Prakṛti* which are as follows:[15]

(a) All individual things in this world are limited, dependent, conditional and finite. The finite cannot be the cause of the universe. Logically we have to proceed from the finite to the infinite, from the limited to the unlimited, from the temporary to the permanent, from the many to the one. *Prakṛti* is infinite, unlimited, eternal and all-pervading which is the source of this universe (*bhedānām parimāṇat*).

(b) All worldly things possess certain common characteristics by which they are capable of producing pleasure, pain and indifference. Hence there must be a common source composed of three *guṇas*, from which all worldly things arise (*samanvayāt*).

(c) All effects arise from the activity of the potent cause. Evolution means the manifestation of the hitherto implicit as the explicit. The activity which generates evolution must be inherent in the world-cause. And this cause is, *Prakṛti* (*kāryatah pravṛttescha*).

(d) The effect differs from the cause and hence the limited effect cannot be regarded as its own cause. The effect is the explicit and the cause is the implicit state of the same process. The effects, therefore, point to a

---

[14] Sharma, *Indian Philosophy: A Critical Survey*, 140-141.

[15] Sharma, *Indian Philosophy: A Critical Survey*, 141-142.

world-cause where they are potentially contained (*kāranakāryavibhāgāt*).

(e) The unity of the universe points to a single cause. This cause is *Prakṛti* (*avibhāgāt vaishvarūpyasya*).

Prakṛti is said to be the unity of the three *guṇas* - *sattva*, *rajas*, and *tamas* - held in equilibrium (*guṇānām sāmyāvasthā*). These *guṇas* themselves possess qualities such as lightness, activity, heaviness, etc. They are extremely fine and ever-changing elements. They constitute *Prakṛti*, which is nothing apart from them. *Sattva* literally means 'real' or 'existent' and is responsible for the manifestation of objects in consciousness. It is called goodness and produces pleasure. It is light and bright, buoyant (*laghu*) and illuminating (*prakāśaka*). Luminosity of light, power of reflection, upward movement, pleasure, happiness, contentment, and bliss are all due to it. Its colour is white. *Rajas*, which literally means 'foulness,' is the principle of motion. It produces pain. Restless activity, feverish effort, and wild stimulation are its results. It is mobile (*chala*) and stimulating (*upastambhaka*). Its colour is red. *Tamas*, which literally means 'darkness,' is the principle of inertia. It produces apathy and indifference. Ignorance, sloth, confusion, bewilderment, passivity, and negativity are its results. It is heavy (*guru*) and enveloping (*āvaraṇaka*) and, as such, is opposed to *sattva*. It is also opposed to *rajas* as it arrests activity. Its colour is dark. These three *guṇas*, which constitute *Prakṛti*, are never separate. They conflict and yet cooperate with one another and are always found intermingled.[16]

The nature of a thing is determined by the predominance of a particular *guṇa*. Objects and beings are classified as good, bad, or indifferent; intelligent, active, or slothful; pure, impure, or neutral, based on the dominance of *sattva*, *rajas*, or *tamas*, respectively. When these *guṇas* are in a state of equilibrium, this state is called *Prakṛti*, where the evolution of worldly objects does not occur. These *guṇas* are inherently dynamic and cannot

[16] Sharma, *Indian Philosophy: A Critical Survey*, 142.

remain static even for a moment. Evolution occurs when one *guṇa* predominates over the other two, leading to the unfolding or development of the material world.[17]

Sāṃkhya's concept of Prakṛti offers a systematic and rational explanation for the origin and transformation of the universe, emphasizing an eternal, dynamic material principle governed by the interplay of the three *guṇas*. This framework provides a compelling account of cosmic evolution, influencing later Indian philosophical traditions. However, it's strict dualism—separating *Puruṣa* and *Prakṛti* as independent realities, raises questions about their interaction and the role of consciousness in the material world. Additionally, while Sāṃkhya avoids the need for a creator God, its reliance on an uncaused *Prakṛti* as the fundamental source of existence leaves room for debate on whether this explanation is entirely satisfactory. Despite these challenges, Sāṃkhya remains one of the most influential and nuanced philosophical systems in Indian thought.

2.3. *Puruṣa* (Self)

According to Sāṃkhya, there are many souls, each independent of the others. If there were oneness of soul, the birth of one would imply the birth of all, and the death of one would imply the death of all. Unlike Jainism, which asserts that the soul possesses *anantajñāna* (infinite knowledge), *anantadarśana* (infinite perception), *anantasukha* (infinite bliss), and *anantavīrya* (infinite power or energy), Sāṃkhya holds that the soul (or self) does not possess any of these attributes. Instead, the self has pure consciousness (*cit*) as it essence, devoid of qualities. Sāṃkhya differs from Vedānta in its view of the self. While Vedānta often attributes pure intelligence and bliss to the self, Sāṃkhya maintains that bliss is a property of *prakṛti* (matter) and not an intrinsic quality of the soul. Moreover, in contrast to Advaita Vedānta, which posits a singular, unified

---

[17] Sharma, *Indian Philosophy: A Critical Survey*, 143.

reality, Sāṃkhya asserts that the soul/self is real, distinct, and inherently plural in nature.[18]

According to Sāṃkhya, the soul (*Puruṣa*) is the ultimate knower which is the foundation of all knowledge. It is the pure subject and as such can never become an object of knowledge. It is the silent witness, the emancipated alone, the neutral seer, the peaceful eternal. It is beyond time and space, beyond change and activity. It is self-luminous and self-proved. It is uncaused, eternal and all- pervading.

Sāṃkhya School gives the following five proofs for the existence of the *Puruṣa*:[19]

(a) Teleological (*Sanghātaparārthatvāt*): All compound objects exist for the sake of the *Puruṣa*. The body, the senses, the mind and the intellect are all means to realize the end of the *Puruṣa*. The three *guṇas*, the *Prakṛti*, the subtle body - all are said to serve the purpose of the self. *Prakrti* evolves itself in order to serve the *Puruṣa*'s end. This proof is teleological (*Sanghātaparārthatvāt*).

(b) Logical (*Triguṇādiviparyayāt*): All objects are composed of the three *guṇas*, which logically presuppose the existence of *Puruṣa*, the witness who observes these *guṇas* yet remains beyond them. The existence of the three *guṇas* inherently suggests the concept of *niṣtraiguṇya* - that which transcends and is unaffected by the *guṇas*.

(c) Ontological (*Adhiṣṭhānāt*): There must exist a transcendental synthetic unity of pure consciousness to harmonize and coordinate all experiences. The very act of knowing inherently presupposes the existence of the self. The self serves as the foundation or basis (*adhiṣṭhāna*) and the fundamental premise underlying all empirical knowledge. Both affirmations and

[18] S. N. Dasgupta, *A History of Indian Philosophy: An Introduction to the Eight Major Philosophies of Ancient India*, Vol. 1, (Cambridge: Finger Print Classic, 2024), 275-276.

[19] Sharma, *Indian Philosophy: A Critical Survey*, 144-145.

negations inevitably presuppose its presence. Without the self, experience would lack coherence and would not qualify as experience. This reasoning constitutes an ontological proof (*adhiṣṭhānāt*).

(d) **Ethical (*Bhoktṛbhāvāt*):** Non-intelligent *Prakṛti* cannot experience its own products, which necessitates the presence of an intelligent principle to perceive and experience the worldly manifestations of *Prakṛti*. *Prakṛti* is the 'enjoyed' (*bhogyā*), and therefore, there must be an 'enjoyer' (*bhoktā*). All objects in the world possess the characteristics of producing pleasure, pain, and bewilderment, but these attributes hold significance only in relation to a conscious principle capable of experiencing them. Thus, the existence of *Puruṣa* is essential.

(e) **Mystical or Religious (*Kaivalyārtham pravṛtteḥ*):** Some individuals seek to attain freedom from the sufferings of the world. The desire for liberation and emancipation inherently suggests the existence of a person capable of striving for and achieving it. Every aspiration presupposes the presence of an aspirant.

Sāṃkhya's concept of *Puruṣa* presents a distinctive non-theistic dualism that emphasizes the plurality and independence of selves, setting it apart from other Indian philosophical traditions such as Vedānta and Jainism. By portraying the self as pure consciousness, devoid of qualities or attributes, Sāṃkhya avoids anthropomorphic notions of the soul and instead focuses on its role as the passive observer of *Prakṛti*'s transformations. This perspective offers a logical and systematic framework for explaining consciousness and experience. However, the doctrine raises certain philosophical challenges. The strict separation between *Puruṣa* and *Prakṛt*i, while elegant in theory, leaves unresolved questions about the actual mechanism of their interaction – how an entirely passive *Puruṣa* becomes entangled in *Prakṛti*'s evolution. Despite these complexities, Sāṃkhya's theory of *Puruṣa* has had a profound influence on Indian thought, particularly in its impact on Yoga philosophy and later Vedāntic developments. It remains a crucial contribution to the discourse on selfhood, perception, and liberation, offering a rigorous, albeit sometimes abstract, model of consciousness and existence.

2.4. Bondage and Libration

Bondage, according to Sāṃkhya, arises due to the misidentification of *Puruṣa* with *Prakṛti*. Though *Puruṣa* is pure consciousness, eternal, and unaffected by the activities of *Prakṛti*, its close association with *Prakṛti* creates the illusion of attachment and entanglement in worldly existence. The *Puruṣa* mistakenly identifies itself with the body, mind, and senses, which are products of *Prakṛti*. Bondage causes *Puruṣa* to falsely experience the pleasure, pain, and delusion produced by the interaction of the three *guṇas* of *Prakṛti* (*sattva, rajas, tamas*). This misidentification perpetuates the cycle of birth, death, and rebirth (*saṃsāra*), keeping the soul in a state of suffering.

Liberation in Sāṃkhya philosophy is the realization of the true nature of *Puruṣa* as distinct from *Prakṛti*. It is a state of complete separation between the two, leading to freedom from bondage and the cycle of *saṃsāra*. Liberation is achieved through the knowledge (*jñāna*) of the distinction between *Puruṣa* (the conscious self) and *Prakṛti* (the material world). This discriminative knowledge eliminates the false identification of *Puruṣa* with the products of *Prakṛti*. Liberation is referred to as *kaivalya*, meaning "isolation" or "aloneness." It denotes the state where *Puruṣa*, having realized its independence from *Prakṛti*, abides in its own pure nature as eternal, self-luminous consciousness. In the state of liberation, the *guṇas* of *Prakṛti* cease to influence *Puruṣa*. While *Prakṛti* continues to exist, its activity no longer affects the liberated *Puruṣa*.

For Sāṃkhya, liberation is simply cessation of pain and suffering or freedom from suffering where *Puruṣa* achieves this state by realizing its true nature as a passive, non-participatory observer, separate from *Prakṛti*. Unlike many other Indian

Philosophical Schools, it has no positive aspect of liberation like bliss, happiness, etc. In Sāṃkhya, *Puruṣa* is described as pure consciousness (*cit*) that is completely devoid of attributes or qualities (*nirguṇa*). Unlike other schools that see bliss (ānanda) as an essential quality of the liberated self, Sāṃkhya argues that the liberated self or *Puruṣa* is beyond all experiences, whether of pleasure, pain, or bliss. In Sāṃkhya's view, pleasure and bliss are the products of *Prakṛti*. They arise due to the interplay of the three *guṇas* (*sattva*, *rajas*, *tamas*). Since liberation involves complete disassociation from *Prakṛti*, *Puruṣa* cannot experience pleasure and bliss in any form. Thus, liberation in the Sāṃkhya system is *not a positive attainment* but *merely the cessation of pain and suffering*, achieved through the realization of the absolute distinction between *Puruṣa* and *Prakṛti*.

2.5. The Problem of God

Whether Sāṃkhya is theistic, atheistic or agnostic has been a point of contention for many centuries, even among its commentators. Some of the commentators out rightly rejected the belief in God while some others argue that Sāṃkhya is no less theistic than the Nyāya.[20]

We can say confidently that the original Sāṃkhya was monistic and theistic.[21] The classical Sāṃkhya moved away from this and became atheistic. The arguments put forward against the existence of God are as follows:[22]

(a) God cannot be the cause of the world, because God is said to be eternal and immutable and such a thing cannot be the active cause of anything. The cause of anything should be the eternal but ever-changing like that of *Prakṛti*.

(b) There is an argument that non-intelligent matter, *Prakṛti*, requires an intelligent being to direct and control it in

---

[20] Chaterjee and Datta, *An Introduction to Indian Philosophy*, 268.

[21] Sharma, *Indian Philosophy: A Critical Survey*, 152.

[22] Chaterjee and Datta, *An Introduction to Indian Philosophy*, 268.

the production of the material world. Since individual selves are limited and incapable of controlling *Prakṛti*, this reasoning leads to the conclusion that an unlimited, wise being, God must guide and govern *Prakṛti*. However, Sāṃkhya refutes this idea as untenable. If God is the controller of *Prakṛti*, a fundamental question arises: who or what motivated God to control *Prakṛti* and create the world? It cannot be God Himself or Herself, as a perfect being would not have unfulfilled desires or unattained purposes to necessitate creation. Furthermore, the existence of a world filled with suffering and sin contradicts the idea of creation by a perfect being. Such a flawed world cannot reasonably be attributed to an omniscient, omnipotent, and benevolent God.

(c) The belief in God is inconsistence with the distinctive reality and immorality or individual selves. If the selves (*jiva*) are part of God, they ought to have some of the divine powers which is not the case. If they are created by God, they must be subject to destruction, which is also not the case.

So, the conclusion drawn from these arguments is that God does not exist and that Prakrti creates the world unconsciously like the milk of the cow flows unconsciously through her udder.

Concluding Remarks

Sāṃkhya philosophy stands as a cornerstone of Indian philosophical thought, offering a profound and systematic exploration of reality. Its dualistic metaphysics, centered on the distinct yet interdependent principles of *puruṣa* (soul) and *prakṛti* (matter), provides a framework for understanding the nature of existence, the dynamics of the universe, and the path to liberation. By rejecting the need for a creator God, Sāṃkhya emphasizes a rational, self-evolving cosmos, grounded in cause-and-effect relationships within *prakṛti*. However, the absence of a theistic element has led some critics to argue that Sāṃkhya lacks an ultimate source of moral order or purpose, reducing the universe to a mechanical process rather than a teleological system.

The epistemological foundation of Sāṃkhya, which relies on Perception, Inference, and Testimony, reflects its commitment to an integrative pursuit of knowledge, balancing empirical observation, logical reasoning, and scriptural authority. However, its heavy reliance on inference to establish the existence of *puruṣa* and *prakṛti* raises questions about its empirical verifiability. Additionally, while its doctrine of the three *guṇas* provides a compelling explanation of psychological and physical diversity, the deterministic nature of *prakṛti*'s evolution may seem to undermine individual agency, a point that has been contested by later Indian philosophical traditions.

The analysis of bondage and liberation further illustrates Sāṃkhya's practical focus, with bondage arising from ignorance of the *puruṣa-prakṛti* distinction and liberation achieved through discriminative knowledge (*viveka*). However, unlike Vedānta, which offers a more affirmative vision of *mokṣa* as a state of blissful realization, Sāṃkhya presents liberation as merely the cessation of suffering, with no positive state of fulfillment beyond the disengagement from *prakṛti*. This negative conception of liberation has been critiqued as an inadequate end goal for human existence, lacking the richness of spiritual fulfillment found in other traditions.

Thus, while Sāṃkhya philosophy remains a highly influential and intellectually rigorous system, its deterministic cosmology, heavy reliance on Inference, and negative conception of liberation present challenges that invite further philosophical reflection. Nonetheless, its insights into the nature of reality, self-awareness, and the mechanisms of bondage continue to inspire intellectual inquiry and spiritual practice for those seeking a deeper understanding of existence and the ultimate goal of freedom (*mokṣa*).

Chapter 8

Yoga School of Philosophy

Patañjali assumed the role of systematizing the Yoga tradition, structuring it into a coherent school of philosophy. While the notion of yoga possesses antiquity congruent with that of the Vedas, its diverse manifestations are discernible within the Upaniṣads and the Bhagavad Gītā. However, it is Patañjali who ascended the mantle of endorsing yoga as a preeminent philosophical school within the Indian context. Patañjali's *Yoga Sutra* is frequently acknowledged as the culmination of multifarious yoga doctrines, drawn from sources such as the Upaniṣads, Bhagavad Gītā, as well as Buddhist and Jain scriptures. This magnum opus not only codified these teachings but also synthesized them into a singular cohesive narrative.

Patañjali's exposition of Yoga has not garnered prominence primarily due to its metaphysical tenets. In its metaphysical underpinnings, Yoga largely aligns itself with the Sāṃkhya School, diverging primarily in its conception of God - where Yoga acknowledges the existence of a divine entity, a departure from the atheistic stance held by Sāṃkhya. This distinction has led to the nomenclature of "theistic Sāṃkhya" being attributed to the Yoga school.

The fundamental aspiration of Patañjali's Yoga is to bestow liberation upon the individual soul. The goal of Yoga is to give freedom to the individual soul. According to Patañjali, there are two entities in human being – soul (called *puruṣa* in Yoga School) and body (*prakṛti*). Inherent to this perspective is the recognition of the soul's true essence as perfect, pristine, and untarnished. Yet, the veils of ignorance (*avidya*) have trapped the soul within the confines of the body, resulting in its confinement within this physical vessel. Gradually, the soul identifies itself exclusively with the body, perceiving itself as the body. This condition persists until the moment when the soul disentangles itself from the body, thereby achieving emancipation.

The central objective of Patañjali's yoga lies in the separation of the soul from the body. This process of discernment serves to augment the soul's autonomy and liberty. The culmination of this endeavour is the segregation of the soul (*purusa*) from the body (*prakṛti*), heralding the soul's attainment of liberation - referred to as "*mokṣa*." Consequently, we may say that the ultimate aspiration of Yoga revolves around severing the bonds that bind the soul and body, culminating in their complete separation. To achieve this, Patañjali prescribes the eightfold paths (*aṣṭāṅga yoga*):

1. The Eight Limbs of Patañjali's Yoga

There are eight limbs in the Patañjali's yoga – five external limbs which are visible and observable from outside, and three internal limbs which are not visible from outside as they are operated internally. The following are the eight limbs of Patañjali's yoga:

- *Yama* – restraint from evil
- *Niyama* – cultivation of good habits
- *Āsana* – body postures
- *Prāṇāyāma* – control of breath
- *Pratyāhāra* – withdrawal of senses
- *Dhāraṇā* – focus on intended object
- *Dhyāna* – meditation
- *Samādhi* – ultimate concentration

1.1. *Yama*

In Patañjali's *Yoga Sūtras*, the eightfold path (*aṣṭāṅga yoga*) is presented as a systematic approach to attaining spiritual liberation (*mokṣa*). The first limb, *Yama*, consists of ethical restraints that serve as the foundation for a disciplined and harmonious life. These restraints are universal moral principles that transcend cultural and religious boundaries, guiding individuals toward a life of integrity, compassion, and non-harm. The *Yamas* focus on controlling one's behavior in relation to others and the external world, ensuring that actions align with higher spiritual goals. Patañjali outlines five Yamas, which are as follows:

(a) ***Aḥimsā* (Non-violence):** *Aḥimsā* is the principle of non-violence in thought, word, and action. It requires individuals to avoid causing harm to any living being, whether through physical aggression, harmful speech, or destructive intentions. This practice fosters compassion, empathy, and a sense of interconnectedness with all life. *Aḥimsā* is considered the cornerstone of ethical living in yoga.

(b) ***Satya* (Truthfulness):** *Satya* emphasizes honesty and sincerity in communication and actions. It involves speaking the truth while ensuring that it does not cause harm to others. Satya is more than mere factual accuracy; it calls for alignment between thoughts, words, and deeds, promoting authenticity and trustworthiness.

(c) ***Asteya* (Non-stealing):** *Asteya* refers to refraining from taking what does not belong to oneself, whether material possessions, ideas, or time. It encourages contentment and respect for the rights and efforts of others. By practicing *asteya*, individuals cultivate a sense of abundance and gratitude, reducing the desire for unnecessary accumulation.

(d) ***Brahmacharya* (Moderation/Chastity):** *Brahmacharya* is often interpreted as celibacy, but its broader meaning involves moderation and self-restraint in all aspects of life, including sensory pleasures and desires. It encourages the redirection of energy toward spiritual growth and higher goals rather than indulgence in transient pleasures.

(e) ***Aparigraha* (Non-possessiveness):** *Aparigraha* advocates freedom from greed and attachment to material possessions. It involves letting go of the tendency to hoard or cling to objects, relationships, or ideas. By practicing *aparigraha*, individuals learn to embrace simplicity and focus on their inner journey rather than external accumulation.

The famous yoga expert, B.K.S. Iyengar said that in order to reach *Samadhi*, the final spiritual experience, the *yogin* (one who practices yoga) must practice restraint of senses.[1] The *Yamas* are not merely external rules but are deeply tied to the cultivation of inner virtues and attitudes. Practicing these ethical principles prepares the individual for higher stages of yoga by purifying the mind and fostering harmony within oneself and with the world. By adhering to the *Yamas*, the *yogi* establishes a firm moral foundation, ensuring that their spiritual progress is rooted in ethical living and compassionate action.

1.2. *Niyama*

Niyama is the second limb of the eightfold path (*aṣṭāṅga yoga*), which focuses on personal discipline and self-regulation. While *Yama* deals with external ethical principles, *Niyama* emphasizes cultivating positive habits and attitudes to nurture inner growth. These observances help create a disciplined and harmonious lifestyle conducive to spiritual advancement and self-realization. Patañjali identifies five *Niyamas*, each representing a specific practice to guide individuals toward inner purity and alignment with their higher self:

---

[1] B. K. S. Iyengar, *Light on Yoga*, Revised Edition, (New York: Schocken Books, 1979), p. 31.

(a) ***Śauca* (Purity):** *Śauca* refers to cleanliness and purity, both external and internal. External cleanliness involves maintaining hygiene and a clean environment, while internal purity pertains to cleansing the mind of negative emotions such as anger, greed, and jealousy. Practicing śauca prepares the body and mind for higher spiritual practices by promoting clarity and focus.

(b) ***Santoṣa* (Contentment):** *Santoṣa* emphasizes cultivating contentment and satisfaction with one's circumstances. It encourages individuals to accept life as it is, without excessive desires or dissatisfaction. By practicing *santoṣa*, one develops inner peace and resilience, recognizing that true happiness comes from within rather than external possessions or achievements.

(c) ***Tapas* (Discipline):** *Tapas* signifies disciplined effort, self-control, and perseverance in the pursuit of spiritual goals. It involves enduring discomfort or challenges for the sake of self-transformation. Tapas cultivates willpower and determination, helping individuals overcome obstacles and stay committed to their practice.

(d) ***Svādhyāya* (Self-study):** *Svādhyāya* means self-reflection and the study of sacred texts. It involves gaining a deeper understanding of oneself and one's purpose by introspecting on thoughts, actions, and motivations. Additionally, studying spiritual scriptures or teachings helps align personal growth with universal truths and fosters a connection with the divine.

(e) ***Īśvarapraṇidhāna* (Surrender to God):** *Īśvarapraṇidhāna* represents devotion and surrender to a higher power, acknowledging the presence of the divine in all aspects of life. It involves letting go of ego and control, trusting in the wisdom and guidance of the universe. This practice instills humility and helps individuals stay grounded in their spiritual journey.

The *Niyamas* provide a framework for cultivating inner strength, self-awareness, and spiritual focus. By integrating these observances into daily life, practitioners create a foundation for deeper yoga practices, ensuring that their spiritual progress is rooted in discipline, contentment, and surrender. *Niyama*, together with *Yama*, forms the ethical and personal bedrock upon which the subsequent limbs of yoga are built, leading ultimately to self-realization and liberation.

Looking at the first and second limbs of yoga, it can be assumed that these two limbs are adopted from the teachings of Jainism and Buddhism. It appears that Patanjali, who is the author of yoga philosophy, was deeply influenced by the teachings of Buddhism and Jainism. It is reasonable to think that yoga philosophy is the amalgamation of various religious teachings – both Vedic and non-Vedic.

1.3. *Asana*

In Patañjali's *Yoga Sūtras*, *Āsana*, the third limb of the eightfold path (*aṣṭāṅga yoga*), refers to the practice of physical postures. While modern yoga often emphasizes the elaborate physical aspects of *āsana*, Patañjali's focus was more on the stability and comfort of the body to facilitate meditation and spiritual discipline. *Āsana* serves as a preparatory step, enabling the practitioner to develop a firm, healthy body and a calm mind, essential for the higher limbs of yoga.

Patañjali defines *āsana* succinctly in *Yoga Sūtra 2.46:* "*Sthira-sukham-āsanam*", meaning "Posture should be steady and comfortable." This definition underscores that *āsanas* are not meant merely for physical exercise but are a means of creating a stable and relaxed body, conducive to prolonged meditation and introspection. This is in contrast to many of the yoga postures practiced today, which are extremely difficult to perform.

The significance of *āsana* in Patañjali's yoga is twofold: *Physical Preparation - āsanas* prepare the body for the rigors of spiritual practice by cultivating strength, flexibility, and endurance. A strong and healthy body minimizes physical distractions, allowing the mind to focus on deeper meditative states. *Mental Stability* - Practicing āsanas encourages mental discipline and the ability to remain calm under stress. The balance and stillness achieved through physical postures mirror the steadiness required in the mind for advanced yogic practices.

While Patañjali does not elaborate on specific postures, the later *Hatha Yoga* traditions expanded on this concept, introducing various *āsanas* to enhance physical health, purify the body, and control the flow of energy (*prāṇa*). However, in the context of Patañjali's philosophy, the primary goal of *āsana* is to create a body-mind harmony that supports the journey toward self-realization. In essence, *āsana* is not an end in itself but a means to cultivate stability, comfort, and focus, forming a crucial foundation for the higher stages of yoga, including concentration (*dhāraṇā*), meditation (*dhyāna*), and liberation (*samādhi*). By mastering the physical body, one creates a stable vessel for the transformative journey of the mind and spirit.

1.4. *Pranayama*

Prāṇāyāma is the fourth limb focusing on the regulation and control of breath. The word *prāṇa* refers to life force or vital energy, often equated with the breath, and *āyāma* means control or extension. Therefore, *prāṇāyāma* involves both the conscious control of the breath and the expansion of *prāṇa*, with the aim of harmonizing the body and mind. Patañjali's treatment of *prāṇāyāma* is not just about the physical act of controlling the breath, but also about directing and regulating the flow of *prāṇa* within the body. *Prāṇāyāma* purifies and balances the energy systems, calming the mind and preparing the practitioner for deeper meditation and spiritual practice.

The practice of *prāṇāyāma* is rooted in the understanding that the breath is intimately connected to mental states. When the breath is shallow or irregular, the mind tends to be restless; when the breath is controlled and deep, the mind becomes still and focused. Therefore, by mastering the breath, one can also gain mastery over the mind.

Patañjali does not describe specific techniques in detail but outlines the purpose of *prāṇāyāma* as controlling the rhythm of the breath in a way that directly influences *prāṇa* and enhances physical and mental well-being. It is traditionally practiced in three stages: Inhalation (*Puraka*) – the act of drawing the breath in, which brings *prāṇa* into the body; Exhalation (*Rechaka*) – the process of expelling the breath, which helps expel toxins and negative energy from the body; and Retention (*Kumbhaka*) – holding the breath, which is said to intensify the flow of *prāṇa* and promote mental clarity and concentration.

Patañjali emphasizes that *prāṇāyāma* helps purify the mind and body, preparing one for deeper meditation (*Sūtra* 2.49–2.53). A steady, controlled breath calms the fluctuations of the mind, facilitating concentration (*dharana*), meditation (*dhyāna*), and ultimately leading to a state of mental stillness and liberation (*samādhi*).

1.5. *Pratyāhāra*

Pratyāhāra, the fifth limb of Patañjali's *aṣṭāṅga yoga* (eightfold path), marks a pivotal transition from the external practices of yoga to the inner, meditative disciplines. Derived from the Sanskrit roots *prati* (against or away) and *āhāra* (intake or nourishment), *Pratyāhāra* refers to the withdrawal or control of the senses from external stimuli. This practice is designed to help the practitioner turn their awareness inward, preparing the mind for deeper concentration and meditation. In daily life, the senses are constantly engaged with the external world, pulling the mind in multiple directions and creating distractions. *Pratyāhāra* is the process of detaching the senses from their objects, allowing the practitioner to regain control over their mind and redirect their focus toward the inner self. This withdrawal is not about suppressing the senses but about mastering them so they no longer dominate the mind or hinder spiritual growth.

Patañjali emphasizes that *Pratyāhāra* is essential for achieving mental stillness, as it breaks the habitual cycle of sensory engagement. The *Yoga Sūtras* describe this process as the senses "following" the mind inward, rather than outwardly engaging with their usual objects of perception. For instance, instead of being absorbed by the sight of a beautiful landscape or the sound of music, the senses become dormant, allowing the mind to concentrate on subtler realities.

Pratyāhāra serves as the gateway to the higher limbs of yoga, particularly *dhāraṇā* (concentration), *dhyāna* (meditation), and *samādhi* (liberation). By mastering *Pratyāhāra*, the *yogin* learns to quiet the external distractions that often dominate the mind, creating a still and receptive inner state conducive to spiritual progress.

1.6. *Dhāraṇā*

Dhāraṇā or 'focused attention' is a mental discipline involving the fixation of the mind (*citta*) on a chosen object.[2] Derived from the Sanskrit root *dhṛ*, meaning 'to hold' or 'to support,' *dhāraṇā* involves holding the mind steady on a single object, thought, or point of focus. This practice is foundational for meditation (*dhyāna*) and ultimately leads to the state of absorption (*samādhi*). The *Yoga Sūtras* define *dhāraṇā* as the binding of consciousness to a particular locus. It requires the practitioner to withdraw attention from all distractions and direct the mind unwaveringly toward a chosen object, whether external or internal. The practitioner selects an object and directs their full concentration toward it. This 'object' can be anything. According to Sage Vyāsa, the esteemed commentator on Patañjali's *Yoga Sūtras*, one may focus on specific parts of the body, such as the navel, the space between the eyebrows, the tip of the nose, or the tongue. Alternatively, the object of focus could be external, like the moon, an image of a deity, or any other suitable symbol.[3] Once the object is chosen, the

---

[2] Chatterjee and Datta, *An Introduction to Indian Philosophy,* 304.

[3] Gerald James Larson, "Introduction to the Philosophy of Yoga", in *Encyclopedia of Indian Philosophies, Vol. XII: Yoga – India's Philosophy of Meditation*, (Delhi: Motilal Banarsidass Publishers, 2008), p. 120.

practitioner must channel all their thoughts and mental energy toward it.

The purpose of *dhāraṇā* is to discipline the wandering mind and develop one-pointedness (*ekāgratā*), which is essential for deeper meditative states. In everyday life, the mind is often scattered, shifting rapidly between thoughts and external stimuli. *Dhāraṇā* trains the practitioner to overcome this restlessness by anchoring the mind to a single point, fostering mental clarity, stability, and inner peace. The benefits of *dhāraṇā* extend beyond spiritual pursuits. It enhances cognitive abilities, improves memory and decision-making, and fosters emotional resilience. By mastering concentration, practitioners develop the mental fortitude to remain calm and focused even in challenging situations.

In the context of Patañjali's yoga system, *dhāraṇā* represents a critical turning point where the practitioner begins to transcend the external world and delve deeply into the inner self. It bridges the practices of sensory withdrawal (*pratyāhāra*) and meditation (*dhyāna*), forming a crucial step on the journey toward self-realization and liberation (*mokṣa*). Ultimately, *dhāraṇā* trains the mind to become a tool for spiritual awakening, leading the practitioner closer to the profound stillness of *samādhi*.

1.7. *Dhyāna*

Dhyāna, the seventh limb of Patañjali's *aṣṭāṅga yoga* (eightfold limb), represents the practice of meditation or sustained contemplation. Derived from the Sanskrit root *dhyai*, meaning 'to think,' 'to contemplate,' or 'to meditate,' *Dhyāna* "means the even flow of thought about, or rather, round about, the object of attention. It is the steadfast contemplation of the object without any break or disturbance."[4] It refers to an uninterrupted flow of awareness toward a single object or point of focus. When the mind is calm, fully absorbed, and fixed on the selected

[4] Chatterjee and Datta, *An Introduction to Indian Philosophy*, p. 304.

object for an extended period, one reaches the state of *Dhyāna*.[5] It is the natural progression from *dhāraṇā* (concentration), where the effort to focus the mind transitions into a seamless and effortless meditative state. In the *Yoga Sūtras*, *dhyāna* is described as the continued and unbroken focus on the chosen object of meditation. While *dhāraṇā* involves a deliberate effort to concentrate, *dhyāna* emerges when the mind becomes steady and absorbed in the object without distraction. It is a state of profound mental stillness and clarity, where the boundaries between the observer and the observed begin to dissolve.

The purpose of *dhyāna* is to transcend the fluctuations of the mind (*citta vṛtti*) and to connect with the deeper layers of consciousness. Achieving this level of concentration allows the mind to become enlightened, enabling the practitioner to discern the distinction between the soul (*jīva*) and the body (*prakṛti*). This ability to separate the soul from the body marks a crucial step in the yogic path, leading to the final stage of Yoga practice, *Samādhi*, where ultimate realization is attained.

1.8. *Samādhi*

Samādhi is often translated as 'absorption' or 'meditative absorption.' It refers to a state of deep, unbroken concentration in which the mind becomes so focused on the object of meditation that the individual self merges with it. There is no duality of subject and object; they become one. In *Samādhi* one experiences complete absorption where the practitioner's attention is so intense and focused that they lose awareness of everything else, including the body and ego. In *Samādhi*, there are no distractions or fluctuations in the mind (*vṛttis*). The mind is fully still, and external stimuli no longer affect the meditator. Then the practitioner experiences his or her true nature as pure consciousness, distinct from the body and mind. This realization brings freedom from suffering and ignorance (*avidyā*). Attaining *Samādhi* leads to *mokṣa* - liberation from the cycle of birth and rebirth (*saṃsāra*). The *yogin* is no longer bound by the dualities

[5] Iyengar, *Light on Yoga*, p. 51.

of life and death, pleasure and pain, and the attachments of the material world.

When a *yogin* reaches the final state, he or she is believed to acquire certain extraordinary powers. It is claimed that the *yogin* can tame ferocious animals, obtain objects merely by wishing for them, directly perceive the past, present, and future, produce supernatural sights, sounds, and smells, and perceive subtle entities. Additionally, the *yogin* may be able to see through closed doors, pass through stone walls, disappear from sight, appear in multiple places simultaneously, and perform other miraculous feats. But the Yoga system warns the practitioner not to practice yoga having this ends in mind. "The yogin must not get entangled in the quagmire of supernormal power," rather he or she must move on till he or she "comes to the end of the journey, viz. liberation."[6]

Thus, the Eight Limbs of Patañjali Yoga (*Aṣṭāṅga Yoga*) provide a comprehensive and structured approach to achieving physical, mental, and spiritual well-being. Each limb, beginning with the ethical guidelines (*yama* and *niyama*), gradually leads the practitioner through a process of purification, discipline, and self-realization. The physical postures (*āsana*) strengthen the body, while breath control (*prāṇāyāma*) and sensory withdrawal (*pratyāhāra*) help refine the mind and create an environment conducive to inner peace. Concentration (*dhāraṇā*), meditation (*dhyāna*), and ultimately *samādhi* - the final state of deep, undisturbed absorption - lead the practitioner to spiritual enlightenment and self-realization. These steps together guide individuals towards a life of balance, harmony, and liberation (*mokṣa*), transcending the limitations of the ego and the material world.

By following the Eight Limbs, yoga becomes not just a physical practice but a path of wholistic transformation, enabling practitioners to cultivate inner peace, awareness, and a profound connection with the divine and the universe. In this

---

[6] Chatterjee and Datta, *An Introduction to Indian Philosophy*, 305.

way, Patañjali's system of yoga offers a timeless and practical framework for achieving ultimate freedom and self-mastery.

2. The Place of God in Yoga

Yoga and Sāṁkhya philosophies share significant similarities. Yoga adopts the epistemology and most of the metaphysical teachings of Sāṁkhya, with one key difference: the concept of God. For this reason, Yoga is often referred to as 'theistic Sāṁkhya.' Unlike Sāṁkhya, Yoga acknowledges the existence of God on both practical and theoretical grounds, emphasizing the practical value of devotion to God as a key aspect of its practice.[7]

According to Yoga, God (*Īśvara*) is the Supreme Person, transcending all limitations and free from any defects. He is described as all-pervading, omnipotent, and omniscient - an immortal and perfect spirit, untouched by afflictions or actions. As the supreme ruler of the world, God is recognized as the ultimate reality and the Supreme Self. The existence of God is affirmed in the Vedas, the Upaniṣads, and other authoritative scriptures, which consistently speak of Him in these terms. Furthermore, the existence of God can be logically deduced from the law of continuity. In the universe, there are gradations of lower and higher, smaller and greater, as well as varying degrees of knowledge and power - facts universally acknowledged. If this is the case, there must exist a being who possesses perfect knowledge and ultimate power, one who is the highest and greatest. Such a being is God, the Supreme Person, the highest and the greatest reality.[8]

Devotion to God is not only part of the practice of Yoga but the best mean for attainment of concentration and restraint of mind (*Samādhi-yoga*). God is the Supreme Lord who, by His grace, purges away the sins and evils in the life of His devotees and makes the attainment of liberation easier for them.[9]

---

[7] Chatterjee and Datta, *An Introduction to Indian Philosophy*, (2007), 285.

[8] Chatterjee and Datta, *An Introduction to Indian Philosophy*, (2007), 286.

[9] Chatterjee and Datta, *An Introduction to Indian Philosophy*, (2007), 287.

Īśvara is the Supreme Person who is eternal and free from all imperfections. *Īśvara* is not bound by the cycle of birth and death, nor affected by *karma*, afflictions, or the limitations of time. He represents a state of perfect freedom (*kaivalya*) and is considered the ultimate guide for spiritual aspirants. God governs the world and upholds the cosmic order. Yoga philosophy uses the term *Īśvara* to refer to God. The term appears prominently in Patañjali's *Yoga Sūtras*, the foundational text of classical Yoga. In *Yoga Sūtra* 1.23-24, *Īśvara* is described as a special being (*puruṣa-viśeṣa*) who is untouched by the limitations of human existence, such as afflictions (*kleśas*), actions (*karmas*), or the results of *karma* (*vipāka*). Īśvara represents an eternal, all-knowing, and ever-liberated entity.

In Yoga, God, who is a personal God, is both a theoretical ideal and a practical necessity. Īśvara represents the ultimate reality, serving as a source of inspiration, a guide for spiritual growth, and a symbol of perfection. While liberation is primarily achieved through self-effort and disciplined practice, devotion to God enriches the practitioner's journey, providing a powerful means to attain spiritual fulfillment and ultimate freedom.

Concluding Remarks

Yoga philosophy, particularly as articulated in Patanjali's *Yoga Sūtras*, presents a profound and systematic approach to mental, physical, and spiritual well-being. The *Eight Limbs of Yoga* (*Aṣṭāṅga Yoga*) offer a wholistic framework that guides practitioners in ethical conduct and disciplined practice toward the ultimate goal of self-realization and liberation (*kaivalya*). These limbs, encompassing moral observances (*yamas*), personal disciplines (*niyamas*), physical postures (*āsanas*), breath control (*prāṇāyāma*), withdrawal from the senses (*pratyāhāra*), concentration (*dharanā*), meditation (*dhyāna*), and pure contemplation (*samādhi*), collectively offer a pathway toward harmony and balance within the individual and their relationship with the world. This structured approach not only emphasizes spiritual development but also integrates mental and physical health, thus offering a well-rounded approach to human flourishing.

The place of God (*Īśvara*) in Patanjali's system adds a significant and profound dimension to the philosophy. Unlike the Sāṃkhya system, which shares many similarities with Yoga but rejects belief in God, Patañjali's inclusion of *Īśvara* (God) as a distinct, transcendent consciousness introduces a theistic dimension to Yoga. *Īśvara*, in Patanjali's framework, is not merely an abstract concept but a specific, eternal, and all-knowing being who plays an essential role in the spiritual journey of the practitioner. *Īśvara* serves as a catalyst for liberation, offering divine guidance and grace to those whose personal efforts alone may not suffice. In this sense, the belief in *Īśvara* provides an important metaphysical foundation, linking the individual's struggle for spiritual progress with divine support. This makes the path of Yoga not purely a human endeavour but also one that engages a divine dimension, suggesting that spiritual liberation (*kaivalya*) is ultimately achieved through the cooperation of personal discipline and divine guidance.

However, despite its comprehensive system, Yoga philosophy has its share of criticisms. The emphasis on renunciation and the suppression of the body's natural desires, especially in the early stages of practice, may be seen as overly ascetic and disconnected from the lived realities of modern existence. The strict discipline and long-term commitment required to progress through the stages of Yoga can be daunting, and for many, the goal of achieving *kaivalya* may seem abstract or even unattainable within a single lifetime. Additionally, the philosophical underpinnings of Patañjali's Yoga, particularly in its reliance on the control and transcendence of the mind, may overlook the complex, subjective nature of human experience. The strict separation between the self (*puruṣa*) and the mind (*citta*) can lead to an oversimplified view of the mind-body connection and may not fully account for the intricate interplay between consciousness, emotions, and mental states in a more integrated, wholistic sense.

The inclusion of *Īśvara* in Yoga also raises significant questions regarding the nature of divinity and its relationship with the individual soul. *Īśvara* is not just a passive force but is described as an eternal, omniscient being who transcends time and space. His presence in the system provides an essential avenue for the practitioner to tap into a higher source of wisdom and power. However, some critics argue that the incorporation of divine guidance into the practice of Yoga complicates the system by introducing an element of dependence that may challenge the otherwise self-reliant nature of Yoga. The tension between personal discipline and reliance on divine intervention might be perceived as a contradiction, potentially leading to ambiguity regarding the true nature of liberation in the Yoga system. Yet, for those who embrace this theistic dimension, *Īśvara* provides a clear and comforting path to spiritual fulfillment, reaffirming Yoga's wholistic approach to personal and divine integration.

Nevertheless, Yoga philosophy's profound influence on both Eastern and Western thought, its practical application for mental and physical well-being, and its deep spiritual insights continue to make it a timeless system of personal transformation. While its goals may seem lofty and its practices rigorous, the principles of Yoga still offer valuable tools for cultivating self-awareness, mindfulness, and emotional resilience in a world that often feels fragmented and disconnected. Despite its limitations, Yoga remains a significant and influential philosophical tradition, offering a pathway to a deeper understanding of the self and the universe.

The influence of Patañjali's Yoga is evident in contemporary yoga practices across both the East and the West. Most of the numerous yoga systems we see today are deeply rooted in Patañjali's teachings. These modern forms of yoga are essentially modifications and variations of the foundational principles laid out in Patañjali's Yoga which is reverently called as "*Raja Yoga.*"

Chapter 9

Mīmāṁsā Philosophy

Mīmāṁsā, also referred to as 'Pūrva Mīmāṁsā' is one of the six orthodox (*āstika*) schools of Indian philosophy, forming a critical part of the Vedānta tradition. The term 'Pūrva Mīmāṁsā,' literally meaning 'prior inquiry,' refers to the school's focus on the first part of the Vedas -specifically the *Karma Kanda* (ritualistic sections) - which deals with the performance of rituals, ethical duties, and the methods for attaining spiritual and material benefits through these practices. At its core, Mīmāṁsā is concerned with the correct interpretation of the Vedic texts, offering a systematic framework for understanding the principles underlying ritual actions and their significance. It emphasizes the importance of following Vedic prescriptions with precision and devotion, claiming that the performance of rituals is a crucial means for both worldly well-being and ultimate liberation.

Mīmāṁsā is traditionally attributed to Sage Jaimini, an ancient philosopher whose work is encapsulated in the *Mīmāṁsā Sūtras*. These *sūtras* form the foundation of the school's methodology and establish its central concerns with ritual actions *(karma*) and the means through which these actions yield results (*phala*). Mīmāṁsā was significantly developed by later commentators who enriched its philosophical depth and solidified its status as an orthodox school of Indian philosophy. Śabara (2nd-3rd century CE) provided an early and crucial commentary on Jaimini's *sūtras*, elaborating on the interpretation of rituals. Kumārila Bhaṭṭa (7th century CE) made substantial contributions with his *Ślokavārttika*, emphasizing the necessity of Vedic rituals for liberation and introducing the theory of *Apūrva* to explain the causal link between actions and results. Prabhākara (7th century CE), with his *Prabhākara Bhāṣya*, offered a more lenient interpretation, focusing on the role of doubt in understanding Vedic injunctions. These commentators collectively expanded and systematized Mīmāṁsā, ensuring its lasting influence in Indian philosophy.

Mīmāṁsā is distinct from Uttara Mīmāṁsā or Vedānta, the latter of which primarily addresses the philosophical teachings found in the Upaniṣads and focuses on the nature of the ultimate reality (Brahman) and the nature of self (*ātman*). The distinction between Pūrva Mīmāṁsā and Uttara Mīmāṁsā is crucial in understanding the differences in their approach: Pūrva Mīmāṁsā centers on the *ritualistic portions* of the Vedas, while Uttara Mīmāṁsā (Vedānta) focuses on the *philosophical teachings* contained in the Upaniṣads. Although both schools fall under the umbrella of Vedic tradition, their emphasis and methodologies differ significantly.

1. Theory of Knowledge (*Pramāṇa*)

The Mīmāṁsā school of Indian philosophy, particularly its Kumārila Bhāṭṭa and Prābhākara sub-schools, is one of the most rigorous systems of epistemology in Indian thought. It primarily focuses on the correct interpretation of the Vedas and emphasizes the performance of rituals as the path to *dharma*. In this framework, the Mīmāṁsā philosophers developed a sophisticated theory of knowledge to establish the validity of scriptural testimony and human cognition.

Jaimini, the founder of Mīmāṁsā philosophy recognized three sources of valid knowledge – Perception, Inference and *Śabda* (Testimony); Prābhākara accepts apart from the above three, *Upamāna* (comparison) and *Arthāpatti* (Implication or Postulation); Kumārila Bhāṭṭa adds one more to the above five *pramāṇas* – *anupalabdhi* (non-recognition).[1] Thus, we have six sources of valid knowledge (*pramāṇa*) recognized by the Mīmāṁsā school of philosophy: Perception (*pratyakṣa*), inference (*anumāna*), postulation (*arthāpatti*), comparision (*upamāna*), authority or testimony (*śabda*), and non-perception or non-cognition (*anupalabdhi*). The last one, non-perception or non-cognition (*anupalabdhi*) is accepted by Kumārila Bhāṭṭa but rejected by Prābhākara. It may be noted here that these six *pramāṇas* are also accepted by Vedanta School of Philosophy. We shall elaborate these sources of valid knowledge as follows:

1.1. Perception (*Pratyakṣa*)

Perception is defined as knowledge that arises from the direct interaction of the sense organs with objects. "Prabhäkara defines perception as direct apprehension (*sâksât pratîtih pratyaksam*). Kumārila defines it as direct knowledge produced by the proper contact of the sense-organs with the presented objects, which is free from defects."[2] The Bhāṭṭa school follows a realist perspective, asserting that perception is the result of contact between the sense organ and the external object, mediated by the mind. According to Mīmāṁsā, there are two types of perception – *indeterminate* and *determinate*. We know the object with the help of any one of our sense organs, but we have not yet understood what it is. This type of knowledge we gained through perception is called indeterminate, immediate knowledge (*nirvikalpaka pratyakṣa* or *ālocana-jñāna*). In the next stage, we interpret the object in the light of our past knowledge and come to the conclusion that "this is a man", "this is a table", etc., we have the second type of perception, the determinate (*savikalpaka*) perception.

---

[1] S. Radhakrishnan, *Indian Philosophy Vol. II*, (New York: The Macmillan Company, 1958), 378-379

[2] Chandradhar Sharma, *Indian Philosophy: A Critical Survey*, (New York City: Barnes & Noble, Inc. 1962), 206.

1.2. Inference (*Anumāna*)

As the theory of inference in Mīmāṁsā is more or less similar with Nyāya school of philosophy, we may not give elaborate discussion here. In Mīmāṁsā philosophy, inference (*anumāna*) is a crucial means of knowledge that derives conclusions from observed relationships, particularly through the principle of *vyāpti* (invariable concomitance). It is defined as reasoning based on the consistent association between a sign (*liṅga*) and what it signifies, such as the presence of fire being inferred from the observation of smoke. Mīmāṁsā emphasizes the role of inference in practical matters, especially in interpreting the Vedas and understanding unseen entities like *dharma*. While recognizing inference as a valid *pramāṇa* (means of knowledge), Mīmāṁsā philosophers, particularly the Bhāṭṭa and Prābhākara schools, subordinate it to *śabda* (verbal testimony), considering the Vedas as the ultimate and most reliable source of knowledge about *dharma*. Thus, inference in Mīmāṁsā serves primarily to support and validate scriptural interpretation.

1.3. Comparison (*Upamāna*)

Mīmāṁsā recognizes comparison (*upamāna*) as a valid source of knowledge. According to this view, knowledge arises from comparing a known object from the past with a present object. For instance, upon seeing a rat, one recalls a mouse perceived earlier and recognizes the similarity between the two. This leads to the knowledge that the remembered mouse resembles the perceived rat. Similarly, someone who has previously seen a cow at home might encounter a *gavaya* (wild cow) in the forest and, noticing its similarity to the domestic cow, gains the knowledge that the gavaya resembles the cow at home. This process of understanding relationships through similarity exemplifies the role of comparison in acquiring knowledge.[3]

Śabarasvāmī, a well known interpreter of Mīmāṁsā philosophy, understands *upāmana* in line with Western logic

[3] Satishandra Chaterjee and Dhirendramohan Datta, *An Introduction to Indian Philosophy*, (New Delhi: Rupa, 2007), 293-294.

analogical argument. According to him, the existence of another self is established from your feeling of your own self. By analogy, you can believe that as you have self, others humans should also feel the existence of their own self. So, he defines *upāmana* as 'knowledge of an unperceived object as being similar to some known object.'[4]

According to Mīmāṁsā philosophy, comparison (*upamāna*) facilitates understanding through relational cognition, where a present perception triggers a memory of a past experience, leading to a comparison and new knowledge. This knowledge is not directly perceptual but arises from comparing and correlating past and present observations. Mīmāṁsā emphasizes the practical significance of *upamāna*, especially in understanding and categorizing the world based on relational awareness.

1.4. Testimony (*Śabda*)

Śabda (testimony) has got the greatest importance in Mīmāmsā philosophy. It refers to verbal authority and is the means of acquiring knowledge about supra-sensible objects through understanding the meanings conveyed by words. Kumārila classifies testimony into two types: personal (*pauruṣeya*) and impersonal (*apauruṣeya*). Personal testimony refers to the statements of trustworthy individuals (*āptavākya*) and is not intrinsically valid; its validity depends on the reliability of the speaker, making it susceptible to doubt, error, and later contradiction. In contrast, impersonal testimony refers to the Vedas (*Vedavākya*), which Kumārila asserts are intrinsically valid, eternal, and authorless. The Vedas are not the creation of any being, human or divine, and the sages are regarded as mere seers, not authors. Even God is not considered the composer or speaker of the Vedas. Since the Vedas pertain to *dharma*, which cannot be known through perception, inference, comparison, or any other *pramāṇa* (valid means of knowledge), their injunctions are infallible and cannot be contradicted by

[4] Chaterjee and Datta, *An Introduction to Indian Philosophy*, 295.

any subsequent knowledge. This intrinsic validity underscores the Vedas' supreme authority in matters of *dharma*.[5]

For the Mīmāṁsākas, Vedas are eternal, not created by God. They hold that the Vadas exist forever in their own right. God who is incorporeal has no organ of speech and therefore, cannot utter the words of the Vedas.[6] They classified the content of the Vedas into injunction (*vidhi*), hymns (*mantras*), names (*nāmadheya*), prohibition (*niṣedha*), and explanatory passages (*arthavāda*). Mīmāṁsākas attempt to prove that every part of the Vedas refers to acts of duty.[7]

The value of the Vedas, according to Mīmāṁsākas, is that they give direction for performance of sacrifice because for them Vedic sacrifice is the sole and sure way for liberation.

1.5. Postulation (*Arthāpatti*)

Postulation (*arthapatti*) is the necessary supposition of an unperceived fact which alone can explain a phenomenon that demands explanation so as to reconcile apparent contradictions between two known facts.[8] In other words, *Arthāpatti* is the process by which a previously unobserved fact is presumed to explain two contradictory observations.

Prābhākara and Kumārila Bhāṭṭa recognize Postulation (*arthāpatti*) as an independent and valid means of knowledge. Arthāpatti refers to the act of presumption or implication, where an unperceived fact is assumed to reconcile two seemingly contradictory observed facts. For instance, if Devadatta is observed to be fat and is also known not to eat during the day, one presumes he must eat at night to resolve the apparent contradiction between 'being fat' and 'not eating during the day.' While the Naiyāyika school reduces this presumption to a form of inference, the Mīmāṃsaka considers it an independent *pramāṇa*. According to Prābhākara, the distinguishing factor

---

[5] Chandradhar Sharma, Indian Philosophy, 208.

[6] S. Radhakrishnan, *Indian Philosophy Vol. II*, 392.

[7] S. Radhakrishnan, *Indian Philosophy Vol. II*, 388.

[8] Chaterjee and Datta, *An Introduction to Indian Philosophy*, (2007), 299.

between presumption and inference lies in the element of doubt. In presumption, there is doubt about the truth of the two perceived facts, and this doubt is resolved through postulation. In contrast, inference operates without such doubt. Kumārila, however, disagrees with the role of doubt in presumption. He argues that its foundation lies in the mutual inconsistency of the two observed facts, which is resolved by the act of postulation.[9]

The Mīmāṃsakas argue that *arthāpatti* is distinct from other *pramāṇas* like perception (*pratyakṣa*) or inference (*anumāna*). While inference involves establishing a conclusion based on a universal concomitance (*vyāpti*) between the middle term and the predicate, *arthāpatti* relies on logical necessity rather than formal reasoning. It directly addresses the inconsistency between two observed facts ('being fat' and 'not eating during the day') and resolves it by introducing a plausible assumption (he must eat at night).

Arthāpatti plays a crucial role in Mīmāṃsā epistemology by highlighting the importance of logical necessity in human cognition. It demonstrates the ability of the human mind to infer unseen realities based on observed contradictions, thereby expanding the scope of knowledge beyond mere perception or formal inference. Mīmāṃsakas use *arthāpatti* in various philosophical and theological contexts, particularly in scriptural interpretation, where apparent contradictions in sacred texts are resolved through postulation.

1.6. Non-cognition (*Anupalabdhi*)

This is a very unique source of knowledge which is accepted by some of the famous commentator of the Mīmāṃsā philosophy. While Kumārila Bhāṭṭa (and also the Advaita Vedānta School) admits Non-apprehension (*anupalabdhi*) as the sixth independent *pramāna*, Prabhākara (along with *Naiyāyikas*) rejects it. It is primarily concerned with the cognition of absence or non-existence (*abhāva*). Unlike other *pramāṇas*, which deal with the presence of entities or phenomena, *anupalabdhi* facilitates the

[9] Chandradhar Sharma, *Indian Philosophy*, 210.

understanding of their absence, providing an epistemological foundation for negation. According to S. Radhakrishnan, "Non-apprehension is a means of knowledge (*mānam*) with reference to the object negated."[10] For example, when we look at a table and observe that there is no jar on it, this absence cannot be known through perception, as perception requires the presence of an object to be apprehended by the senses. Similarly, it cannot be established through inference, as the principle of *vyāpti* (invariable concomitance) does not apply in this case. According to the Mīmāṃsakas, the absence of the jar on the table can be known solely through *anupalabdhi* (non-apprehension).

The Bhāṭṭas and Advitins accept that the non-existence of the jar on the table is known from the absence of its cognition. We are sure that there is no jar on the table because it is not perceived. This phenomenon cannot be explained by any other means; so, to explain the direct knowledge of the jar's non-existence, we have to recognize non-perception or non-cognition (*anupalabdhi*) as a separate and an independent source of knowledge.[11]

The Mīmāṃsā theory of knowledge represents a sophisticated and systematic approach to epistemology, deeply rooted in the quest for precision and reliability in human cognition. By identifying six independent *pramāṇas* - perception (*pratyakṣa*), inference (*anumāna*), comparison (*upamāna*), postulation (*arthāpatti*), testimony (*śabda*), and non-apprehension (*anupalabdhi*) - Mīmāṃsā scholars have provided a comprehensive framework for understanding the diverse ways in which valid knowledge (*pramā*) can be acquired. This inclusiveness reflects the Mīmāṃsā school's commitment to accounting for the complexity of human experience and the diversity of contexts in which knowledge arises. Furthermore, their recognition of *anupalabdhi* and *arthāpatti* as independent *pramāṇas* highlights their pioneering contribution to Indian

[10] S. Radhakrishnan, *Indian Philosophy Vol. II*, 394.

[11] Chaterjee and Datta, *An Introduction to Indian Philosophy*, (2007), 301.

epistemology, setting them apart from other schools that often subsume these under perception or inference.

At its core, the Mīmāṃsā theory of knowledge is not merely an abstract exercise but is deeply practical, designed to support the interpretation and application of *Vedic injunctions* in ritual and ethical contexts. This pragmatic orientation reinforces the idea that valid knowledge must ultimately serve a purpose, whether in guiding actions, resolving contradictions, or affirming truths.

2. Authority of the Vedas

Mīmāṁsā philosophy regards the Vedas as eternal and authorless revelations that contain timeless truths about ritual, duty, and the nature of the universe. It places utmost importance on the textual authority of the Vedas and emphasizes the need for meticulous interpretation to derive correct meanings and injunctions from the scriptures. Mīmāṁsā focuses primarily on the *Karma Kanda* section of the Vedas, which deals with rituals (*karma*), sacrifices (*yajna*), and religious duties (dharma). Chandradhar Sharma notes, "Greatest importance is attached to the *Brähmaṇa* portion of the Veda to which both the *Mantras* and the *Upaniṣads* are subordinated. The aim of the Mīmāṁsā is to supply the principles according to which the Vedic texts are to be interpreted and to provide philosophical justification for the views contained therein."[12] It provides elaborate rules and guidelines for performing rituals and fulfilling religious obligations prescribed in the Vedas.

Mīmāṁsā scholars meticulously analyze Vedic texts to understand the precise procedures and meanings of rituals. A significant aspect of Mīmāṁsā philosophy is its methodology of interpretation, known as hermeneutics. Mīmāṁsā scholars developed sophisticated principles of interpretation to extract meaning and injunctions from the Vedas. They classified Vedic sentences into different categories (e.g., injunctions, statements of fact) and formulated rules for understanding their intended

[12] Chandradhar Sharma, *Indian Philosophy,* 200.

meanings. Unlike some other Indian philosophical schools like Vedānta, Mīmāṁsā does not explicitly focus on metaphysical concepts such as the nature of the self (*ātman*) or the existence of God. Instead, it prioritizes the understanding and performance of rituals and duties prescribed in the Vedas as the means to achieve worldly prosperity and spiritual fulfillment. Mīmāṁsā scholars were known for their rigorous debate and logical reasoning. They engaged in philosophical debates with proponents of other schools, particularly Vedānta, Nyāya, and Buddhism, defending the authority of the Vedas and the efficacy of Vedic rituals.

3. Supremacy of Vedas and Vedic Rituals

The Mīmāmsā School of philosophy is based on the ritualistic side of the Vedas. As pointed out earlier, it places greater emphasis on the Brāhmaṇas than on the Mantras, viewing the Vedas primarily as a text of rituals.[13] There are two ways by which Mīmāmsā tries to help and support ritualism – (a) to supply methodological tools for understanding, harmonizing and following the complicated Vedic rituals, (b) to foster a philosophical justification of the beliefs on which ritualism depends.[14] To support its emphasis on ritualism, Mīmāmsā School claims that Vedas are eternal and self-existing and are not the handiwork of human beings - implying the necessity of following what are there in them. For Mīmāmsākas, human responsibility is to do his/her duty that includes ritual performance. However, "ritual enjoined by the Vedas should be performed not with the hope of any reward but just because they are so enjoined", because only "the disinterested performance of the obligatory rites… gradually destroys the *karmas* and bring

[13] M. Hiriyanna, *Outlines of Indian Philosophy*, (Delhi: Motilal Banarsidass, 2000), p. 299.

[14] Satishandra Chaterjee and Dhirendramohan Datta, *An Introduction to Indian Philosophy*, (Calcutta: University of Calcutta, 2004, Eight Edition), p. 313.

about liberation after death."[15] Obligatory rite is to be performed not because it will benefit the performers, but it is because we ought to perform it as it is the injunction of the Vedas.[16] The Mīmāmsā also admits that when any person performs any ritual, there arises in his/her soul potency (*apūrva*) which produces in future the fruit of action that he or she will enjoy.[17]

The Mīmāmsā School does not ignore the necessity of knowledge, but maintains that knowledge is subservient to rites and is part of the rites. They argue the validity of rites by stating that it is the injunction of Upaniṣads. A variety of Upaniṣadic texts show that rites are important – "Janaka, emperor of Videha, performed a sacrifice in which gifts were freely distributed" (Bṛ.U. 3.1.1), "Sir, I am about to perform a sacrifice" (Ch.U. 5.11.5). "If liberation can be achieved through knowledge alone, why should they have undertaken (the householder's) duties involving strenuous effort, for proverbially it is known, 'Why should one go to a hill if one has honey at hand.'"[18] Śaṅkara, one of the foremost critics of the Mīmāṁsā school, articulates the Mīmāṁsākas' position on the primacy of ritual action over knowledge, saying that the Upaniṣads proclaim that "rite becomes more powerful that is done along with meditation, faith, and sacred knowledge" (Ch.U. 1.1.10). Therefore, knowledge is heard of as forming a part of some rites hence knowledge by itself cannot be the cause of liberation. Knowledge cannot be independent in the text, "It (i.e. the departing soul) is followed by knowledge, work, (and past experience) (Bṛ.U. 4.4.2.), so, knowledge and work are seen to act in association in producing the result."[19]

Mīmāmsā maintains that according to Upaniṣads one who is possessed of the knowledge of all the things revealed in the

[15] *Ibid.*, p. 44.

[16] *Ibid.*, p. 337.

[17] *Ibid.*, p. 45.

[18] *B.S.B*. 3.4.3. in Śaṅkara, *Brahma Sūtra Bhāṣya* (*B.S.B*) translated by Swami Gambhirananda, (Calcutta: Advaita Ashrama, 1993), p. 761.

[19] *B.S.B*. 3.4.4. & 3.4.5 in *Ibid.*, pp. 761-762.

Vedas is qualified for undertaking rites for it is said, "One who comes back from his teacher's house after duly reading (i.e. reciting) the Vedas… and then enters the householder's life and continues the study of the Vedas in a holy place and performs other prescribed duties, attains the world of Brahman" (Ch.U. 8.9.1). From this also it follows that knowledge cannot produce its result independently. That which is known as the *Agnihotra* is a sacrifice that has to be followed till decrepitude and death, for one gets released from it either through decrepitude or death. It follows that knowledge is a subsidiary of rites.[20]

From this it is cleared that Mīmāmsā School stands for three things in connection with the relationship between work and knowledge –

- Knowledge is part of rites,
- Knowledge alone does not produce liberation,
- Knowledge is in fact subservient to rites.

The Mīmāṃsā philosophy underscores the supremacy of the Vedas as eternal, self-existent scriptures and advocates the centrality of Vedic rituals as the essence of human duty. By providing methodological tools for understanding and performing the intricate rituals and offering a philosophical justification for their importance, Mīmāṃsā establishes rituals as indispensable to spiritual and moral life. The school emphasizes that rituals must be performed not with a desire for rewards but as obligatory duties prescribed by the Vedas. Such disinterested action gradually leads to the destruction of *karmas* and, ultimately, liberation. While Mīmāṃsā acknowledges the value of knowledge, it asserts that knowledge is subservient to and a component of Vedic rituals. According to this view, liberation cannot be attained through knowledge alone but through its integration with prescribed rites.

In essence, Mīmāṃsā upholds a vision of life centered on the diligent and selfless performance of Vedic injunctions,

[20] *B.S.B.* 3.4.6 and 3.4.7. in *Ibid.*, pp. 762-763.

reaffirming the inseparable connection between duty, ritual, and spiritual fulfillment.

4. The Idea of *Apūrva*

The term *Apūrva* literally means 'unprecedented' or 'new' or 'not existing previously.' In the Mīmāṃsā framework, it refers to the invisible, intermediary force or link that connects the performance of a ritual (*karma*) to its eventual fruit or outcome (*phala*). It acts as the metaphysical causal factor that ensures the fruition of ritualistic actions.

As pointed out earlier, Mīmāṃsā philosophy, founded by Jaimini, primarily focuses on interpreting the *Karma Kanda* (ritualistic portion) of the Vedas and emphasizes the importance of performing prescribed rituals (*yajnas*). Mīmāṃsā philosophers faced a philosophical challenge: How can an act performed here and now produce a result much later and somewhere else (e.g., going to heaven)? Does it not violate the law of cause and effect? So, there had to be an explanation for the delayed connection between the action and its fruit.

To address this problem, Mīmāṃsā evolved the concept and theory of *Apūrva*. This objection is addressed through the formulation of the theory of *śakti* (potential energy). Just as a seed contains an imperceptible power that enables it to produce a sprout, the soul similarly possesses the power to manifest the results of Vedic rituals. Upon the completion of these rituals, they generate within the soul this *śakti* or power. Since this power did not exist previously (*a-pūrva*, meaning 'not existing previously') and is created as a consequence of the rites, it is termed *apūrva*. This *apūrva* is eventually expended after producing its intended results.[21] *Apūrva* acts as a bridge, storing the potency of the ritual and releasing it at the appropriate time.

Kumārila Bhaṭṭa, one of the most renowned exponents of Mīmāṃsā philosophy, provides the following explanation of *apūrva*: The potential that was absent before the performance

---

[21] Swami Harshananda, "Apurva" in *https://www.hindupedia.com/en/Apurva* (15.01.2025).

of a ritual and is generated afterward is referred to as *apūrva*. Before the ritual is performed, it cannot serve as a means to attain heaven (*svarga*), nor is the performer capable of achieving such a result. Thus, it becomes necessary to accept that the performance of a ritual generates a specific potential. Without acknowledging this potency, there would be no distinction between performing and not performing the ritual. Therefore, in the Mīmāṃsā system, the potential inherent in both the performer and the act itself is termed *apūrva*.[22]

The next question arises: how is *apūrva* known? Kumārila asserts that it is understood through *śrutyarthāpatti* (presumption based on the meaning of the Vedic texts). *Arthāpatti* refers to implication or presumption. According to Kumārila, perception and other means of knowledge are insufficient to grasp *apūrva*. Its existence must be inferred through implication.[23]

Thus, *Apūrva* serves as the intermediate causal link between the performance of a ritual and its result, providing an explanation for their relationship. The concept of *apūrva* bridges the apparent gap between the cause (ritual performance) and its effect (the result). Without this theory, it would be challenging to establish a causal relationship between ritual actions and their future outcomes. Furthermore, the absence of *apūrva* would undermine the authority of the Vedic injunctive sentences (*vidhi-vākya*), which form the core of the Veda's guidance. These Vedic injunctions, both positive (prescriptive) and negative (prohibitive), are crucial in directing human behaviour - encouraging the performance of righteous acts and discouraging wrongful ones. Thus, the *apūrva* theory not only resolves the issue of causality between rituals and their results but also upholds the foundational authority of the Vedic directives.[24]

---

[22] Ujjwala Jha, "Mīmāmasā theory of apūrva," *Journal of East-West Thought* in *http://journals.calstate.edu* (15.01.2024), 14.

[23] Ujjwala Jha, "Mīmāmasā theory of apūrva," 15.

[24] Ujjwala Jha, "Mīmāmasā theory of apūrva," 16-17.

Nature and role of Apūrva may be given as follows:

(a) ***Invisible Force***: *Apūrva* is not directly perceivable but is inferred from the efficacy of rituals.

(b) ***Causal Power***: It is considered the potential energy (*śakti*) created by performing rituals. For example, if one performs an *Agnihotra*, a Vedic fire ritual, with proper adherence to Vedic prescriptions, the *Apūrva* generated ensures the fulfillment of the desired result.

(c) ***Eternal Connection***: Mīmāṃsā believes in the eternal connection (*nityatva*) between *karma* (action) and its result (*phala*), mediated by *Apūrva*.

The concept of *Apūrva* is a cornerstone of Mīmāṃsā philosophy, providing a metaphysical explanation for the connection between the performance of rituals and their delayed results. By introducing *Apūrva* as an unseen causal force, Mīmāṃsā bridges the apparent temporal and spatial gap between *karma* (ritual action) and *phala* (result), ensuring the continuity and efficacy of ritual practices.

This theory not only addresses the philosophical challenges surrounding causality but also reinforces the authority of the Vedic injunctions that guide ritualistic practices. *Apūrva*, as an invisible potential energy, upholds the belief in the efficacy of Vedic rituals while emphasizing the necessity of their precise and faithful execution. In doing so, it solidifies the foundational role of rituals in the Mīmāṃsā system and affirms the eternal connection between action and its outcome.

Concluding Remarks

Mīmāṁsā philosophy, with its rigorous epistemological framework and unwavering commitment to the authority of the Vedas, remains one of the most foundational schools of Indian thought. Its epistemology, grounded in the reliability of perception, inference, and most importantly, verbal testimony (*śabda*), reinforces the idea that the Vedas are the ultimate source of knowledge. Unlike other schools that seek metaphysical truths or ultimate liberation, Mīmāṁsā prioritizes the preservation and correct interpretation of Vedic injunctions, establishing the supremacy of the Vedas as eternal and self-validating.

A key contribution of Mīmāṁsā is its doctrine of *Apūrva*, which explains how the unseen potency of Vedic rituals ensures the fruition of prescribed actions. By introducing *Apūrva* as the causal link between ritual performance and its results, Mīmāṁsā provides a philosophical justification for the effectiveness of Vedic rites, even when their outcomes are not immediately perceivable. This concept reinforces the school's emphasis on duty (*karma*) and the necessity of faithfully following Vedic prescriptions.

However, this rigid adherence to scriptural authority and ritual formalism raises questions about its adaptability in an evolving intellectual and spiritual landscape. While its meticulous hermeneutical approach ensures the continuity of the Vedic tradition, it also risks prioritizing textual fidelity over philosophical flexibility. The insistence on the eternality and infallibility of the Vedas, coupled with a deterministic view of *karma*, can be seen as limiting in contrast to later philosophical developments that sought a balance between scriptural authority and experiential wisdom.

Despite these limitations, Mīmāṁsā provides a strong intellectual defense of the Vedic worldview, demonstrating how ritual action, scriptural authority, and the principle of *Apūrva* form the foundation of *dharma*. While later schools, such as Vedānta, adapted and reinterpreted Mīmāṁsā principles, its emphasis on the infallibility of the Vedas and the necessity of ritual action remains a defining feature of Hindu thought. The enduring legacy of Mīmāṁsā lies in its profound influence on Indian hermeneutics, jurisprudence, and the broader philosophical discourse on knowledge, duty, and ritual efficacy - though its applicability in a world increasingly shaped by rational inquiry and spiritual pluralism remains an open question.

Chapter 10

Vedānta School of Philosophy

Vedānta, one of the most profound and influential schools of Indian philosophy, derives its name from the Sanskrit words *Veda* (knowledge) and *Anta* (end or conclusion), signifying the culmination of Vedic wisdom. Rooted in the Upaniṣads, which form the philosophical core of the Vedas, Vedānta seeks to explore the ultimate reality (*Brahman*), the nature of the self (*Ātman*), and their interrelation. The teachings of Vedānta have shaped the spiritual, theological, and intellectual traditions of India and continue to resonate in contemporary discourses on metaphysics and spirituality.

Vedānta is not a monolithic or uniform tradition but encompasses diverse interpretations and doctrinal expositions by various *ācāryas* (teachers). Among the prominent figures who systematized and developed Vedāntic philosophy are Ādi Śaṅkarācārya, Rāmānujācārya, and Madhvācārya. These philosophers, while drawing from a common scriptural foundation, articulated distinct perspectives on the nature of reality and the path to liberation: Śaṅkara's Advaita Vedānta emphasizes the non-dualistic essence of existence. He endorses *jñāna* as the ultimate way for Self-Realization. Rāmānuja's *Viśiṣṭādvaita* introduces a qualified non-dualism, positing that the ultimate reality is *Brahman* with attributes, comprising both the world and individual souls as integral parts of its divine body. Rāmānuja emphasizes devotion (*bhakti*) as the means to achieve union with the personal God, Viṣṇu. Madhva's *Dvaita* presents a dualistic interpretation, maintaining a clear distinction between the independent reality of God (*Viṣṇu*) and the dependent reality of individual souls and the material world. Madhva's philosophy underscores the eternal separateness of the finite and the infinite, advocating worship (*upāsanā*) as a path to grace and liberation.

1. Vedānta Critique of Mīmāṁsā Philosophy

As the primary opponent of Mīmāmsā philosophy, Śankara's Advaita Vedānta stands in direct refutation of its core tenets. Śankara's writings serve two fundamental purposes: first, to establish the oneness of reality in opposition to the dualism proposed by the Sāṃkhya system, and second, to critique the Mīmāmsā system, which advocates Vedic rituals as the path to liberation for the bound soul. Indeed, Śaṅkara's primary opposition was directed against the Mīmāmsākas, so, we will look here Śaṅkara's refutation to Mīmāmsā School.

Śaṅkara gives an elaborate refutation to Mīmāmsā School as we shall present here below:

Śaṅkara starts his argument by pointing out that the thing to realized is much greater than the embodied soul, which is free from the mundane attributes as agenship – the Supreme Self, so His knowledge cannot supply any impulsion for work, on the contrary it uproots all works, because it is stated in the aphorism, "Knowledge is independent of rites, since it uproots all worldly distinctions."[1] So, what the teacher Bādarāyaṇa had expressed in *Brahma Sūtra* 3.4.1, "Liberation results from this knowledge of the Self, because the Vedic texts declare

[1] Śaṅkara, *Brahma Sūtra Bhāṣya*, (hereafter *B.S.B*) translated by Swami Gambhirananda, (Calcutta: Advaita Aśrama, 1993), 3.4.8., 763-764.

so" remains as it is, and it cannot be shaken by the fallacious arguments that knowledge is subsidiary of rites.[2]

The Mīmāmsā School's emphasis on works sprung from its belief that individual self is real in itself because the transmigrating soul is indicated by terms like "lovable", etc. Śaṅkara on the other hand, argues that this text should not be understood as referring to the absolute difference between the individual self and Brahman, for it is said "That thou art" (Ch.U. 6.8.7), "There is no other witness but this", etc. In its real nature, the embodied soul is but God Himself, while its state of embodiedness is a creation of limiting adjuncts.[3]

In reply to the stand taken by the Mīmāmsā School that for the enlightened humans it follows that knowledge is subservient to rites, Śaṅkara maintains, "Upaniṣadic mention of the conduct of enlightened men (*sic*) is equally in evidence to show that knowledge is not subservient to rites."[4] He quotes verses like, "The Kāvaṣeya seers who has known this very entity says, 'Why need we study, why need we perform sacrifices… the enlightened of yore ceased to perform the *Agnihotra* sacrifice" (Kau. 2.5); "Knowing this very Self the Brāhmaṇas renounce the desires for sons, for wealth, and for worlds, and lead a mendicant life" (Bṛ.U. 3.4.1); "'This much indeed is immortality, my dear', saying this Yājñavalkya embraced a mendicant's life" (Bṛ.U.4.5.15).[5] However, it is to be remembered that Śaṅkara never negates the importance of works even for the enlightened ones, on the contrary he suggests that the enlightened one may continue performing his/her usual acts for setting an example to others.[6]

---

[2] *B.S.B*, 764.

[3] *B.S.B*,

[4] *B.S.B*, 765.

[5] *B.S.B*, 3.4.9, 765

[6] Cf. Śaṅkarāchārya, *Bhagavad Gītā Bhāṣya*, (hereafter *B.G.B*), Translated by A. Mahadeva Shastri, (Mysore: Government Oriental Library, 1901), 3.20, 93.

In connection with the Upaniṣadic text that states: "That rites become more powerful that is done along with meditation, faith and secret knowledge" (Ch.U. 1.1.10) which the Mīmāmsākas take it as indicating the superiority of rite over knowledge, Śankara replies – this does not refer to all kinds of knowledge, it being confined to the relevant meditation that forms the topic. The topic under discussion was the meditation on Udgītha as contained in, "One shall meditate on the letter *Om* as Udgītha" (Ch.U. 1.1.1).

Śaṅkara drives home his concluding part of the refutation by stating that knowledge is not inferior to rites, on contrary knowledge is by itself sufficient for liberation and in fact, is the only mean for attaining Brahman. But, rite (work) also has its own value – these two means: Knowledge and Work are but meant for two distinct people, the different stages of life. He says, "A division is to be noted here to the effect that knowledge follows one, and work another" (*B.S.B.* 3.4.11). Whereas knowledge applied mainly to the mendicants, works applied to the householders. But, he firmly believes that works (rites) do not produce the necessary result of liberation by *itself* whereas knowledge does; works leads to knowledge which finally leads to liberation. So, in a way rites are for the glorification of knowledge (*B.S.B.* 3.4.14). Works (rites) are useful for liberation in an indirect manner whereas knowledge has a direct result of producing the realization of Brahman.

Thus, knowledge cannot be a subsidiary of rites (*B.S.B.* 3.4.15). According to scriptures, knowledge destroys the whole world of manifestations which are the creation of ignorance as it is stated, "But when to the knower of Brahman everything has become the Self, then what should one smell and trough what", and so on (Bṛ.U. 2.4.14). So, this also follows that knowledge is independent of rites (*B.S.B.* 3.4.16). According to Śaṅkara, as knowledge belongs to the monks (the final stage of *Aśrama Dharma*), knowledge cannot become subsidiary to rites since in that order rites are absent as the monks are not required to perform Vedic rites like *Agnihotra*, etc. Monasticism is not only meant for the last stage of life, but for all stages of life according to the individual commitment (cf. Ch.U. 2.23.1; Ch.U. 5.10.1; Mu.U. 1.2.11; Bṛ. 4.4.22; Jābāla 4), for this reason also knowledge is independent of rites (*B.S.B.* 3.4.17).

Finally, Śaṅkara comes to the concluding section of his refutation by stating the value and necessity of religious activities like rites, etc. thereby highlighting the integral relationship between *Karma* (work) and *Jñāna* (knowledge) for self realization. He says, "Knowledge needs the help of all the duties of the various stages of life, and it is not a fact that there is absolutely no dependence on them" but "once knowledge has emerged, it does not depend on any other factor for producing its (own) result (viz. liberation); but it does depend on others for its own emergence."[7] He continues,

> On the strength of the Upaniṣadic texts prescribing sacrifice etc. … there occurs the text, 'The Brāhmaṇas seek to know it through the study of Vedas, sacrifices, charity, austerity consisting in a dispassionate perception of sense object' (Bṛ. 4.4.22), which shows the helpfulness of sacrifices etc. to the attainment of knowledge. Moreover, it is understood from their association with "seeking to know" (Bṛ. 4.4.22), that they act as a means for the emergence of knowledge… the duties of the different stages of life are helpful to the acquisition of knowledge. *Smṛti* texts also support this, for instance, "The duties result in scorching away sins; the supreme goal being knowledge, when sins are scorched by duties, knowledge begins to emerge," and so on.[8]

The integral relationship between *jñāna yoga* and *karma yoga* is further explicated by Śaṅkara in the following lines –

[7] *B.S.B.* 3.4.26, 781.

[8] *B.S.B.* 3.4.26, 783.

> And in the Gītā and other *Smṛti* it has been stated elaborately that sacrifices etc., when performed without any motive for fruits, become the means for the attainment of knowledge by an aspirant who desire liberation. Hence sacrifices etc. and self control etc., which are the duties of the respective stages of life, are all but means for the emergence of knowledge. And yet among these, such means as self-control etc. which are connected with knowledge by the clause, "He who knows it as such" (Bṛ. 4.4.23), are proximate to knowledge, while the other means, viz. sacrifices etc. are external (i.e. remote), they being connected with the seeking to know (Bṛ. 4.4.22). This is how these are to be distinguished.[9]

The main position of Mīmāmsā School is that rites are superior to knowledge which is but a part of rites and that knowledge alone does not produce the needed result i.e. liberation and is subservient to rites. Śaṅkara gives elaborate reply to this and maintains that knowledge is independent of rites and produces the needed result of liberation all by itself once it is emerged. It is neither part of the rites nor inferior to rites but is the only mean for attaining Brahman which is beyond the grasp of visible external human religious practices like rites, etc. He makes a distinction between works and knowledge by stating that they are meant for two separate classes of people; work is assigned mainly to the householders whereas knowledge is for the mendicants.

However, Śaṅkara does not neglect to relate these two – work and knowledge but maintains that knowledge, though it needs no help when it is emerged, alone could not lead people to liberating stage without the help of work. The importance and necessity of Vedic rites, therefore, is to elevate the seekers to a stage where they could be fit for knowledge to attain Brahman. Work has no direct excess to liberation and knowledge, though

---

[9] *B.S.B.* 3.4.27, 785.

has direct access to liberation, needs the help of work for its emergence. Thus, according to Śaṅkara, *Jñāna Yoga* and *Karma Yoga* have integral relationship for the realization of Brahman.

2. Major Schools of Vedānta

There are three major schools within Vedānta system – Advaita Vedānta, *Viśiṣṭādvaita*, and *Dvaita*.

2.1. Advaita Vedanta of Śaṅkara

Śaṅkara is undoubtedly the most influential thinker and religious genius in medieval and modern India. He is endowed with supernatural gift: "metaphysical genius, faultless acumen, dexterous logic, incomparable eruption and unshakeable faith."[10] His contribution towards the resurgence of Hinduism is so great that it is no wonder that he is described as 'the greatest intellect of the world' and 'the most towering personality of Hinduism in its renaissance period.'[11] Due to his significant influence on Hindu philosophy and theology, we will explore Śaṅkara and his teachings in greater depth.

2.1.1. The Life of Śaṅkara

There is hardly any agreement among scholars concerning the facts of Śaṅkara's life though plenteous traditions are with us narrating contradictory stories about him. C. N. Krishnaswami Aiyer may be right when he says, "Few of the facts of his life can be narrated with certainty, not even the time and the place of his birth.[12] It is beyond the purview of this book to go deep into the various arguments concerning his life and attempt to deduce

[10] R. De Smet, "Śaṅkara's Non-dualism (Advaita-Vāda)", in *Religious Hinduism*, edited by R. De Smet and J. Neuner, Fourth Revised Edition, (Mumbai: St. Pauls, 1997), p. 81.

[11] W. S. Urquhart, *The Vedanta and Modern Thought*, (London: Oxford University Press, 1928), p. 51

[12] C. N. Krishnaswami Aiyer, "Life and Time of Saṅkara", in *Three Great Acharyas: Śaṅkara, Ramanuja, Madhwa: Critical Sketches of their Life and Times, an Expositions of their Philosophical System*, (Madras: G.A. Natesan & Co., Publishers, No year of publication), p. 1.

the most obvious one, but we shall discuss a brief account of his life which is more or less accepted by most of the scholars and specialists in the study of Śaṅkara's life and thought with a reservation that what has been reproduced here is also subject to disagreement.

Sources

There are ten *Śaṅkara-Vijaya* (Biographies of Śaṅkara) identified by T. S. Narayana Sastri in his book *The Age of Saṅkara.*[13] These *Śaṅkara-Vijayas* are accepted generally as the source book for the life of Śaṅkara. However, out of these ten,[14] only five are printed and even most of them are very rare to find. The five printed *Śaṅkara-Vijaya* are - *Śaṅkara-Vijaya* of Aanntānandagiri, *Śaṅkara-Vijaya* of Govindanātha, *Śaṅkara-Vijaya* of Villisahāyakavi, *Śaṅkara-Vijaya* of Chitvilāsa, *Śaṅkara-Vijaya* of Mādhava.[15] Those unprinted manuscripts are not available to us any longer. According to Narayana Sastri, there are some other sources preserved by various Advaitic Maths which talk about Śaṅkara,[16] but scholars are not interested in them, as their authenticity cannot be verified. It is to be noted here that most of the books and materials concerning the life of Śaṅkara are based on the above five *Śaṅkara-Vijaya*, of which the latest one, considered to be written by the great Mādhavācharya, is the most popular and widely circulated.

[13] T. S. Narayana Aier, *The Age of Saṅkara*, (Madras: B. G. Paul & Co., 1971; first published in 1916), p. 32.

[14] The ten *Śaṅkara-Vijaya* are – (1) *Śaṅkara-Vijaya* of Sri Chitsukhāchārya, one of the direct disciple of and co-student of *Śaṅkara*, (2) *Śaṅkara-Vijaya* Ānandagiri, (3) *Śaṅkara-Vijaya* of Vidyā Śaṅkara or Śaṅkarānanda, (4) *Śaṅkara-Vijaya* of Govindanātha, (5) *Śaṅkara-Vijaya* of Chūdāmani Dikshita, (6) *Śaṅkara-Vijaya* of Aanntānandagiri, (7) *Śaṅkara-Vijaya* of Villisahāyakavi, (8) *Śaṅkara-Vijaya* of Sadānanda, (9) *Śaṅkara-Vijaya* of Chitvilāsa, (10) *Śaṅkara-Vijaya* of Mādhava. In Narayana Aier, *The Age of Saṅkara*, 32-33.

[15] Cf. Swami Tapasyananda in the "Introduction" to Madhva-Vidyaranya, *Śaṅkara-Dig-Vijaya: The Traditional Life of Sri Śaṅkarācharya*, translated by Swami Tapasyananda, (Madras: Sri Ramakrishna Math, No year of publication), p. ix.

[16] T. S. Narayana Aier, *The Age of Śaṅkara*, p. 33.

However, this account is not a historical piece but more of philosophical treatise full of legends in need of filtering to get the historical facts of Śaṅkara's life.

A Brief Sketch of His Life

There is no consensus among scholars regarding the time of Śaṅkara's birth and death except that he is considered to have had a short life. Amidst several suggestions, the most accepted date is 788-820 A.D. but this is not without disputation. Swami Tapasyananda, in his Introduction to *Śaṅkara-Dig-Vijaya*, after discussing at length the possible date of Śaṅkara, concludes in a dejected mood thus, "Vastly varied are the views about Śaṅkara's date, ranging from 509 B.C. to 788 A.D., i.e., more than a millennium and a half."[17] This indicates that we do not know for sure the exact date of Śaṅkara's birth and death. He was probably born in a small village known by the name Kaladi in Kerela. His father Śivaguru and mother Aryamba were endowed with all good things of life but a son. The traditions maintain that the couple went to a Śiva Temple for *bhajanam* – worship and prayer. While spending their time in the temple, Lord Śiva in the form of an old man appeared in the dream of Śivaguru to fulfill his heart-felt desire – a baby boy. He asked him to choose between several dull-witted sons who would live long or a single brilliant and virtuous but short-lived one. He chose the latter.[18] This is how the life of Śaṅkara[19] had started. He was considered no ordinary human being but the incarnation of Śiva – Lord Śiva comes with human flesh.

In his fifth year *Upanayana* ceremony was performed for Śaṅkara and as early as at the age of eight he had completed

---

[17] Swami Tapasyananda in the "Introduction" to Madhva-Vidyaranya, *Śaṅkara-Dig-Vijaya,* p. xxiii.

[18] T. M. P. Mahadevan, *Śaṅkarācharya*, (New Delhi: National Book Trust, India, 1968), 4-5.

[19] His father gave him the name Śankara which means the bestower (*kara)* of happiness (*sam*), Cf. Madhva-Vidyaranya, *Śaṅkara-Dig-Vijaya: The Traditional Life of Sri Śaṅkarācharya*, p. 17.

his Vedic learning and return home from the house of his guru. His father was not fortunate enough to witness his son's extraordinary skill and knowledge and his subsequent fame as he died when Śaṅkara was only three years old. Śaṅkara became a *Sannyāsin* after a reluctant mother, who could not bear to lose her only son to asceticism was persuaded. According to various traditions, he became the disciple of sage Govinda who was the disciple of the great Gaudapada, the founder of Vedānta philosophy. After several years of training under his guru, Śaṅkara departed from him for Varanasi (Benares) which was the center of religious learning and propagation during that time and stayed there for several years, gathering disciples and devoting to writing commentaries. Madhava maintains that it was his guru Govinda who sent him to Varanasi to proclaim the message of *advaita*, in spite of his desire to be with him and serve him throughout his life.[20] Tradition maintains that at Varanasi, Śaṅkara received a commission to proclaim the unity of reality to the whole country from Lord Śiva himself who appeared before him in disguise as a *Chandala* (out-caste).[21] He faithfully followed his Master's wish in bringing the gospel of unity of reality to the four corners of the country untill his death at the early age of 32 or 38.[22]

2.1.2. His Works

Just like his life, there is confusion and contention concerning the works of Śaṅkara. There is a vast body of literature piling up that bears the name of Śaṅkara. According to De Smet, considered as one of the specialists in Śaṅkara's study, the list of writings attributed to Śaṅkara comprises of 433 titles. Modern scholarship rejects most of these as spurious and recognizes the following as the genuine works of Śaṅkara:[23]

---

[20] Madhva-Vidyaranya, *Śaṅkara-Dig-Vijaya,* 56.

[21] Madhva-Vidyaranya, *Śaṅkara-Dig-Vijaya,* 59.

[22] Krishnaswami Aiyer, "Life and Time of Śankara", in *Three Great Acharyas: Śaṅkara, Ramanuja, Madhwa,* 58.

[23] R.De Smet, "Śaṅkara's Non-dualism (Advaita-Vāda)", 82.

(a) The commentary (*bhāṣya*) on nine Upaniṣads[24] – such as *Bṛhadāranyaka, Chāndogya, Aitareya, Taittīriya, Īśa, Kena, Kaṭha, Praśna and Muṇdaka*
(b) The commentary on *Bhagavad Gītā*
(c) The Commentary on *Brahma Sūtra* or *Vedānta Sūtra*
(d) A non-commentarial treatise – the *Upadeśa-Sāhasrī.*

2.1.3. The Main Teachings of Śankara

Śaṅkara's teachings presented by the Indologists and Indian scholars in a number of books are misleading as they misrepresented Śaṅkara's original teachings. Some of the most common misinterpretations of Śaṅkara's Advaita Vedānta include – Brahman alone is real, the world is false, or the world is *māyā*, the illusory manifestation of Brahman, human soul is identical with Brahman, some of the Upaniṣadic statement like – *sarvam khalvidam Brahma* (verily this whole world is Brahman), *Aham Brahmāsmi* (I am Brahman) should be understood literally, Brahman is *nirguṇa* which means Brahman is impersonal so no proper personal relationship is possible with Brahman.[25] Another prominent misinterpretation is that for Śaṅkara there is only one genuine path for Self-realization, that is, *Jñāna* (knowledge) and that *Karma* (work) has no ontological value for humans' liberation.

Over against such misinterpretations, we make attempt here to present in brief the main theological teachings of Śaṅkara.

(a) Brahman

According to Śaṅkara, Brahman is the non-dual *(A-dvaita)* absolute, who alone is Being (*sat*) in the supreme sense of the term (*paramārthatah*). It cannot be expressed by the primary meaning (*mukhyārtha*) of words but only indicated (*lakṣita*)

[24] Many scholars and even contemporary researcher put the total of Śaṅkara's commentary on Upaniṣad to ten. Cf. Roger Marcaurelle, *Freedom through Inner Renunciation: Śaṅkara's Philosophy in a New Light*, (Delhi: Sri Satguru Publications, 2002), 12.

[25] R.De Smet, "Śaṅkara's Non-dualism (Advaita-Vāda)", 81-82.

by the secondary meaning (*lakṣyārtha*) of terms.[26] For Śaṅkara the Upaniṣadic explanation of Brahman as *neti neti* designates that Brahman, unaffected by its *upādhis* (limiting adjuncts or extrinsic denominator) is beyond the grasp of speech and mind, "When, however, we wish to describe Its true nature, free from all differences due to limiting adjuncts, then it is an utter impossibility. Then, there is only one way left, viz. to describe It as 'Not this, not this,' by eliminating all possible specifications of It that one may know of" (Bṛ.U.B. 2.3.6).[27]

However indescribable It might be, Śaṅkara uses a number of adjectives to indicate Brahman, such as: Brahman is eternal, pure, intelligent, free by nature, all-knowing, all-powerful, unchangeably permanent, devoid of all modifications (*vikriyā*), partless (*niravayavam*), birthless (*ajaḥ*), undecaying (*ajaraḥ*), fearless (*abhayaḥ*), etc.[28]

Śankara explains Brahman in relation to Its creations as follows –

> Therefore, the unconditioned Self, being beyond speech and mind, undifferentiated and one is designated as "Not this not this"; when it has the limiting adjuncts of the body and organs which are characterized by ignorance, desire and work, it is called the transmigrating individual self; when the Self has the limiting adjuncts of the power of eternal and unlimited knowledge, it is called Internal Ruler and *Īsvara*. The same Self as by nature transcendent, absolute and pure, is called the Immutable and Supreme Self. Similarly, having the limiting adjuncts of the bodies and organs, the Undifferentiated, the gods, the species, the individual, men, animals,

---

[26] K.P. Aleaz, *The Relevance of Relation in Śaṅkara's Advaita Vedānta*, (Delhi: Kant Publications, 1996), 27.

[27] Śaṅkara, *Bṛihadāraṇyaka Upaniṣad Bhāṣya*, translated by Swami Mahavananda; (Mayavati: Advaita Aśrama, 1950), 344.

[28] K. P. Aleaz, *The Relevance of Relation in Śaṅkara's Advaita Vedānta*, 37-38.

> spirits, etc., the Self assumes those particular names and forms (Bṛ.U.B. 3.8.12).[29]

The '*neti neti*' definition sets Brahman apart from all other realities by asserting, "It is not this, not this." These limitations are only its *upādhis* or extrinsic denominators, or limiting adjuncts.[30] This means that Brahman, the ultimate reality, is the underlying essence of everything in the world, yet the world appears to limit or obscure Brahman's true, infinite nature.

(b) Human Being

According to Śaṅkara a human being is nothing but Brahman with the *upādhis* (limiting adjuncts or extrinsic denominators) (Bṛ.U.B. 3.8.12),[31] or in other words, the Self (*Ātman*) presiding over the cage of body and senses and associated with the fruit of action is called individual soul (*jīva*) (B.S.B 2.3.16).[32] So, it is cleare that though *jīva* is the prototype of Brahman, it is not identical with Brahman. A person is a *jīvātman* plus inner senses, outer senses, and body conjoined. It is a reflection (*ābhāsa*) of the Supreme Ātman in the mirror-like ego-sense. As Brahman is real, a human being is also real, but its reality is derived from Brahman. Human being is not an illusion but an ontologically relative and dependent contingent entity. In other words, for Śaṅkara, human being is an integrated contingent being totally dependent on the Absolute, the Brahman.[33]

(c) Creation

Śaṅkara says that Brahman created the entire universe in due order but without the help of any substance other than Itself. So, the whole universe is Brahman alone and is real, but its reality is

---

[29] Śaṅkara, *Bṛihadāranyaka Upaniṣad Bhāṣya*, 528-529.

[30] R.De Smet, "Śaṅkara's Non-dualism (Advaita-Vāda)", 87.

[31] Śaṅkara, *Bṛihadāranyaka Upaniṣad Bhāṣya*, 528.

[32] Śaṅkara, *Brahma Sūtra Bhāṣya*, 472.

[33] K.P. Aleaz, *The Relevance of Relation in Śaṅkara's Advaita Vedānta*, 27-28.

a derived reality, derived from Brahman. The world originates, lives and is absorbed in Brahman. At all these three points in time, the world remains in Brahman. In other words, the entire universe is the *upādhis* of Brahman, the effect (*kārya*) and name and form (*nāma rūpa*) of Brahman.[34] As Brahman is real, Its name and form, which are Its limited adjuncts should also be real. K. P. Aleaz notes, "Left to themselves, they are unreal. Our ignorance lies in identifying the extrinsic denominators as real in themselves."[35]

When Śaṅkara says that the entire universe is the name and form (*nāma rūpa*) of Brahman, he refers to the idea that the entire universe, including all its objects and beings, is a manifestation of Brahman in the form of names and forms. The universe is essentially a manifestation of Brahman, but it appears to us in the form of names and forms (*nāma rūpa*). In this view, Brahman itself does not undergo any change or transformation. While we perceive the world as a multitude of different objects with distinct names and forms, in reality, these names and forms are not separate from Brahman. They are simply manifestations of the one underlying Brahman. The names and forms have no independent reality of their own; they are merely different ways in which Brahman appears to our senses. For Śaṅkara, Advaita Vedānta teaches that the material world is not absolutely real (*paramārthika satya*) but only relatively real (*vyāvahārika satya*).

(d) Māyā

One of the important themes of Śaṅkara's theology/Philosophy which is widely misunderstood is his concept of *māyā*. Many interpretations label that the world is *māyā*, the illusory manifestation of Brahman. However, according to Śaṅkara, *māyā* "is the power of the Supreme Lord (*parameśvaryah śakteh*) ...

---

[34] K. P. Aleaz, *The Relevance of Relation in Śaṅkara's Advaita Vedānta*, 28.

[35] K. P. Aleaz, *The Relevance of Relation in Śaṅkara's Advaita Vedānta*, 50.

which creates the whole universe (*samastajagadvidhāyinyā*)."[36] For Śaṅkara *māyā* does not mean total 'illusion' that makes the material world looks real, he calls the universe the product of *māyā* only when it is misapprehended by the ignorant as independently real, apart from Brahman.

We must remember that Śaṅkara does not equate *māyā* with mere 'illusion'. Rather, he views *māyā* as the creative power of Brahman, responsible for the appearance of the universe as diverse and multifaceted, while ultimately remaining non-different from Brahman. According to Śaṅkara, *māyā* is not a force independent of Brahman but rather an inherent power of Brahman that enables the appearance of the world. In this sense, *māyā* is what allows Brahman - the formless, infinite, and absolute reality - to manifest as the diverse world of names and forms (*nāma-rūpa*). It is the mechanism through which the one, non-dual Brahman appears as the many in the empirical world.

Therefore, in Śaṅkara's Advaita Vedānta, *māyā* should not be understood as the 'total illusion' that makes the world appears real. Rather, it is the 'creative power of Brahman' that gives rise to the appearance of multiplicity. The world, as it is experienced by the ignorant, is a misapprehension - an appearance of reality as independent of Brahman, though in truth, the world is non-different from Brahman. The appearance of duality and multiplicity is due only to the veiling power of *māyā*, and with the removal of ignorance, the non-duality of Brahman is realized. Thus, *māyā* is not the cause of non-existence but the cause of the misapprehension of the world's true, non-dual nature.

(e) Bondage and Liberation

The goal of Śaṅkara's theology/philosophy is the liberation of the bound soul in order to regain its original purity. Śaṅkara himself attests thus, "There is no other attainment higher than that of the Self. For that is the purpose for which the teachings

[36] K. P. Aleaz, *The Relevance of Relation in Śaṅkara's Advaita Vedānta*, 63.

of the Vedas, the *Śmṛitis* and the actions (described in the work-portion of the Vedas) are there" (U.S.17.4).[37] Śaṅkara accepts the general conception of transmigration of soul from one body to another – i.e. *jīva* transmigrates into another body at death. This is the result of the past accumulated actions, so the condition of the new body would also be determined by the past life. Śaṅkara is very specific that when the Self passes form one body to another there is no change in the Self (B.G.B. 2:13).[38] For Liberation to occur Śaṅkara suggests four things as a prerequisites – (a) to get the help of a competent guru, (b) to learn and study Vedānta, (c) to be able to control senses (d) to be able to discriminate between what is real and what is unreal (B.G.B. 18.50).[39]

(f) The Place of Works (Rites)

That Śaṅkara consistently upholds in his *Bhagavad Gītā* Commentary that there are two means/paths for liberation – knowledge (*jñāna*) and work (*karma*). Following this, he says that these two paths should not be conjoined, as they are fundamentally different and distinct; conjunction is not possible. [40] He even argues that if they were to be conjoined they would become one and not two; the fact that they are made two negates the possibility of conjunction (B.G.B. 3:1). These two paths – *Jñāna Yoga* and *Karma Yoga* are for two distinct classes of aspirants. *Jñāna Yoga* is only for those who are wise and enlightened[41]; it is for the *Sānkhyas*, for those who possessed a clear knowledge of the Self and the not-Self, who renounced the world from *Brahmacharya*, who belonged to the highest class of *sannyāsins* known as the *Paramahaṃsas*, whose thought ever dwelt on Brahman only (*B.G.B.* 3:3). It is evident that this path

[37] Śaṅkara, *Upadeśa Sāhasrī*, translated by Swami Jagadananda, (Madras: Sri Ramakrishna Math, 1989), p. 192.

[38] Śaṅkarāchārya, *B.G.B.*, p. 25.

[39] *B.G.B.*, 442.

[40] *B.G.B.*, 19, 72, 77-78, 80, 456-457.

[41] *B.G.B.*, 38.

is not intended for common people, but for *sannyāsins* only as Śaṅkara says, "It must also be true that the path of knowledge is intended from *Sannyāsins* only" (B.G.B. 3:3).[42] If it is so, does it mean that for Śaṅkara, householders or people in other stages of life (*Aṣramas*) have no hope for salvation unless they reach the stage of *synnyāsya* or complete renunciation? The answer is found when he said that Janaka and Asvapati who did not renounce their householder duties but "tried by action alone to attain *mokṣa*" were still considered as liberated;[43] that shows the possibility of salvation for the householder; or in other words, physical renunciation of all actions is not mandatory for attaining Brahman because, salvation is attainable even for those who actively fulfill their worldly duties.

Śaṅkara's position is that these two means are for separate classes of people – *Jñāna yoga* is for the *sannyāsins* who renounced physically the world, and *Karma yoga* is for the rest of the stages, especially the householder, who, while performing their holder duties tread the path of salvation via *Karma Yoga*.[44] He also says, "The *Karma-yoga*, devotion to action, is indeed meant for the ignorant only, not for the wise."[45] In that case, *Karma yoga* is also a valid path of salvation. However, Śaṅkara maintains that *Karma yoga* i.e. works (Vedic rites) *by itself* cannot lead people to a liberating stage. In other words, work alone does not result in liberation; rather, it eventually leads to the discipline of knowledge, which purifies the mind and enables Self-knowledge, ultimately yielding liberation. Here, Roger Marcaurelle is worth quoting:

> From Śaṅkara's perspective, even though the yoga of action cannot lead directly to liberation by reason of its basic involvement with the sense of doership, nevertheless, since it can be accompanied by the

[42] *B.G.B.*, 82.

[43] *B.G.B.*, 92, cf. 22.

[44] *B.G.B.*, 85, 90.

[45] *B.G.B.*, 85.

> discipline of knowledge, together with the latter, it can produce the purity necessary for the mind to access, trough the scriptures, that experiential steadfastness in Self-knowledge (*jñānaniṣṭhā*), which alone is free from doership and yield liberation.[46]

So, according to Śaṅkara, *Karma Yoga* in itself does not yield liberation directly. However, if practiced without expectation of results (*niṣkāma karma*), it leads to purity of mind, which, in turn, paves the way for knowledge to arise, ultimately resulting in liberation.

(g) Relationship between Knowledge (*Jñana*) and Work (*Karma*)

Śaṅkara maintains that knowledge and works are two distinct paths and cannot be combined together in a person at the same time. Moreover, knowledge and works are for two different types of aspirants. It is the teaching of the Lord "that knowledge and action are intended for two distinct classes of men respectively on the ground that a simultaneous devotion – on the part of one man – to knowledge and action was impossible owing to their mutual opposition."[47] So, the path of knowledge is assigned to the wise such as *sannyāsins* whereas the path of *karma* is assigned to the ignorant. Prithipal notes, "It is true that the path of knowledge is prescribed for the *Sannyāsin* and that of action for the man still bound to discharge his social duties. But devotion to action is a means to an end."[48]

These two paths are designed in accordance with the phenomenal and absolute reality of the world and Brahman, respectively. Karma is valid insofar as the phenomenal reality of this world is concerned, whereas *Jñāna* applies to the

---

[46] Roger Marcaurelle, *Freedom through Inner Renunciation: Śaṅkara's Philosophy in a New Light*, (Delhi: Sri Satguru Publications, 2002), 129-130.

[47] Roger Marcaurelle, *Freedom through Inner Renunciation,* 78.

[48] D. Prithipal, *Advaita Vedānta: Action and Contemplation*, (Varanasi: Bharatiya Vidhya Prakasan, 1969), 55.

absolute reality of Brahman. From the transcendental standpoint (*pāramārthika*), when we consider Brahman as the sole reality - undifferentiated, immutable, and so on - works (rites, etc.) have no actual significance because in Brahman there can be no activity. However, from the perspective of the phenomenal realm or common-sense viewpoint (*vyāvahārika*), when the world is considered real because it exists within Brahman, and Brahman is real, the worship of *Īśvara* with rites and rituals is considered significant, important, and obligatory. Thus, states Śaṅkara, "Now, listen to the teaching concerning *Yoga* (path of works), which is the means of attaining wisdom concerning *Sāṇkhya* (path of knowledge): this *yoga*, which constitutes the worship of *Īśvara*, consists in practicing *Samādhi* or in performing works without attachment, after killing the pairs of opposites (such as heat and cold)" (B.G.B. 2:39).

Performance of rites is obligatory before the dawn of knowledge, and as long as humans remain in the stage of ignorant. Śaṅkara maintains, "A man who is qualified for works it is necessary to perform works before he becomes fit for the path of knowledge" (B.G.B. 2:46). The positive aspect of Śaṅkara's teaching on *Karma-yoga* is that it purifies the mind so that it makes the devotees qualify to tread the path of *Jñāna-yoga*. K. N. Tiwari may be worth quoting, "Śaṅkara accepts the purificatory function of *karmas* without which the spiritual attainment is regarded as impossible. The Vedānta does not go further than that, but restricts the role of *karma* to the purificatory level."[49] In this sense, *Jñāna-yoga* and *Karma-yoga* work together for the liberation of human soul. Tiwari continues, "However paradoxical it may sound, yet it is eminently true that freedom from action is attained by the right performance of action (B.G.B 3:3). Mere renunciation of action, i.e., simple and total inaction, is not in any way conducive to adherence to the path of knowledge."[50] In other words, renunciation of

---

[49] Kapil N. Tiwari, *Dimensions of Renunciation in Advaita Vedānta*, (Delhi: Motilal Banarsidass, 1977), 85.

[50] Kapil N. Tiwari, *Dimensions of Renunciation in Advaita Vedānta*. 56.

works is attained only when the devotee performs selfless and pure action. So, works and knowledge, though recognized as distinct means of salvation, are integrally related. Here, A. G. Krishna Warrier, who had earned doctoral degree for his research on Saṅkara's concept of *Mukti* is worth quoting, he says, "Commenting on *Brahmasūtra* III.4.26 Śaṅkara discusses the important question of the relation between action and knowledge. Without performance of actions of four stations in life, the saving knowledge of identity cannot dawn at all; for thus alone the mind becomes fit for such knowledge."[51]

The birth of a human is the consequence of past *Karmas*, which is due to *avidyā (*ignorance), and therefore, any child born is born with ignorance. So, according to Śaṅkara, every human being has to start his/her religious journey toward the end, i.e., liberation, with rites and rituals (works), as he/she is not fit for the higher path - the path of Knowledge. But Works alone cannot liberate a human; only in company with knowledge do works have liberative capacity. When knowledge dawns in an individual, because of the purity of mind resulting from works done without attachment, liberation is attained.

Thus, we may conclude that for Śaṅkara, there is an integral and inseparable relationship between *Karma-yoga* and *Jñāna-yoga* for Self-realization. Here, Subrahmanya Iyer is worth quoting when he says,

> The best interpretation of Śaṅkara's philosophy is that furnished by his own life which illustrates how action (*Karma*) and Thought (*Jñāna*) are "inseparable," and that *Jñāna* (thought, wisdom or philosophy) does not "in the least" imply inaction nor does "*mithyatwa*" (illusoriness) justify indifference to life, or callousness…he never sought any cave or temple or monastery for refuge or retirement or mystic realization, as so many *Yogis*, *Sadhus* and *Sannyāsis*

[51] A. G. Krishna Warrier, *The Concept of Mukti in Advaita Vedānta*, (Madras: University of Madras, 1981), 432.

> do. He was 'ever' moving about the whole continent of India, 'organizing' and 'teaching,' with a view to helping all men to realise the underlying oneness or 'unity.'[52]

A brief survey of the life and teachings of Śaṅkara reveals the challenges faced by scholars and experts in uncovering the truth about his life and philosophy. The more we examine various accounts, the greater the confusion becomes. The facts about Śaṅkara's life that are widely accepted by scholars are so limited that they barely suffice to meaningfully reconstruct his biography. The *Śaṅkara-Vijayas*, which serve as our primary sources for reconstructing his life, are often filled with fanciful and whimsical narratives, making it difficult to distinguish fact from legend.

Similar difficulties arise when identifying Śaṅkara's authentic writings. Contemporary scholarship generally agrees that Śaṅkara authored commentaries on nine or ten principal Upaniṣads, the Brahma Sūtras, and the Bhagavad Gītā. In addition, he composed a non-commentarial philosophical and theological treatise, the *Upadeśa Sāhasrī.*

Śaṅkara's philosophy emphasizes the absolute oneness of reality, asserting that Brahman alone is real. The world, including human beings, is understood as *nāma-rūpa* (name and form) and *upādhi* (limiting adjunct) of Brahman. In this sense, the world is real, but its reality is not independent - it is derived from Brahman. The world, with all its diversity, is real only in relation to Brahman; without Brahman, it is unreal. According to Śaṅkara, the fundamental human problem lies in the mistaken identification of the soul with the material world, a confusion caused by ignorance (*avidyā*). Since ignorance is the root cause, its remedy is knowledge (*jñāna*). While Śaṅkara does not deny the importance of religious rites (*karma*), he asserts that Vedic

---

[52] V. Subrahmanya Iyer, "Śankara's Philosophy and Action" in http://www.yabaluri.org/TRIVENI/CDWEB/ShankarasPhilosophyandAction1941.htm (22.11.2011).

rituals alone cannot lead to liberation. True liberation can only be attained through knowledge.

2.2. *Viśiṣṭādvaita* of Rāmānuja

Rāmānuja (1017–1137 CE), a distinguished Tamil Brāhmaṇa, was a renowned theologian, philosopher, and Bhakti saint. His primary philosophical teachings are encapsulated in his celebrated commentary on the *Brahma Sūtra*, where he presented a systematic critique of Śaṅkara's *Advaita Vedānta*. Rāmānuja's philosophy, known as *Viśiṣṭādvaita* (Qualified Non-Dualism), upholds the oneness of ultimate reality (*advaita*) while emphasizing that this singular reality is characterized by numerous distinct and interrelated attributes (*viśiṣṭa*). According to him, the one supreme reality, Brahman, encompasses both conscious souls (*cit*) and unconscious matter (*acit*) as integral parts of Him. Thus, while Brahman is non-dual, it is not a homogeneous unity but a dynamic reality enriched by diversity, making it both transcendent and immanent in all existence. Rāmānuja's ideas laid a strong foundation for Bhakti traditions, advocating an intimate, personal relationship with the divine.

2.2.1. God

God or Brahman is the Absolute Reality, which is one, but in Him, there are two integral parts—unconscious matter (*acit*) and the conscious but finite soul (*cit*). Brahman is the only reality, and outside of Him, there is no other reality. But God contains within Himself the material objects as well as finite souls, both of which are real. Unlike Śaṅkara's conception of the oneness of reality as non-dual, Rāmānuja's oneness is not a distinctionless unity. The Absolute God contains the many. His system is called *Viśiṣṭādvaita*, which means the unity (*Advaita*) of Brahman, possessed (*viśiṣṭa*) of real parts - the conscious and the non-conscious. Brahman is devoid of any external distinction because there is nothing besides God, either similar or dissimilar to Him. However, God is possessed of internal distinction (*svagata-bheda*), as there are within Him different conscious and unconscious substances, which can be mutually distinguished.[53]

For Rāmānuja, God or the Absolute is this whole. He is the immanent inner controller, the Supreme Real who holds together in unity the dependent matter and individual souls as His body. Rāmānuja recognizes three things as ultimate and real (*tattva-traya*): matter (*acit*), souls (*cit*), and God (*Īśvara*). Though all are equally real, the first two are absolutely dependent on God. Though they are substances in themselves, yet in relation to God, they become His attributes. They are the body of God, who is their soul. God is the soul of nature. God is also the soul of souls. Our souls are souls in relation to our bodies, but in relation to God, they become His body, and He is their soul.[54]

Though One in Himself, God manifests Himself in *five forms* in order to help His devotees. *First form* - As the immanent soul of the universe, He is *Antaryāmī*. *Second form* - As the transcendent personal Lord, *Nārāyana* or *Vāsudeva*, He is Para or Supreme. *Third form* - As the creator, preserver and destroyer, He reveals Himself through four-fold *Vyūha* (God as creator - *Pradyumna*, God as Lord – *Vāsudeva*, God as destroyer - *Saṅkarṣaṇa*, God as preserver – *Aniruddha*). *Fourth form* – As *Vibhava* or *Avatāra* – incarnation in order to protect the good, punish the wicked and restore the *dharma*. The *fifth and the last form* of God is when out of His extreme mercy He takes the form of the holy idols (*archāvatāra*) enshrined in the recognized temples like *Shriraṇgam* so that His devotees might get opportunities to serve Him physically.[55]

For Rāmānuja, God is not characterless (*nirguṇa*) or indeterminate, but possessed of an infinite number of good qualities (*saguṇa*) such as omnipotence, omniscience,

---

[53] Satishandra Chaterjee and Dhirendramohan Datta, *An Introduction to Indian Philosophy*, (New Delhi: Rupa, 2007), 387.

[54] Chandradhar Sharma, *Indian Philosophy: A Critical Survey*, (New York City: Barnes & Noble, Inc. 1962), 334.

[55] Chandradhar Sharma, *Indian Philosophy: A Critical Survey*, (2007), 337.

benevolence, etc. God is the Supreme Person who is in all things and beings of the world and also remains beyond them. Thus, He is both immanent and transcendent. He is the highest object of love and the goal of our religious life and devotion. It is by pleasing God through devotion and prayer that we can obtain salvation.[56] So, in Ramanuja's theological teaching we see emphasis on devotion, love, prayer, grace of God, and God's mercy.

2.2.2. The World

Rāmānuja holds that God or Brahman created the world out of unconscious matter (*acit*) which exists in God. The world is real as Brahman is real. The source of material objects is called *prakṛti* which is unconscious. But unlike Saṃkhya system where *prakṛti* is considered as existing independent of God eternally, Rāmānuja holds that *prakṛti* is part of God and controlled by God. God created out of *prakṛti* the world of diverse objects. Regarding the Upaniṣadic texts and Śaṅkara's Advaita which deny the multiplicity of objects and assert the unity of all things, Rāmānuja argues that these texts do not mean to deny the reality of the many objects, but only teach that in all of them there is the same Brahman, on which all are dependent for existence, just as all gold articles dependent on gold.[57]

Prakṛti (matter), *kāla* (time), *śuddhatattva* (pure matter) are the three non-conscious substances. They are object of experience (*bhogya*), liable to changes and indifferent to the ends of human. *Prakṛti* has three qualities – *sattva* (purity/goodness), *raja* (activity/passion) and *tamas* (darkness/illusion) which are evolved at the time of the world-creation. *Kāla* or time is given an independent place. It is the form of all existence which is an object of perception. Distinction of days, months, years, etc. is based on the relation of time. Unlike *Prakṛti*

---

[56] Chaterjee and Datta, *An Introduction to Indian Philosophy*, (2007), 388, 390.

[57] Chaterjee and Datta, *An Introduction to Indian Philosophy*, (2007), 383.

(matter), *Śuddhatattva* or pure matter has only *sattva.* All these non-conscious entities work in obedience to the will of God. They are not in themselves good or bad, but happen to please or pain the individual according to their *karma*. While both souls and matter constitute the body or the attributes of God, matter is more completely dependent on Brahman than the souls, which have freedom of choice.[58]

According to Rāmānuja, the word '*māyā*' stands for god's power of creating wonderful objects. It also stands sometimes for *prakṛti* to signify her wonderful creativity. So, he denies that the creation and the created world are illusory.[59]

2.2.3. Human Being

According to Rāmānuja the self of human is limited and finite like the body. The body is made up of matter which is a part of God. The soul is eternally existing but finite. As it is finitely small or very subtle it can penetrate into every material substance but not all-pervassive. Consciousness is not the essence of self as held in Advaita Vedānta, but it is the eternal quality/character of the self. Rāmānuja identified the self with what we call the "I" (*aham*) – 'I am.' Even after liberation, the human self is not identical with God but similar with God. In other words, human self does not achieve union with God, but it is not different from God - God pervades and controls human self even after liberation.

Though the individual soul is an attribute or mode (*prakāra*) of God and forms part of His body, yet it is also a spiritual substance in itself and is absolutely real. It is an eternal point of spiritual light and beyond destruction. In the state of creation, it is embodied according to its *karmas*, while in the state of dissolution and in the state of liberation, it remains in itself. Though it is eternal, real, unique, uncreated and imperishable, yet it is finite and individual, being only a part or a mode of

[58] S. Radhakrishnan, *Indian Philosophy Vol. II*, 696-697.

[59] Chaterjee and Datta, *An Introduction to Indian Philosophy*, (2007), 384.

God. Though it is really subjected to earthly existence and to the various imperfections, defects and miseries which the worldly life implies, yet these do not affect its essence.[60] The soul remains unchanged in its essential nature through all the processes of birth and death. It is born many times into the world and departs from it again; but throughout it maintains its identity.[61]

Unlike Śaṅkara, Rāmānuja maintains that the *jīva* (soul) is not one with God, it differs in essential character from Him. As mentioned before, the soul is part (*aṁśa*) of Brahman, but not in the sense of cutting out of the whole since there is no existence Brahman and there is no real division in Brahman. The soul is part of Brahman in the sense of *viśeṣaṇa* – qualified form or attribute or mode of Brahman. It is regarded as the effect of Brahman.[62]

The soul is different from its body, sense-organs, mind, vital breaths and even cognition. In *saṁsāra*, it wrongly identifies itself with these due to ignorance and *karma*. There are innumerable individual souls which are essentially alike. The soul is conceived as a real knower (*jnātā*), a real doer (*kartā*) and a real enjoyer (*bhoktā*). Action and enjoyment are simply different modes in which knowledge, which constitutes the very essence of the soul, manifests itself. The soul is a self-luminous substance as well as a self-conscious subject.[63]

While the self is in bondage, its knowledge is obscured by its *karmas* and thus it functions in a restricted manner. At liberation (*mokṣa*), all the *karmas* are destroyed and there remains no impediment in the way of knowledge, then it becomes all-comprehensive. The liberated soul becomes omniscient because its *dharma-bhūta-jñāna* (knowledge or consciousness of the self) is restored to its original state and in the absence

[60] Chandradhar Sharma, *Indian Philosophy: A Critical Survey,* 338.

[61] S. Radhakrishnan, *Indian Philosophy Vol. II*, (New York: The Macmillan Company, 1958), 691.

[62] S. Radhakrishnan, *Indian Philosophy Vol. II*, 692.

[63] Chandradhar Sharma, *Indian Philosophy: A Critical Survey,* 338.

of karmic obstructions, it comprehends all objects. Bliss is the essence of the soul, so, in its essence, the soul is *ānandarūpa* or ever blissful. The imperfections and miseries of *saṁsāra*, do not touch its essence. In liberation, it enjoys infinite knowledge and everlasting bliss.[64]

Though the individual soul is absolutely real, yet it is not independent. It is utterly dependent on God. The individual soul is the body of God and God is its soul. It is supported, controlled and utilized by God. It is the supported (*dhārya*) and God is its support (*dhartā*). It is the controlled (*niyāmya*) and God is its controller (*niyantā*). It is the means (*shesa*) and God is its end (*shesī*). It is a mode (*prakāra*) and God is its substance (*prakāri*). It is a part (ārṣa) and God is the Whole (*aṁśi*). It is the body (*śarīra*) and God is its soul (*śarīri*). And yet it is a real agent and performs and reaps the fruits of its actions. Its defects and imperfections and miseries do not affect God.[65]

Rāmānuja describes three classes of souls. The *first* are the ever - free (*nitya-mukta*) souls which were never bound. They are ever free from *karma* and *prakṛti* and live in *Vaikuntha* (eternal heavenly realm) in constant service of the Lord. The *second* ones are the liberated (*mukta*) souls who were once bound but who obtained liberation through their action, knowledge and devotion. The third ones are the bound (*baddha*) souls who are wandering in *saṁsāra* on account of ignorance and bad *karmas*. These are further divided into four classes: superhuman, human, animal and immobile.[66]

2.2.4. Bondage and Liberation

Though human soul is not identical with the body, due to ignorance and the fruit of his/her actions, the soul identifies itself with the body and regards it as itself, it becomes subject to the limitations of the body and is in bondage. For liberation one should first perform the obligatory rituals enjoyed by the

---

[64] Chandradhar Sharma, *Indian Philosophy: A Critical Survey,* 339.

[65] Chandradhar Sharma, *Indian Philosophy: A Critical Survey,* 339.

[66] Chandradhar Sharma, *Indian Philosophy: A Critical Survey,* 339.

Vedas which purify the heart. Rāmānuja prescribes the study of Mīmāmsā philosophy for the correct knowledge concerning Vedic sacrifices. Liberation is not attained by mere study or reasoning nor by rites and rituals, but by the grace of God. For this, there must be a steady, constant remembrance of God as the dearest object of love with meditation, prayer and devotion. Constant remembrance of God with devotion and self surrender (*bhakti*) ultimately matures into the realization of God. He/she who realizes God is liberated from all bondage to the body for ever. Liberation is not becoming identical with God; the liberated soul having pure consciousness becomes similar with God. Free from bondage of every kind, the liberated soul enjoys infinite joy born of complete communion with God.[67]

Rāmānuja acknowledges that knowledge is the immediate cause of liberation. However, this knowledge is not ordinary verbal or intellectual understanding; it is real knowledge, which he equates with the highest form of *bhakti* (devotion). This highest *bhakti* is attained through *prapatti* (self-surrender) and *dhruvā smṛtiḥ* (constant remembrance of God as the sole object of devotion). Such remembrance, also referred to as *upāsanā* (pure meditation) or *dhyāna*, serves as a preparatory practice. It is important to note that constant meditation is not itself the highest *bhakti* (real *jñāna*); rather, it is a means to achieve it. This ordinary *bhakti*, expressed through *prapatti* and *upāsanā*, ultimately leads to the realization of the highest *bhakti*, which is pure *jñāna* - the immediate and intuitive knowledge of God. According to Rāmānuja, this intuitive knowledge is the direct cause of liberation and is possible only through the grace (*prasāda*) of God.[68] Thus, Rāmānuja emphasizes that liberation cannot be attained by human effort alone; divine grace is indispensable.

For this realization two things are necessary: *firstly*, the utter destruction of the *karmas* by which the soul acquires its

---

[67] Chaterjee and Datta, *An Introduction to Indian Philosophy*, (2007), 397-398.

[68] Chandradhar Sharma, *Indian Philosophy: A Critical Survey,* 340.

innate purity, and *secondly*, the dawning of the Divine Grace which transforms constant meditation into the immediate intuition of God. For Rāmānuja, there is no *jīvanmukti* for as long as the soul remains associated with the body, the *karmas* persist; and as long as the *karmas* persist, the soul cannot acquire its innate purity. There is no liberation without God's grace because unless the Divine grace dawns, the constant meditation cannot mature into real *bhakti* or *jnāna* - the immediate intuitive knowledge of God. Unless true knowledge dawns, liberation cannot take place. The removal of all *karmas* and the dawning of immediate knowledge of God take place simultaneously and not successively and both are produced at once by the Divine grace.[69]

Unlike Śaṅkara's Advaita Vedānta, liberation, according to Rāmānuj, is not the merging of the individual soul into Brahman, the Absolute. The liberated soul does not become *identical* with Brahman, but only *similar* to Brahman (*Brahmaprakāra*). It realizes itself as the body of Brahman and ever dwells in direct communion with God, enjoying infinite consciousness and infinite bliss like God. But it retains its individuality for otherwise enjoyment of bliss in communion with God is not possible.[70]

Rāmānuja's *Viśiṣṭādvaita* philosophy stands as a profound and harmonious synthesis of metaphysics, theology, and devotion. By emphasizing the inseparable relationship between the individual soul (*jīva*), the material world (*prakṛti*), and the supreme reality (*Brahman*), Rāmānuja presents a deeply relational worldview where God is both the immanent and transcendent reality. The doctrine of *saguṇa Brahman* - a personal God with attributes - offers a practical and accessible pathway for spiritual realization, centered on devotion (*bhakti*), surrender (*prapatti*), and Divine grace (*prasāda*).

Viśiṣṭādvaita emphasizes that liberation (*mokṣa*) is not merely a state of impersonal absorption into Brahman

[69] Chandradhar Sharma, *Indian Philosophy: A Critical Survey,* 341.

[70] Chandradhar Sharma, *Indian Philosophy: A Critical Survey,* 341-342.

but an eternal, blissful communion with the personal God, characterized by love and service in His divine presence. This vision of liberation elevates the relational aspect of existence, valuing the individual's distinct identity even in the state of ultimate union with God.

Rāmānuja's theology also underscores the indispensability of ethical living, humility, and unwavering devotion as essential components of spiritual practice. His insistence on God's grace as the ultimate enabler of liberation offers both hope and humility, reminding individuals of their dependence on the divine while affirming the dignity of human effort through self-surrender and meditation.

Thus, *Viśiṣṭādvaita* provides a great philosophical and theological framework that integrates reason, faith, and devotion. Its emphasis on the personal, dynamic, and loving relationship with God has not only shaped the *Bhakti* traditions of India but also continues to inspire spiritual seekers with its profound message of divine love and grace.

2.3. *Dvaita* of Madhva

Madhva (1238–1317 CE), also known as Ānandatīrtha, was a prominent philosopher and theologian who founded the *Dvaita Vedānta* (dualistic school of Vedānta). He was born in a village called Pajaka, near Udupi in present-day Karnataka. Madhva was deeply influenced by Vaiṣṇavism, and his philosophy strongly emphasizes devotion to Viṣṇu as the Supreme Being. Madhva considered himself an incarnation of Vayu (the wind god) and a servant of Vishnu. He is also remembered for establishing the Kṛṣṇa Temple in Udupi, which remains a central site for followers of his tradition.

Madhva's philosophy, *Dvaita*, offers a stark contrast to Śankara's Advaita Vedānta, which asserts the non-duality of Brahman. Instead, Madhva emphasized an unbridgeable dualism between God and the individual souls (*jīvas*), asserting that they are eternally distinct. In his early days, Madhva is believed to have been inclined towards Śaṅkara's *Advaita Vedānta*.

However, he eventually diverged from it and developed his own distinctive theological and philosophical system. A prolific writer, Madhva is credited with authoring 37 works, collectively known as the *Sarvamūla Granthas*. While he strongly refuted Śaṅkara's *Advaita Vedānta*, it is noteworthy that he did not present a direct or comprehensive critique of Rāmānuja's *Viśiṣṭādvaita Vedānta*.

His Main Teaching

Madhva strongly asserted that by the very fact that a being is itself, it is different from all other beings. Things are diverse by their very nature (*padārtha-svarūpatvād bhedasya*). From this assumption, Madhva proposes fivefold difference – (a) difference between Lord and Souls (*jīva*), (b) difference between Lord and world (*prakṛti*), (c) difference between soul and souls, (d) difference between souls (*jīvas*) and world (*prakṛti*), (e) difference between each entity of the world and all other material entities.[71]

(a) God: The Lord is completely independent Being (*svatantra*), His deepest essence is pure consciousness (*tat sārabhūtam cinmātram*). He possesses an infinite number of excellent differences which, though found distinct in other beings, are found in Him in perfect identity. God is omnipotent and possess of the eternal soul and eternal *prakṛti* through them He gives existence to all particular beings. He penetrates into souls and resides there as their inner witness (*antaryāmin*) and guardian, and also enters natural worlds as its inner controller (*niyāmaka*).[72] Madhva identifies Viṣṇu (*Nārāyaṇa*) as the Supreme Being, distinct from all other realities, and holds that worship of Viṣṇu alone leads to liberation. He also rejects the idea of a formless, impersonal Brahman, emphasizing that God possesses eternal attributes (*guṇas*) such as bliss, knowledge, and power, which make Him both transcendent and immanent.

---

[71] R. De Smet, "Rāmānuja and Madhva" in *Religious Hinduism*, edited by R. De Smet and J. Neuner, (Mumbai: St. Pauls, 1997), 104.

[72] De Smet, "Rāmānuja and Madhva", 105.

(b) Natural World: According to Madhva, nature (*prakṛti*) exists eternally without the help of God for its existence, but it is not a conscious substance. It is just the instrument of God. God created the natural world using *prakṛti*, but He can do without it what He does with it.[73] The material world is real in itself but dependent on God. Madhva strongly rejects Śaṅkara's idea of the world and asserts that the physical universe is objectively real and eternally distinct from Brahman. However, because it is under God's control, the world functions in accordance with divine will, and *karma* operates within this framework. The world is not a place of illusion but rather a stage where souls undergo experiences based on their past deeds, progressing towards salvation or deeper bondage.

(c) Soul: Unlike *prakṛti*, the soul is essentially conscious, which is essentially similar to God, yet dependent on Him. Unlike God, the soul is finite, though eternal. God is the perfect model of which the soul is an image (*ābhāsa*), a reflection (*pratibimba*), or a broken-off particle, but it is a self-subsistent, though dependent, image (*nirupādhika*).[74] Madhva emphasizes the eternal distinction between God and the soul, rejecting the Advaitic view that the soul can merge with Brahman. He also classifies souls into a hierarchical structure (*jīva-taratamya*), where some are destined for liberation, others for eternal rebirth, and some for eternal damnation. Unlike Rāmānuja, who views all souls as ultimately capable of attaining liberation, Madhva insists that some souls (like demons and the spiritually ignorant) are eternally doomed to suffering. This classification is based on inherent differences among souls, which are not changeable even through spiritual practice.

(d) Liberation: Madhva emphasizes *bhakti* (devotion) as the primary means of attaining *mokṣa* (liberation). He views devotion as a selfless surrender to God. Liberation requires both God's grace and the individual's devotion and righteous conduct. The highest form of *bhakti* is complete surrender

[73] De Smet, "Rāmānuja and Madhva", 105.

[74] De Smet, "Rāmānuja and Madhva", 105.

to Viṣṇu, which leads to His grace (*anugraha*), the ultimate determinant of liberation. He maintains that in liberation, the soul retains its individuality (*sva-svarūpa*) and experiences eternal bliss in service to Viṣṇu in *Vaikuṇṭha* (blissful abode of Viṣṇu). Unlike Advaitin, which sees *mokṣa* as identity with Brahman, and Viśiṣṭādvaita, which sees it as unity with God while maintaining individuality, Dvaita Vedānta defines *mokṣa* as eternal enjoyment of God's presence in a hierarchical order, where liberated souls experience different levels of bliss based on their spiritual merit.

In conclusion, we may say that Madhva's *Dvaita Vedānta* stands as a bold affirmation of dualism, where God (*Viṣṇu*), souls (*jīvas*), and the material world (*prakṛti*) exist as eternally distinct realities. Unlike Śaṅkara's Advaita, which dissolves individual identity into an impersonal Brahman, and Rāmānuja's Viśiṣṭādvaita, which sees the universe as God's body, Madhva emphasizes an unbridgeable gap between the Creator and the created. His doctrine of *pañca-bheda* (fivefold differences) underscores the absolute distinction between (a) God and souls, (b) God and matter, (c) souls and matter, (d) one soul and another, and (e) one material object and another.

Madhva's philosophy is deeply theo-centric, with *bhakti* (devotion) to Viṣṇu as the sole path to liberation. Unlike Śaṅkara's *jñāna*-centered approach, Madhva asserts that only divine grace (*anugraha*) can free the soul from bondage, though individual effort in righteousness (*dharma*) is also necessary. His doctrine of *jīva-taratamya* (hierarchical classification of souls) uniquely distinguishes Dvaita Vedānta, emphasizing that not all souls are equal - some are destined for liberation, others for eternal rebirth, and some for eternal damnation.

In his realist metaphysics, Madhva firmly defends the ontological reality of the world, rejecting Advaita's theory of contingent reality of the world. For Madhva, the world is a true creation of Viṣṇu, sustained and governed by Him. This emphasis on objective reality, personal devotion, and divine sovereignty makes Dvaita Vedānta highly compatible with *Vaiṣṇava Bhakti* traditions, influencing movements such as Haridāsa Bhakti and later Bhāgavata traditions in Karnataka.

Madhva's contribution to Indian philosophy lies in his unyielding defense of dualism, his strong emphasis on divine grace, and his hierarchical understanding of reality. His teachings challenge monistic interpretations and offer a deeply personal, theistic vision of *mokṣa*, where the liberated soul eternally serves and enjoys the bliss of Viṣṇu in *Vaikuṇṭha*. Thus, Dvaita Vedānta remains a distinct and powerful voice in the broader Vedāntic discourse, providing an alternative to non-dual and qualified non-dual perspectives on ultimate reality.

Concluding Remarks

The Vedānta school of philosophy represents one of the richest and most influential traditions in Indian thought, offering profound interpretations of the nature of reality, the self, and ultimate liberation. The teachings of Śaṅkara, Rāmānuja, and Madhva, while rooted in the same foundational texts of the Vedanta (primarily the Upaniṣads, Bhagavad Gītā, and Brahma Sūtra), diverge significantly in their perspectives, providing a spectrum of philosophical insights.

Śaṅkara's *Advaita Vedanta* views Brahman as the sole, undivided reality, asserting that there is no reality beyond Brahman. Liberation (*mokṣa*) is the realization of one's identity with Brahman through knowledge (*jñāna*). In contrast, Rāmānuja's *Viśiṣṭādvaita Vedanta* presents a vision of Brahman as both transcendent and immanent, with the world and individual souls being real yet inseparable parts of God. He emphasizes devotion (*bhakti*) as the means to achieve eternal communion with God, where the soul retains its individuality while participating in divine bliss. Madhva's *Dvaita Vedanta* takes an explicitly dualistic stance, maintaining the eternal distinction between God, individual souls, and the world. He highlights the supremacy of God and the necessity of divine grace for liberation, which allows the soul to experience eternal service to God without merging with Him.

Together, these philosophies encapsulate the diversity and depth of Indian metaphysical thought. Śaṅkara's focus on the oneness of existence, Rāmānuja's emphasis on relational harmony between God and the individual, and Madhva's insistence on the individuality of souls offer complementary paths to understanding ultimate reality. Each philosophy provides a unique framework to address spiritual and existential questions, catering to different temperaments and aspirations. The enduring relevance of these systems lies in their ability to engage both intellectual minds and spiritual seekers, offering pathways to transcendence while embracing the richness and complexity of human existence.

Chapter 11

Tribal Worldview

The Tribal or indigenous worldview is deeply rooted in a holistic understanding of existence, where the human, the divine, and the natural world are intricately interconnected. Unlike Western dualistic thought, which often separates humanity from nature and the sacred from the secular, indigenous traditions perceive reality as a web of relationships. At the heart of this worldview lies *communitarianism*, a way of life that emphasizes collective identity, shared responsibility, and reciprocity among humans, the divine, and the natural world.

In primal religious worldview, the relationship between God (or the divine), humanity, and creation is not one of domination but of mutual coexistence and reverence. This triadic relationship is central to indigenous spiritual life, where sacred myths, rituals, and oral traditions affirm the interconnectedness of all beings. The land is not merely a resource but a living entity with spiritual significance, animals are often considered kin, and the divine presence is experienced in every aspect of nature.

We will explore communitarianism as a defining characteristic of the tribal or indigenous worldview, highlighting how indigenous societies structure their existence around collective well-being rather than individualism. We also examine the *God-human-creation relationship* in the tribal worldview, demonstrating how indigenous cosmologies offer a vision of harmony that challenges exploitative approaches to nature.

1. Communitarianism among the Tribal or Indigenous People

Communitarianism is a fundamental characteristic of tribal or indigenous societies, shaping their social, economic, religious, and ecological outlook. Unlike the individualistic orientation found in many modern societies, tribal communities emphasize collective well-being, shared responsibilities, and reciprocal relationships. This worldview fosters social cohesion, moral responsibility, and sustainable living, making communitarianism an essential aspect of indigenous identity.

1.1. The Foundations of Communitarianism in Tribal Societies

Tribal communitarianism is deeply rooted in the belief that human existence is meaningful only in relation to the community. The individual is not seen as an isolated entity but as an integral part of a larger social and cosmic order. Several key principles define communitarian life in tribal societies:

(a) **Collective Identity:** In many indigenous traditions, identity is derived from the community rather than personal achievements. A person's worth is measured by their contributions to communal welfare rather than individual success.

(b) **Mutual Support and Reciprocity:** A strong sense of interdependence exists within tribal societies. Resources, labour, and knowledge are shared among members to ensure that no one is left behind. This is evident in practices such as communal farming, collective decision-making, and kinship-based support systems. If a family is unable to work in the *jhum* fields due to illness, the entire village comes together to complete the work on their behalf. Similarly, if someone is too poor to build a house, the community unites to construct it for them. This practice of mutual support and solidarity continues to this day.

(c) **Oral Tradition and Ancestral Wisdom:** Indigenous knowledge, history, and moral values are transmitted orally from generation to generation. Storytelling, folklore, and myths serve as educational tools that reinforce communal responsibilities and ethical living. These oral tradition and ancestral wisdom are community-oriented and help the new generation to continue the communitarian tradition.

(d) **Sacred Kinship with Nature:** Tribal communitarianism extends beyond human relationships to include the land, animals, and spirits. Nature is not seen as a commodity but as a sacred entity that must be protected for future generations. This aspect will be further discussed shortly.

1.2. The Role of Kinship and Clan Systems

Kinship plays a central role in tribal societies, forming the foundation of communitarian values. Clans and extended families function as the primary units of social organization, where duties and responsibilities are collectively shared. Unlike nuclear family structures in modern society, tribal kinship networks provide *social Security*. In times of crisis, such as illness or food shortage, the entire community comes together to support affected members. This kinship network helps in *conflict resolution*. Disputes are settled through communal discussions led by elders or tribal councils, ensuring that justice is restorative rather than punitive. It also enhances *shared leadership***.** Leadership in many tribal societies is not based on hierarchical authority but on wisdom and experience. Elders and spiritual leaders guide the community through consensus rather than coercion.

1.3. Economic and Ecological Dimensions of Communitarianism

Indigenous economic systems are often based on subsistence rather than profit-driven exploitation. The principles of communal ownership and sustainable use of resources shape their economic interactions. Key features include – (a) c*ommunal land ownership* where land is not privately owned but belongs to the entire community. This ensures equitable access to natural resources and prevents environmental degradation; (b) *Barter and exchange systems*: Instead of a market-driven economy, many tribal societies practice reciprocal exchange, where goods and services are traded based on need rather than monetary value. This aspect, of course, much diminished now among the indigenous people due to modernism but still to be seen in many rural places. (c) *Sustainable resource management*: The community takes collective responsibility for the preservation of forests, rivers, and wildlife. Rituals and taboos often regulate hunting, fishing, and agriculture to maintain ecological balance.

1.4. Religion and Spirituality as Expressions of Communitarianism

Tribal spirituality reinforces communitarian values by emphasizing relationships between the divine, humanity, and nature. Indigenous religious beliefs promote: (a) *Collective worship and rituals* - Religious ceremonies are community affairs rather than private expressions of faith. Festivals, harvest celebrations, and rites of passage involve the participation of the entire village. (b) *Ancestral veneration* - The ancestors are regarded as spiritual guardians of the community. Their wisdom and guidance are sought in decision-making, and their memory is honored through rituals. (c) *Sacred responsibility toward nature* - Many indigenous myths and religious narratives depict nature as sacred, reinforcing the moral duty to protect and nurture creation. (d) *Cosmologies* - Many Tribal cosmologies view the universe as a web of relationships, where humans, animals, plants, and even inanimate objects are interconnected. This wholistic perspective fosters a sense of responsibility toward the entire community of life. Rituals and ceremonies often serve to reinforce these connections, bringing the community together to honor their shared heritage and values.

1.5. Challenges and Contemporary Relevance of Tribal Communitarianism

Despite its resilience, tribal communitarianism faces challenges in the modern world, including: (a) *Displacement and Land Alienation* - Economic development and industrialization have disrupted communal land ownership, leading to the erosion of indigenous ways of life. (b) *Western individualism and consumerism* - The infiltration of capitalist and individualistic values threatens the communal ethos of tribal societies, leading to social fragmentation. (c) *Religious and cultural marginalization* - Many indigenous spiritual practices have been suppressed by dominant religious traditions, leading to a loss of traditional knowledge and identity. However, many tribal and indigenous communities are actively resisting these forces, striving to preserve and revitalize their communitarian traditions. Movements for land rights, cultural preservation, and self-determination are gaining momentum worldwide, reflecting a renewed commitment to collective well-being and sustainability. Indigenous leaders and activists are also playing a key role in advocating for communitarian values on the global stage, challenging the dominant paradigms of individualism and exploitation.

Communitarianism is a defining feature of the tribal and indigenous worldview, embodying a profound understanding of interdependence and shared responsibility. It is reflected in their social structures, economic practices, governance systems, and spiritual beliefs, all of which prioritize the well-being of the community over individual interests. While this worldview faces significant challenges in the modern era, it continues to inspire resilience and resistance among tribal and indigenous peoples. Their communitarian ethos offers valuable lessons for a world grappling with the consequences of individualism and environmental degradation, reminding us of the importance of connection, reciprocity, and collective stewardship.

In a time when the world is increasingly divided, the communitarian values of tribal and indigenous communities serve as a powerful reminder of our shared humanity and our responsibility to one another and the planet. By embracing these values, we can work toward a more just, equitable, and sustainable future for all.

2. Divine-Human-Creation Relations in Tribal Worldview

One of the unique features of Tribal or indigenous worldview is the conceived interconnectedness of all realities – Divine, human and creatures. Unlike the Judeo-Roman Christian tradition, which emphasizes various forms of dualism, the tribal community, in its traditional form, holds a holistic worldview that enables its members to perceive and experience the Divine in relation to creation. The term 'divine' is used here instead of the more popular, generic term 'God' for a specific reason. Tribals around the world believe in the existence of one Supreme Being, which can be referred to as 'God.' However, in addition to the Supreme Being, they also believe in the existence and importance of other divine beings and a number of benevolent spirits who play an active and often indispensable role in certain areas of life, sometimes even more so than the Supreme Being. Interestingly, although these spirits are worshipped, prayed to, or invoked, they are seldom considered as 'God.' By using the term 'divine,' we intend to include all of these: the Supreme Being, other divine beings, and the host of benevolent spirits.

Indigenous people all over the world have a unique worldview - which is uncharacteristic of most of other communities - a wholistic, non-dichotomial and relational worldview, the conception of realities as integrally related. According to James Cox, who had done commendable works on African indigenous religions, the African indigenous religions are co-extensive with their societies, because religion is an undifferentiated part of social life. Reciprocity between the community and the spirits marks the central core of indigenous religious activity.[1] John A. Grim of Yale University, talking about Indigenous worldview, says, "Mysticism, although differently expressed in particular indigenous lifeways, manifests the intimate relatedness of person, community, spirits, and ecosystem. This interactive quaternity is ritually embedded in indigenous lifeways and symbolically unfolded in cosmological narratives."[2] Indigenous worldviews do not see the earth as simply an *objective other*, or a reality separate from human beings, but a complex web of persons, communities, and ecosystems charged with spiritual power where "the foundational interaction of humans with their local landscape is the matrix in which indigenous mystical knowledge of the sacred occurs."[3]

In line with this, K. Thanzauva maintains that "the tribal worldview brings together nature and super-nature, space and time, this world and other world. This unity is a unity of continuance in which boundaries between deities, spirit, animals, humans and natural phenomena are more or less obscure or shifting."[4] For instance, the Penan of Sarawak, Malaysia believes that forest is alive; Viliui Sakha tribes of Siberia (Russia) believe that all in nature is spirit possessed, trees, rocks, woods, and all things – animate and inanimate have *ichchi* – the spirit keepers of nature.[5] North America's Indigenous people have an enduring heritage of connections with the natural world and universe. Native spiritual life knows that all forms of life in the natural World are inter-connected.

---

[1] James L. Cox, "Characteristics of African Indigenous Religions in Contemporary Zimbabwe", in *Indigenous Religions: A Companion*, edited by Graham Harvey, (London: Cassell, 2000), 231.

[2] John A. Grim, "Cosmology and Native American Mystical Traditions" in *Theologiques*, (Vol. 9, No. 1, 2001), 115.

[3] John A. Grim, "Cosmology and Native American Mystical Traditions," 141.

[4] K.Thanzauva, *Theology of Community: Tribal Theology in the Making*, (Bangalore: Asian Trading Corporation, 2004), 195.

[5] Rammathot Khongreiwo, "Landscapes and Pre-Christian Naga Belief System: Cosmology, Spirits and 'Land of the Dead'" in *Journal of Tribal studies*, (Vol. XVI, No. 1, Jan-June 2011), 55.

No distinction is made between the spiritual and the secular because it is a holistic totality.[6] According to Joan Hendriks and Gerard Hall, the experience of the sacred and interconnected unity of all beings with the earth, cosmos and ultimate reality is a mystical experience of the Indigenous Australian peoples. One is not separate from this reality; in fact, there is no one - nor for that matter no Other - separate or separable from creation and the natural world.[7]

2.1. Non-dichotomial Worldview

The tribal worldview is primarily characterized by the absence of a dichotomy between what is considered 'the sacred' and 'the secular,' and by the presence of a wholistic vision of reality. The sacred–profane dichotomy, which is now prevalent among tribal communities, is not intrinsic to their traditional worldview but rather an imposition brought about by the process of Westernization. Lalsangkima Pachuau rightly observes that "the onslaught of modern Western thought with its clear dichotomy between what is sacred and what is secular (under "church and state") has deeply influenced existing descriptions of the primal religions of the tribal people. Such a framework is foreign and its imposition fails to do justice to the integrity of the religious concept."[8] Edward E. Dudek also says, "In the tribal worldview, one cannot make a clear-cut distinction between the sacred and secular, between religious and non-religious, between

---

[6] N.A., "Tribal Knowledge, Supernatural & Ceremonies", in *http://www.shannonthunderbird.com/tribal_beliefs.htm*, (11.10.2011), 1.

[7] Joan Hendriks & Gerard Hall SM, "The Natural Mysticism of Indigenous Australian Traditions", in *http://aejt.com.au/__data/assets/pdf_file/0005/158315/Henriks-and-Hall_Indigenous_Mysticism.pdf* (13.11.2014).

[8] Lalsangkima Pachuau, "Mizo '*Sakhua*' Then and Now: Change and continuity between Mizo primal religion and Mizo Christianity", a paper presented in the Faculty Research Seminar, The United Theological College on 12th November, 2003, 1. The same paper with slight modification is published as L. Pachuau, "Mizo 'Sakhua' in Transition: Change and Continuity from Primal Religion to Christianity", in *Missiology*, Vol. 34; No. 1, 2006.

spiritual and material areas of life."[9] Any attempt to study the relationship between divine, human and nature should take this aspect seriously; otherwise, it will not strike the chord correctly.

2.2. Divine-Human-Nature Continuum

Tribal people perceive realities as interconnected harmoniously, so that seemingly different entities are seen as one whole. The divine-human-nature continuum is a striking hallmark of the tribal sacred worldview as Nirmal Minz writes: "A nature-human-spirit continuum is the key to the tribal vision of life. All religious rites, observance, festivities are based on this wholistic vision of reality. Tribal religion accepts the integral relationship of nature, human and spirit in their experiences."[10] Myths, legends, tales, oral epics, proverbs, riddles, rites, and rituals all represent the sacred worldview of tribal people. Each element of folklore, whether verbal or nonverbal, holds purpose and meaning within its socio-cultural context. The functioning of traditional knowledge in sustaining the community is highly structured and communal. Everyone shares this knowledge and applies it in their lives; it forms the foundation of their subsistence.[11] Thus, nature and tribal people are inseparable. Nature has given them a worldview, and their worldview is inherently naturalistic. The supernatural is perceived as present in both the animate and the inanimate. Tribal people acquire their knowledge through close association and interdependence with nature. The earth, forest, river, hills, birds, and animals constitute the life of the tribals, who, dependent upon them,

---

[9] Edward E. Dudek, "Tribal Religious Belief of North East India with special emphasis on Nagaland and the Introduction & Effect of the Gospel" in *GlobeServe Journal of Missions, December 2008, www.globeservejournalofmissions.org* (23.06.2001), 5.

[10] Nirmal Minz, "The Study of Tribal Religion in India", in *Re-Visioning India's Religious Traditions: Essays in honour of Eric Lott*, edited by David C. Scott and Israel Selvanayagam, (Delhi: ISPCK, 1996), 122.

[11] Mahendra K. Mishra, "Sacred Worldview in Tribal Memory: Sustaining nature through Cultural Actions," in *Language & Ecology*, (Vol. 2, no. 4, 2009), 3.

derive their knowledge, shape their identity, and create their folklore, culture, and religion.[12]

It is due to this worldview that the tribal community believes that any harm caused to one entity, such as nature, is disastrous to the entire system and existence. Wati Longchar correctly observes, "All cultural components are closely interrelated. If one element is affected, the whole cultural structure is affected."[13] The destruction of forests, animals, and land can affect not only the equilibrium of the tribal people's peaceful existence with nature but also lead to the annihilation of their culture and religion.

In the tribal worldview, according to M. M. Thomas, "there is the sense of a spiritual continuum within which the dead and the living, natural objects, spirits and gods, the individuals, the clan and the tribe, animal, plants, minerals and man (*sic*) form an unbroken hierarchical unity of spiritual force."[14] K. J. N. Gowtham Shankar also observes, "Tribals believe in the existence of human, nature and spiritual worlds and the continuous interaction between these three worlds is well established and maintained."[15] Tribal people understand spiritual realities not only in otherworldly terms but also conceive spirits as integrally related to humans and creation, present in their paddy fields, trees, rocks, mountains, homes, certain individuals, and peculiar objects that can be possessed, among others.

---

[12] Mahendra K. Mishra, "Sacred Worldview in Tribal Memory: Sustaining nature through Cultural Actions," 1.

[13] A. Wati Longchar, *The Traditional Tribal Worldview and Modernity*, (Jorhat: N. Limla Lkr, 1995), 8.

[14] A. Wati Longchar, *The Traditional Tribal Worldview and Modernity*, pp. 7-8.

[15] KJN Gowtham Shankar, "Endogenous development and Tribal worldviews: Working with Tribal communities in India", a paper presented in the International Conference on Endogenous Development and Bio-Cultural Diversity: The Interplay of Worldviews, globalization and locality, 3-5 October, 2006, Geneva, Switzerland, in *http://www.bioculturaldiversity.net/introduction.htm* (7.10.2011), 1.

2.3. Interconnected Cosmic Order

The Tribals perceive their cosmology in an organic way. In this organic understanding, everything is organically related to each other. Everything is linked together, values everything. Humans see themselves as an integral part of the total cosmic life. Though the sacred power and the Spirit(s) are understood as the creator and sustainer of all living beings, they are also perceived, though distinct, as part of the total cosmic life. This organic relationship is possible because of the earth. The earth is the foundation of cosmo-centric spirituality.[16]

Supreme Being is considered as manifested in natural objects and phenomena. However, there is no sign of pantheistic tendency among the tribals. Natural objects are considered the instruments for the worship of the Supreme Being. Since vegetation signifies the presence of the Supreme Being and the whole of vegetation is perceived as the manifestation of him. The tribals do not erect temples, for them the whole world is the Supreme Being's temple. Since he is an integral part of creation, he cannot be restricted to any location of the earth. This explains why the tribals see the dynamic and active presence of the Supreme Being in all creation, including the wind, sun, trees and rivers.[17]

2.4. The Interconnectedness in Tribal Myths

Myth plays an important role in any religion, may be more in Primal Religion and in fact there is no religion without a myth. Myth is a created story to convey the truth. Mircea Eliade, a well known historian of religion, identified two ways of using the term myth – an usual meaning where it connotes 'fable', 'invention', 'fiction' or 'illusion'. But, it is also used by ethnologists, sociologists, and historians of religions to mean a true story, a story that is a most important because it is sacred,

---

[16] Wati Longchar, "The Uniqueness of Indigenous Spirituality", unpublished paper, 4.

[17] Edward E. Dudek, "Tribal Religious Belief of North East India with special emphasis on Nagaland and the Introduction & Effect of the Gospel", 7.

exemplary, and significant; in the sense of 'sacred tradition, primordial revelation, and exemplary model.'[18] Myth, for the study of Primal Religion, is important because,

> Myth narrates a sacred history; it relates an event that took place in primordial Time, the fabled time of the "Beginnings". In other words, myth tells how, through the deeds of Supernatural Beings, a reality came into existence...In short, myths describe the various and sometimes dramatic breakthroughs of the sacred (or the "supernatural") into the World. It is this sudden breakthrough of the sacred that really *establishes* the World and makes it what it is today.[19]

For David Scott, a well known scholar in Religion, a myth is a story that is sacred to and shared by a group of people who find their most important meanings in it.[20] So, myth is the foundation of religion especially for the tribal as most of the religious truths come down to us in the form of myth. We will explore a few of these myths to understand the intricate interrelationship between the divine, humans, and nature.

Ao-Naga of the Northeast India has several myths concerning the creation of the world or the origin of the universe. One of these myths depicted a total chaos and disorder prevailed in the beginning, and it was the meeting of animals which set the order. A myth of a certain tribe in Arunachal Pradesh describes how human beings are helped by the sun which dispelled darkness so that they can get food. Another Ao-Naga myth talks about a rat giving rice to human beings for

---

[18] Mircea Eliade, *Myth and Reality*, (New York: Happer & Row, Publishers, 1963), p. 1.

[19] Mircea Eliade, *Myth and Reality*, 5-6.

[20] Cited in A. Wati Longchar, *The Tribal Religious Traditions in North East India: An Introduction*, (Jorhat: Wati Longchar, 2000), p. 22. For further study on the meaning and function of Myth ref. G.S.Kirk, *Myth: Its Meaning and Functions in Ancient & Other Cultures*, (London: Cambridge University Press, 1970).

food which was un-known to humans before. The Aos also have another myth that describes how sun was angry and refused to rise and how the cock wisely convinced him to rise again every time he crows in the morning for the benefit of all the living creatures. Still another myth of Ao talks about human beings in want of water but a bird told them where water is and because of that humans survived.[21]

The Mizo community has a rich tradition of myths that explore themes such as creation, the origin of humans, life after death, and the interconnectedness of the divine, humans, and nature. Central to these myths is the idea of a harmonious coexistence among all living beings, as illustrated in the creation story where the goddess *Khuazingnu* creates humans and other beings to live in unity, communicating and thriving together. The myths also delve into moral and social lessons, such as the story of King *Thlanrawkpa*, whose failure to invite his father-in-law, the god *Sabereka*, to a grand feast led to catastrophic consequences, emphasizing the importance of respect and inclusion. Another myth highlights communal cooperation, where animals like the otter, badger, and earthworms work together to restore fertile land, symbolizing the interdependence of all creatures. Additionally, the Mizo flood myth reflects themes of conflict and reconciliation, as well as the consequences of unrequited love, as seen in the story of Ngaitei and the river spirit. These myths not only explain natural phenomena and cultural practices but also reinforce the Mizo worldview, where humans, animals, and the spiritual realm are deeply intertwined.[22] There are several other myths among the Mizos that describe a close relationship between the divine, humans, and nature. The story

---

[21] Cf. A. Wati Longchar, *The Tribal Religious Traditions in North East India* pp. 23-29 where he explains quite a number of myths in details.

[22] Cherrie Lalnunziri Chhangte, "Myth and the Mizo Worldview", the unpublished seminar paper presented at International Seminar on History of Religions, Jawaharlal Nehru University, October 8-10, 2007, 1, 16-17; N.A., *Mizo Thawnthu*, (Aizawl: Tribal Research Institute, Directorate of Art and Culture, Mizoram, 1992), 2-3.

of *Chepahakhata*, who married a witch and had a daughter, is another significant one. His witch wife left him because of his wicked character and went to heaven to be with *Pu Vana*, who is considered one of the divine beings by the Mizos.[23] In all these myths, God, divine beings, spirits, sprites, witches, humans, animals, rivers, trees, flowers, and more are depicted as having a close relationship with one another.

The same types of myths are found among the indigenous people in Africa. John S. Mbiti said that some of the African myths indicated that human being and animals are originated at the same time and in the same way. Many people have a sacred attitude towards their animals. For example, the Herero regards all cattle as sacred and as having originated from their mythical 'tree of life' from where human and other life comes.[24]

The Khasi-Pnar tradition, another Northeast Indian tribe, features myths that highlight the deep connection between the divine, humans, and nature. One creation myth describes how God created sixteen families in heaven, allowing them to travel between heaven and earth via a golden ladder to care for creation. Seven families chose to stay on earth permanently, losing access to the ladder but maintaining communication with God through other means. Another myth explains the origin of religion, where humans and animals mocked the sun and moon during a festival, causing them to leave. Darkness ensued, and after failed attempts by other animals, a cock successfully persuaded the sun to return. Humans then asked God for a religion to prevent such mistakes, and the cock became a central instrument for divination, marking the beginning of religious practices.[25]

---

[23] Cherrie Lalnunziri Chhangte, "Myth and the Mizo Worldview", 29-31.

[24] John S Mbiti, *African Religions and Philosophy, Second Edition*, (Oxford: Heinemann Educational Publishers, 1999), 50.

[25] Bolinkar Sohkhlet, "Phenomenological Study of the Understanding of God (*Blei*) as emerging from selected myth and rituals of the traditional religion of the Khasi Pnar", (Unpublished D.Th. thesis submitted to SATHRI of Senate of Serampore college, 2007, 129-132.

All these myths discussed above emphasize the active role of animals in creation and their personification as wise and discerning beings. Animals are depicted as decision-makers, helpers, and integral to the natural order, challenging the notion of human superiority. Instead, humans are seen as part of nature, with a responsibility to contribute to creation rather than dominate it. Nature is portrayed as a dynamic and essential part of the cosmic system, not merely a resource for exploitation, reinforcing a worldview of interdependence and respect for all life.

Again, these myths demonstrate that gods, spirits, and sprites are actively involved in and are part of the whole system of life on earth, alongside humans and animals. Inter-marriage between these living beings was common. These tribal myths portray human and creatures celebrated feasts together, sang and danced together, built families together, worked together for the rebuilding of the earth, and helped each other in times of need, and so on. Living in harmony with divine beings, spirits, animals, and vegetation is the hallmark of human existence. Wati Longchar aptly said: "The myths portray that it was the divine intention that people, nature, and divinity form one community and live as one family. The myths tell that humans are an integral part of creation. We relate to creation as family members;" these myths "do not make a clear-cut distinction between nature and the supernatural. That is how the tribals understand their history."[26] The tribal myths affirm an organic relationship of all realities as the core of the traditional tribal worldview, where everything – the Supreme Being, the spirits, humans, and nature – is perceived as organically related to each other.[27]

---

[26] Wati Longchar, *The Tribal Religious Traditions in North East India,* 30-31.

[27] A. Wati Longchar, "A Critique of the Christian Theology of Creation", in *Doing Theology with Tribal Resources: Context and Perspective*, edited by A. Wati Longchar and Larry E. Devis, (Jorhat: Tribal Study Centre, ETC, 1999), p. 72.

2.5. The Interconnectedness in Religious Beliefs

Some of the most fundamental religious beliefs of the tribals point to the interconnectedness of the divine, human, and nature, as discussed below:

2.5.1. Mana – Mana is a kind of force or power distinct from physical power that is present in objects such as peculiar stones, trees, plants, animals, or even human beings, such as priests or chiefs. Such a belief indicates the inseparable link between humans, spirits, and created things in a tribal worldview.

2.5.2. Fetish – Closely related to mana is the belief in the power of a fetish. A fetish is an object believed to be inhabited by a spirit and, as such, is supposed to confer its power upon the person who possesses it as their fetish. A fetish may be a stone of peculiar shape, a bright beak of an animal, a stick, a feather, a claw of a beast, a born, or any other curious and peculiar object.[28] The tribals consider the fetish to be semi-human or semi-god, possessing personality and will, and it is sometimes considered an object of worship. The fetish is considered to represent the immanence of the Supreme Being, and as such, it is a clear expression of the relationship between the divine, human, and nature.

2.5.3. Omen and Divination – Another tribal religious belief and practice that clearly points to the interrelationship between the divine, human, and nature is the practice of Omen and Divination. This indicates how much the tribal people depend on other creatures for their safety, survival, and understanding of the divine will. An omen is a sign, warning, or alert given by certain phenomena, indicating that something good or bad is going to happen. This highlights the vital role natural phenomena play in the lives of the tribals. "For the tribals, nature is supernatural in quality, and the supernatural is nature

---

[28] Jonathan H. Thumra, "The Primal Religious Tradition" in *Religious Traditions of India*, edited by P. S. Daniel, et.al., (New Delhi: ISPCK, 2002), 51.

itself," observes Wati Longchar.[29] Sashikaba states, "Omens are mystical signs to which Ao Nagas pay heed for protection, direction, guidance, and blessing in their lives."[30] For the tribal people, these natural phenomena are considered the voices of the divine, telling them beforehand what is going to happen, thus showing how God communicates with humans through natural phenomena.

Divination is a method by which the divine reveals things that are to happen in the future. In other words, "divination is a practice of foretelling the future with supernatural aid."[31] Tribal communities employ various objects for divination, with commonly used items including cocks, bamboo, eggs, and pebbles. For instance, if a cock crows at or before midnight, it is considered a sign of an impending calamity. This unusual behaviour is believed to be divinely directed, serving as a warning to the people. Such practices illustrate how tribal traditions perceive divination and omens as a means through which the divine communicates future events using natural elements. This reflects the deep and inseparable connection between humans, nature, and the divine in tribal worldviews.

2.5.4. Taboo – Taboo in tribal religious tradition refers to a caution or prohibition against certain supernatural objects, plants, animals, or human beings who possess mana. Anything considered taboo should not be touched, smelled, tasted, or heard, as such actions are believed to invite supernatural anger and penalties.[32] Some examples of taboos include: a man should not kill an animal during his wife's pregnancy; during certain sacred days, villagers are prohibited from killing animals; it is

---

[29] Wati Longchar, *The Tribal Religious Traditions in North East India*, 32.

[30] Sashikaba Kechutzar, "Omen, Divination and Dream (Tatakrutsu, Antokdangba/Amsu and Pongmang): Medium for Divine Revelation" in Razouselie Lasetso (ed), *Garnering Tribal Resources for Doing Tribal Christian Theology*, (Jorhat: ETC Programme Coordination, Eastern Theological College, 2008), 325.

[31] Wati Longchar, *The Traditional Tribal Worldview and Modernity*, p. 48.

[32] Jonathan H. Thumra, "The Primal Religious Tradition," 54.

taboo to hunt or set traps during breeding seasons; and it is taboo to cut certain trees, etc. It is taboo to go to the *jhum* for work the day after it has been burnt, as this day is set aside for mourning the animals and insects killed during the burning process, and so on. The preservation of trees, certain animals, and birds through taboos is important not only for the tribal people's wellbeing and survival but also for the protection of the species.

Thus, for tribal communities, taboos and ceremonies serve as powerful symbols of the interconnectedness and interdependence of the entire world. They reflect the belief that every element of existence is woven into a unified whole. When any part of this delicate balance is disrupted or misused, the entire system suffers, highlighting the profound relationship between humans, nature, and the divine. The practice of taboo among the tribals emphasizes the unquestionable inter-relationship between humans, nature, and the divine, where mutual enrichment, respect, and care are the hallmarks of this relationship.

2.5.5. Totem – There may be no single belief or practice that more vividly illustrates the divine-human-nature continuum in tribal worldview than totemism, in which tribal people establish a totemic relationship with certain plants and animals. Totemism is a common socio-religious phenomenon among tribals all over the world, where a people group identifies certain animals, insects, plants, or sometimes, though rarely, inanimate objects as their ancestors or as supernaturally connected with their ancestors.[33] According to Frank Byron Jevons, a fundamental principle in the totem faith is that the human kin and the animal kind are one flesh, one blood, members of the same clan, bound by the sacred tie of blood to respect and assist each other.[34] Some common totem animals include the tiger, tortoise, cobra, monkey, jackal, deer, dog, buffalo, cock, peacock, owl, fish,

---

[33] Jonathan H. Thumra, "The Primal Religious Tradition," 56.

[34] Frank Byron Jevons, *The History of Religion*, (Delhi: Orient Publication, 1985), p. 251.

etc.[35] For the Thadou tribe, the Mithun is their totem; for the Chongthu and Kuki, the Python; for the Zeliangrong Naga, the Pigeon, Tiger, and White Pumpkin; for the Thangkul Naga, the Cock; for the Ao Naga, the Sparrow; for the Rengma Naga, the Tiger; for the Fanai Mizo, the Fish; and for the Garo, the Owl,[36] and so on.

One of the unique features of the indigenous religious experience is the mystical relationship some people have developed with animals, particularly the tiger. Certain 'priests' or 'medicine men/women' have an inexplicable and mysterious bond with tigers, where both the human and the tiger can sense, communicate, and feel each other's emotions, even sharing suffering when one is in pain. These individuals are known as 'tiger men/women.' In this mystical relationship, the human appears to hold a superior position, as he/she can command the tiger to do his bidding. However, if the tiger is hurt, the human will also feel the pain in his/her body, if the tiger is killed, the human will also die instantly. This relationship is deeply mystical and cannot be fully explained in human terms or categories. Such connections were common among several Northeast tribes in the past and still persist today. While the tiger is the most common animal involved in these mystical relationships, other creatures, like pythons, are also part of this unique bond with humans. What we can discern from this mystical phenomenon is the unprecedented closeness that can develop between humans and animals - where human beings regard animals not merely as co-creatures or, in a deeper sense, as part of the family, but as beings with whom they share life in its totality, achieving a profound oneness. Such is the strength of this relationship.

---

[35] Wati Longchar, *The Traditional Tribal Worldview and Modernity,* 59.

[36] Cf. A. Wati Longchar, *The Tribal Religious Traditions in North East India*, pp. 55-56; Budha Kamei, "Belief in Totem among the Tingkao Ragwang Chapriak people", in *http://e-pao.net/epSubPageExtractor.asp?src=manipur.Manipur_and_Religion.Belief_in_Totem_among_the_Tingkao_Ragwang_Chapriak_people,* (14.10.211).

It is evident that the traditional belief systems of tribal communities across India underline the deep interconnectedness between the divine, human beings, and nature. These traditions reflect a worldview where the divine is not distant or separate but is intricately woven into the fabric of life on earth. Through myths, rituals, and practices such as mana, totemism, divination, taboo, and fetishes, the tribes illustrate a profound respect for nature and all its elements, recognizing them as integral participants in the divine order. Humans are not seen as superior to nature; rather, they are part of a larger cosmic system where mutual respect, cooperation, and harmony are essential. This wholistic understanding fosters a sense of responsibility, guiding the tribals to live in balance with the divine, nature, and fellow creatures, ensuring the preservation and continuity of life.

2.6. The Interconnectedness in the Nature and Actions of Divine Beings

Tribals all over the world have one thing in common, that is the belief in the existence of a Supreme Being and other benevolent spirits. Apart from this, they also ascribe importance to and acknowledge the existence of numerous benevolent spirits who are helpful to humans and who are objects of worship in the form of sacrifice and prayer. Their understanding of the Supreme Being and other divine beings clearly depicts a close inter-relationship existing between the divine, human, and nature. The tribals believe that God is in all and all is in God. God is never perceived as wholly other but as the one who participates in the life of the world.

In Mizo tradition, there is a Supreme Being known as *Pathian*, who is considered the creator of everything. He is believed to dwell in high heaven. However, Mizos also worshipped *Khuanu* and *Khuavang* who are known to be closer to human beings than *Pathian*. *Khuanu* is understood to be active in the day-to-day activities of the people, whereas *Khuavang* is never said to have dwelled in high heaven but on the earth, on the hills, and in the mountains. The most significant aspect for our discussion here is that, apart from Pathian, Mizos worshipped a number of spirits or rather 'divine beings.' *Hnuaite* is said to dwell beneath the earth; *Khaltu* takes care of individuals; *Sa* looks after the family or clan, whereas *Khua* is responsible for taking care of the whole community.[37] *Khuavang* is responsible for setting natural boundaries such as rivers, streams, brooks, and ranges of hills. He is also involved with humans by marking them with moles called *Khuavang chhinchhiah* (marks of Khuavang). *Khuavang* is known to have some descendants among human beings.[38] *Lasis*, the benevolent female spirits, are considered the owners of wild animals and would give animals to their human conjugal friends. In short, it can be said that for the Mizos, trees, bamboos, rivers, hills, big rocks, and so on are inhabited by good and bad spirits.

In Khasi-Pnar religion, it is very common to consider God as using nature like hills, rocks and cliffs, rivers, and forests. Many hills are considered sacred as they have supernatural or divine connections with God. Rocks, cliffs, etc., are considered divine tutelary objects; they are regarded as God's servants or agents through which God reveals himself. Rivers are considered sacred as they are the channels by which God empowers the people and blesses them. Khasi-Pnar believes that inter-communication between humans and the divine is possible through natural elements, and forests are the ones through which such interrelationship and communication with the divine are facilitated. They consider forests and groves as the special sanctuaries of *ki ryngkew ki basa* (divine tutelary objects), through which God manifests his/her power. So, forests facilitate a deeper bond between God and human beings.[39]

---

[37] Cf. T. Vanlaltlani, *Tribal Religion: Mizo and Bru*, (Aizawl: Mizo Theological Association, 2009), pp. 58, 85-86. Cf. Zairema, "The Mizos and their Religion" in *Towards a Tribal Theology: The Mizo Perspective*, edited by K. Thanzauva, (Aizawl: Mizo Theological Conference, 1989), p. 37.

[38] T. Vanlaltlani, *Tribal Religion: Mizo and Bru*, 87.

[39] Bolinkar Sohkhlet, Bolinkar Sohkhlet, Bolinkar Sohkhlet, "Phenomenological study of the understanding of God (*Blei*) as emerging from

Ki ryngkew ki basa, the tutelary natural objects of *ki shnong* (villages), *ki raids* (units), and *ki hima* (chiefdoms), are used by God to release His/Her power to help people. This is experienced through natural objects like rocks, boulders, and hills covered by sacred groves. The understanding of this phenomenon is that God works to affirm His/Her relation with people through other objects of His/Her creation. Therefore, humans should acknowledge the relation and power of God through creation and should respect all those tutelary natural objects as their fellow beings. For instance, there is a hill near a village that is helpful in protecting the village. The Khasi regard this hill as *u ryngkew u basa* of the village. This is considered to have power from God, and the people should give due respect to this hill.[40]

Ao Nagas call the Supreme Being '*Lijaba*' – *Li* means 'earth', *zaba* or *jaba* means 'enter', thereby meaning 'the one who enters or indwells the earth'. Every year, Aos observe three days of genna known as *Lijaba za mong* or *Lijaba mong* in the month of March or April, the Ao sowing season. During this season, *Lijaba* is believed to enter the earth just as the seeds enter the earth and rise again after three months, corresponding to the three days. *Lijaba* enters the earth with the seeds and rises again along with the crops.[41]

Therefore, the traditional tribal worldview, which unfortunately is diminishing rapidly due to modernization and urbanization, emphasizes the interrelatedness and interconnectedness of all existence. It stresses the value of wholeness in totality. In this conception of wholeness, each entity participates in the sustenance and well-being of the

selected myth and rituals of the traditional religion of the Khasi Pnar", 100-106.

[40] Bolinkar Sohkhlet, Bolinkar Sohkhlet, "Phenomenological study of the understanding of God (*Blei*) as emerging from selected myth and rituals of the traditional religion of the Khasi Pnar", 88.

[41] Wati Longchar, *The Traditional Tribal Worldview and Modernity*, *op.cit.*, p. 37.

whole. Thus, a community is not composed of human beings alone but is composed of human beings, God, and the whole creation, which are integrally interrelated.

2.7. The Interconnectedness in the Centrality of Land

The post-modern worldview, which deeply affects the life of the tribals, views the land as an object of exploration and exploitation from which humans are destined to gain profits. This utilitarian and materialistic perspective of looking at the land is quite foreign to the traditional tribal worldview, where a deep and inseparable relationship is maintained between the land and the people.

The centrality and importance of 'land' in the tribal worldview is stressed by most of the writers on Primal religion and the proponents of Tribal theology. Wati maintains that most of the tribes in Northeast India, like the Nagas, Mizos, Garos, etc., believe that they were born out of the earth. The earth is conceived symbolically as the spouse of the Supreme Being, the mother of all creatures; the land and everything in it are regarded as having life and power. It is a place that gives an identity to the tribal community, a sacred place, and a temple of the Supreme Being. Thus, the land is an integral part of the Supreme Being.[42] The land is not only the source of their existence, but some tribes, like the Mizos, perceive that the divine dwells on the land and some deities underneath the earth, and many benevolent and malevolent spirits dwell on the surface of the land.[43] According to the Khasi-Pnars' belief, God, the creator of all, fills heaven and earth. Every bit of ground is

---

[42] A. Wati Longchar, *The Traditional Tribal Worldview and Modernity*, *op.cit.*, pp. 64-65; cf. A. Wati Langchar, *An Emerging Asian Theology: Tribal Theology, Issue, Method and Perspective,* (Jorhat: Tribal Study Centre, ETC, 2000), pp. 75-78.

[43] In Mizo traditional religion, we see a Priest invoking a god who is under the earth; and also a god who is known by the name *Khuavang* is known to have dwelt on the mountain, not in heaven above. Cf. Liangkhaia, *Mizo Awmdan Hlui & Mizo Mi leh thil Hmingthangte leh Mizo Sakhua*, (Aizawl: L.T.I Publications, 2008), pp.12, 29.

therefore sacred, and no particular part or portion can be held as holier than the other.[44]

For the tribal people, land is a holy sanctuary, a temple where they worship God, a sacred place animated by spirits.[45] Land is, again, considered a mother. The whole land is the home of the Supreme Being. Symbolically, the land is the spouse of the Supreme Being, as understood by many tribes. The whole creation is the manifestation of the Supreme Being. The Supreme Being is an integral part of the land, and at the same time, the land is not external to God. Without land, the Supreme Being ceases to work. Thus, in the tribal worldview, the land and the Supreme Being are inseparably related.[46]

The land symbolizes the unity of all living beings, the spirit world, and the Supreme Being. Its misuse disrupts this harmony, bringing chaos among creatures - it is akin to harming one's own mother. Many tribes in Northeast India have myths that trace their origins to the earth, believing that their ancestors emerged from stones. Land not only binds clans, villages, and tribes together but also unites the Supreme Being, spirits, ancestors, and creation as one interconnected family. For tribal communities, the entire universe is sacred. Rocks, boulders, trees, and rivers are not mere natural elements but hold deep religious significance. The voices and songs of animals convey spiritual messages, while celestial events like solar and lunar eclipses are not just natural occurrences but signs that communicate with the community, often forewarning of danger or misfortune.[47]

So, for the tribals, God and land and everything in it are inseparably related; destruction of land is directly corresponding

---

[44] Cf. *www.egyankosh.ac.in/bitstream/123456789/25641/1/Unit-18*, (08.10.2011), p. 13.

[45] K. Thanzauva, *Theology of Community*, *op.cit.*, p. 218.

[46] A. Wati Longchar, "Tribal Theology: Nature and Method and Perspective" in *Journal of Tribal study*, (Vol. 5, No. 1, January-June, 2001), pp. 8.

[47] A. Wati Longchar, "Tribal Theology: Nature and Method and Perspective," 9-10.

to the destruction of the relationship between human and God, because it is equivalent to the destruction of the immanence of God or the destruction of the divine presence. As land is so vital, the tribals in their traditional conception have no room for the privatization of land, because human beings are not the owner of land, but the Supreme Being and it is understood that humans are given stewardship responsibility to look after the land.

Our discussion on the 'traditional' worldview of the Tribals clearly demonstrates the absence of a dichotomy between the sacred and the secular, religion and non-religion, and emphasizes the presence of a spirit-human-nature continuum. This wholistic tribal vision of reality is vividly portrayed in the numerous myths that highlight the roles of animals, fish, birds, and trees in creation and in maintaining harmonious life on earth. The spirit-human-nature continuum is further reflected in their understanding of the Supreme Being and other 'divine beings,' who are believed to have a close relationship with the created world. The belief in mana, fetish, taboo, totem, omen, and divination all serve as clear indicators of this interconnectedness. The centrality of land in the tribal worldview underscores the unbroken link between the visible world and invisible supernatural beings.

The tribals' wholistic vision of reality provides a crucial framework for mending the fractured relationship between the divine, human, and nature. The traditional bond that unites the tribal community with its environment - the 'nature-human-spirit continuum,' as Nirmal Minz aptly puts it - must be rediscovered to nurture a harmonious relationship between these elements. Unfortunately, this profound tradition is rapidly diminishing under the influence of modernity, globalization, and urbanization. To counter this, it is essential to revitalize and re-cultivate this tradition within the tribal community. By doing so, the tribal understanding of interconnectedness and interdependence across all forms of existence can become a vital resource and model for addressing contemporary challenges like ecological crisis, etc. and promoting a much-needed wholistic relationship between the divine, human, and nature.

Bibliography

1. Books

Aiyer, C.N. Krishnaswami, "Life and Time of Saṅkara", in *Three Great Acharyas: Śaṅkara, Ramanuja, Madhwa: Critical Sketches of their Life and Times, an Expositions of their Philosophical System*, Madras: G.A. Natesan & Co., Publishers, No year of publication)

Aleaz, K.P., *The Relevance of Relation in Śaṅkara's Advaita Vedānta*, Delhi: Kant Publications, 1996.

Chaterjee, S.C & D.M. Datta, An Introduction to Indian Philosophy, Calcutta: University of Calcutta, 1984.

Chatterjee, Satishchandra and Dhirendramohan Datta, *An Introduction to Indian Philosophy*, New Delhi: Rupa, 2007.

Daniel, P.S., "The Jaina Religious Tradition" in *Religious Traditions of India*, edited by P.S. Daniel, *at.al*, New Delhi: ISPCK, 2002.

Dasgupta, S.N., *A History of Indian Philosophy: An Introduction to the Eight Major Philosophies of Ancient India*, Vol. 1, Cambridge: Finger Print Classic, 2024.

Doshi, Manu, (Tran.) *Tattvartha Sutra*, Ahmadabad: Federation of Jain Associations in North America and Shrut Ratnakar, 2007.

Eliade, Mircea, *Myth and Reality*, New York: Happer & Row, Publishers, 1963.

Gurdon, P.T.R., *The Khasis*, (Delhi: Low Price Publications, 1996.

Harvey, Peter, *An Introduction to Buddhism: Teachings, History and Practices, Second Edition*, Cambridge: Cambridge University Press, 2013.

Hiriyanna, M., *Outlines of Indian Philosophy*, Delhi: Motilal Banarsidass, 2000.

Hminga, C.L., "The traditional Mizo concept of God", in *Towards a Tribal Theology: The Mizo Perspective*, edited by K. Thanzauva, Aizawl: Mizo Theological Conference, 1989.

Iyengar, B.K.S. *Light on Yoga*, Revised Edition, New York: Schocken Books, 1979.

Jaini, Padmanabh S., *The Jaina Path of Purification*, Delhi: Motilal Banarsidass, 1988.

Langchar, A. Wati, *An Emerging Asian Theology: Tribal Theology, Issue, Method and Perspective,* Jorhat: Tribal Study Centre, ETC, 2000.

Liangkhaia, *Mizo Awmdan Hlui & Mizo Mi leh thil Hmingthangte leh Mizo Sakhua*, Aizawl: L.T.I Publications, 2008.

Longchar, A. Wati, "A Critique of the Christian Theology of Creation", in *Doing Theology with Tribal Resources: Context and Perspective*, edited by A. Wati Longchar and Larry E. Devis, Jorhat: Tribal Study Centre, ETC, 1999.

Longchar, A. Wati, *The Traditional Tribal Worldview and Modernity*, Jorhat: N. Limla Lkr, 1995.

Longchar, A. Wati, *The Tribal Religious Traditions in North East India: An Introduction*, Jorhat: Wati Longchar, 2000.

Madhva-Vidyaranya, Śaṅkara-Dig-Vijaya: The Traditional Life of Sri Śaṅkarācharya, translated by Swami Tapasyananda, (Madras: Sri Ramakrishna Math, No year of publication.

Mahadevan, T.M.P., Śaṅkarācharya, New Delhi: National Book Trust, India, 1968.

Mahapatra, Mary D., *Tribal Religion and Rituals: Accounts of Superstition, Sorcery and Spirits*, New Delhi: Dominant Publishers and Distributors, 2001.

Marcaurelle, Roger, *Freedom through Inner Renunciation: Śaṅkara's Philosophy in a New Light*, Delhi: Sri Satguru Publications, 2002.

Mbiti, John S, *African Religions and Philosophy, Second Edition*, Oxford: Heinemann Educational Publishers, 1999.

Minz, Nirmal, "The study of tribal Religion in India", in *Re-Visioning India's Religious Traditions: Essays in honour of Eric Lott*, edited by David C. Scott and Israel Selvanayagam, Delhi: ISPCK, 1996.

N.A., *Mizo Thawnthu*, Aizawl: Tribal Research Institute, Directorate of Art and Culture, Mizoram, 1992.

Narayana Aier, T.S., *The Age of Saṅkara*, Madras: B.G. Paul & Co., 1971; first published in 1916.

Prithipal, D., *Advaita Vedānta: Action and Contemplation*, Varanasi: Bharatiya Vidhya Prakasan, 1969.

Radhakrishnan, S., *et.al.* (Eds.), *A source book in Indian Philosophy,* Princeton: Princeton University Press, 1967.

Radhakrishnan, S., Indian Philosophy Vol I, London: George & Unwin Ltd., 1997.

Radhakrishnan, S., *Indian Philosophy Vol. II*, New York: The Macmillan Company, 1958.

Raju, P.T., *Strutural depth of Indian thought*, (New Delhi:South Asian Publishers, 1985.

Śaṅkara, *Brahma Sūtra Bhāṣya* (*B.S.B*) translated by Swami Gambhirananda, Calcutta: Advaita Ashrama, 1993.

Śaṅkara, *Bṛihadāraṇyaka Upaniṣad Bhāṣya*, translated by Swami Mahavananda; Mayavati: Advaita Aśrama, 1950.

Śaṅkara, *Upadeśa Sāhasrī*, translated by Swami Jagadananda, Madras: Sri Ramakrishna Math, 1989.

Śaṅkarāchārya, *Bhagavad Gītā Bhāṣya*, Translated by A. Mahadeva Shastri, Mysore: Government Oriental Library, 1901.

Sarma, Chandradhar, *A critical Survey of Indian Philosophy,* Delhi: Motilal Benarsidass, 1979.

Sashikaba Kechutzar, "Omen, Divination and Dream (Tatakrutsu, Antokdangba/Amsu and Pongmang): Medium for Divine Revelation" in Razouselie Lasetso (ed), *Garnering Tribal Resources for Doing Tribal Christian Theology*, Jorhat: ETC Programme Coordination, Eastern Theological College, 2008.

Sharma, Chandradhar, *Indian Philosophy: A Critical Survey*, New York City: Barnes & Noble, Inc. 1962.

Sharma, Chansradhar, A critical survey of Indian Philosophy, Delhi: Motilal Benarsidass, 1979

Sinha, Jadunath, Indian Philosophy Vol I, Delhi: Motilal Benarsidass, 1999.

Smet, R. De, "Rāmānuja and Madhva" in *Religious Hinduism*, edited by R. De Smet and J. Neuner, Mumbai: St. Pauls, 1997.

Smet, R.De, "Śaṅkara's Non-dualism (Advaita-Vāda)", in *Religious Hinduism*, edited by R. De Smet and J. Neuner, Fourth Revised Edition, (Mumbai: St. Pauls, 1997.

Thanzauva, K., *Theology of Community: Tribal Theology in the Making*, Bangalore: Asian Trading Corporation, 2004.

Thumra, Jonathan H., "The Primal Religious Tradition" in *Religious Traditions of India*, edited by P.S. Jacob, etc. Delhi: ISPCK, 2010.

Tiwari, Kedar Nath, *Comparative Religion*, Delhi: Motilal Banarsidass, 1992.

Urquhart, W.S., *The Vedanta and Modern Thought*, London: Oxford University Press, 1928.

Vanlaltlani, *Tribal Religion: Mizo and Bru*, Aizawl: Mizo Theological Association, 2009.

Warrier, A.G. Krishna, *The Concept of Mukti in Advaita Vedānta*, Madras: University of Madras, 1981.

Zairema, "The Mizos and their Religion" in *Towards a Tribal Theology: The Mizo Perspective*, edited by K. Thanzauva, Aizawl: Mizo Theological Conference, 1989.

2. Journals

Aleaz, K.P., "A Tribal Theology from a Tribal World-View" in *Indian Journal of Theology*, Vol. 44, nos. 2&3, 2002.

Gupta, Rita, "The Buddhist Doctrine of Momentariness and Its Presuppositions: Dharmakīrti's argument in Hetubindu", *Journal of Indian Philosophy*, Vol. 8, No. 1, March 1980), 47-68.

Gupta, Rita, "The Buddhist Doctrine of Momentariness and Its Presuppositions: Dharmakīrti's argument in Hetubindu", *Journal of Indian Philosophy*, Vol. 8, No. 1, March 1980)

Hoang, Nguyen Quy, "The Doctrine of Not-self (*anattā*) in Early Buddhism," in *International Review of Social Research,* Vol. 9, No. 1, 2019.

Kamal, M. Mostafa, "The Epistemology of the Carvaka Philosophy," *Journal of Indian and Buddhist Studies,* Vol. 46, No. 2, March 1998, 1048-1045.

Khongreiwo, Rammathot, "Landscapes and Pre- Christian Naga Belief System: Cosmology, Spirits and 'Land of the Dead'" in *Journal of Tribal studies*, Vol. XVI, No. 1, Jan-June 2011.

Longchar, A. Wati, "Tribal Theology: Nature and Method and Perspective" in *Journal of Tribal study*, Vol. 5, No. 1, January-June, 2001.

Mishra, Ashok K, "Atomism of Vaisesika-Nyaya VS Jainism – A Scientific Appraisal" in *Indian Journal of History of Science*, Vol. 42, no. 2, 2006), 247-261.

Mishra, Mahendra K., "Sacred Worldview in Tribal Memory: Sustaining nature through Cultural Actions", in *Language & Ecology*, Vol. 2, no. 4, 2009.

Pachuau, L., "Mizo 'Sakhua' in Transition: Change and Continuity from Primal Religion to Christianity", in *Missiology*, Vol. 34; No. 1, 2006.

Internet Sources

https://cdn.ymaws.com/sites/www.jaina.org/resource/resmgr/05042018_ENewsletter/The_Theory_of_Knowledge_in_J.pdf (accessed 15.05.2024)

Hemant Shah, "Types of Knowledge in Jainism," A paper read at a seminar on *Jain Philosophy* and Epistemology organized by the B.L. Institute of Indology, Delhi in December 1990, in *https://www.herenow4u.net/index.php?id=87104* ((15.01.2025).

"The Theory of knowledge in Jainism"" in *https://cdn.ymaws.com/sites/www.jaina.org/resource/resmgr/05042018_ENewsletter/The_Theory_of_Knowledge_in_J.pdf* (15.01.2025).

V. Subrahmanya Iyer, "Śankara's Philosophy and Action" in *http://www.yabaluri.org/TRIVENI/CDWEB/Shankaras-PhilosophyandAction1941.htm* (22.11.2011)

Edward E. Dudek, "Tribal Religious Belief of North East India with special emphasis on Nagaland and the Introduction & Effect of the Gospel" in *GlobeServe Journal of Missions, December 2008*, *www.globeservejournalofmissions.org* (23.06.2001)

KJN Gowtham Shankar, "Endogenous development and Tribal worldviews: Working with Tribal communities in India", a paper presented in the International Conference on Endogenous Development and Bio-Cultural Diversity: The Interplay of Worldviews, globalization and locality, 3-5 October, 2006, Geneva, Switzerland, in *http:// www. bioculturaldiversity. net/introduction.htm* (7.10.2011), p. 1.

N.A., "Tribal knowledge, supernatural & ceremonies", in *http://www.shannonthunderbird.com/tribal_beliefs.htm*, (11.10.2011),

Budha Kamei, "Belief in Totem among the Tingkao Ragwang Chapriak people", in *http://e-pao.net/epSubPageExtractor.asp?src=manipur.Manipur_and_Religion.Belief_in_Totem_among_the_Tingkao_Ragwang_Chapriak_people,*(14.10.2011).

www.egyankosh.ac.in/bitstream/123456789/25641/1/Unit-18, (08.10.2011)

KJN Gowtham Shankar, "Endogenous development and Tribal worldviews: Working with Tribal communities in India", a paper presented in the International Conference on Endogenous Development and Bio-Cultural Diversity: The Interplay of Worldviews, globalization and locality, 3-5 October, 2006, Geneva, Switzerland, in *http:// www.bioculturaldiversity. net/ introduction.htm* (7.10.2011),

Unpublished Papers

Bolinkar Sohkhlet, "Phenomenological study of the understanding of God (*Blei*) as emerging from selected myth and rituals of the traditional religion of the Khasi Pnar", Unpublished D.Th. thesis submitted to SATHRI of Senate of Serampore college, 2007.

Cherrie Lalnunziri Chhangte, "Myth and the Mizo Worldview", the unpublished seminar paper presented at International Seminar on History of Religions, Jawaharlal Nehru University, October 8-10, 2007.

Lalsangkima Pachuau, "Mizo '*Sakhua*' Then and Now: Change and continuity between Mizo primal religion and Mizo Christianity", a paper presented in the Faculty Research Seminar, The United Theological College on 12th November, 2003.

R. Sashikaba, "A phenomenological study of different manifestations of Supernatural powers among the Nagas with Special Reference to the experiences, Beliefs and Practices of the Ao Nagas", Unpublished D.Th. Thesis submitted to SATHRI of Senate of Serampore College (University), 2006.